THE TRUTH

A GUIDE TO MAKING DISCIPLES FOR JESUS

Dr. Christopher Moody

Disciple-Making Disciples

© 2026 by Dr. Christopher Moody

All rights reserved. No part of this book may be reproduced or transmitted in any form or by any means, electronic or mechanical, including photocopying, recording, or by any information storage and retrieval system, without permission in writing from the copyright owner.

Published by DMD Initiative
www.dmdinitiative.com

Scriptures taken from the New American Standard Bible®, Copyright © 1960, 1962, 1963, 1968, 1971, 1972, 1973, 1975, 1977, 1995 by The Lockman Foundation
Used by permission. (www.Lockman.org)

Scriptures taken from THE HOLY BIBLE, NEW INTERNATIONAL VERSION®, NIV® Copyright © 1973, 1978, 1984, 2011 by Biblica, Inc.™ Used by permission. All rights reserved worldwide.

Scriptures taken from the KING JAMES VERSION (KJV): public domain.

Cover Design by Jean-Paul Osteen

Layout Design by Anton Kore

Printed in the United States of America

THE TRUTH

A GUIDE TO MAKING DISCIPLES FOR JESUS

Dr. Christopher Moody

THE TRUTH

This disciple-making tool is dedicated to the local church invested in Jesus' model of personal disciple-making. To the pastors and staff who have sacrificed preconceived standards of ministry success to make authentic disciples who make disciples. To those followers of Christ who love people more than the bricks and beams of a building. This curriculum is dedicated to the Bride of Christ.

Members of DMD Initiative who were involved in the creation of this disciple-making tool.

Dr. Christopher Moody:	Author
Curt Edgerton:	Co-Author
Brittany Miller:	Contributor
Dr. Scott Moody:	Editor
Dr. Gwen Whitehead:	Editor
Angela Kneeland:	Editor
Anton Kore:	Interior Design
Jean-Paul Osteen:	Cover Design

TABLE OF CONTENTS
BELIEF IN CHRIST

008
▌ INTRODUCTION

010
▌ COMMON QUESTIONS

012
▌ DISCIPLE'S COMMITMENT

014
▌ PRACTICAL HELP

016
▌ DISCIPLER'S COMMITMENT

020
▌ WEEK 1
Knowing God
Exodus 3:13-14

039
▌ WEEK 2
The Tri-unity of God
2 Corinthians 13:14,
Deuteronomy 29:29

057
▌ WEEK 3
Made in God's Image
Genesis 1:26-27

075
▌ WEEK 4
Sin
Romans 2:23
Psalm 51:5

093
▌ WEEK 5
Salvation: Justification & Redemption
Romans 3:24-25,
Ephesians 1:7

112
▌ WEEK 6
Salvation: Reconciliation & Propitiation
Romans 5:10,
1 John 4:10

131
▌ WEEK 7
Salvation: Adoption
Romans 8:15-17

TABLE OF CONTENTS
BEHAVIORS IN CHRIST

152
WEEK 8
Spiritual Life & Spiritual Disciplines

Hebrews 12:1-2

171
WEEK 9
Bible Reading & Memorization

2 Timothy 3:16-17

190
WEEK 10
Bible Study & Meditation

Hebrews 4:12

213
WEEK 11
Prayer

Matthew 6:9-13

235
WEEK 12
Worship

Revelation 4:11, Romans 12:1

256
WEEK 13
Witness

Acts 1:8, Romans 6:23

281
WEEK 14
Trust and Obedience

Proverbs 3:5-6

TABLE OF CONTENTS
BODY OF CHRIST

305
WEEK 15
The Church

1 Peter 2:9

327
WEEK 16
Spiritual Gifts

1 Corinthians 12:7

347
WEEK 17
Filled with the Spirit

Ephesians 5:18-20

367
WEEK 18
Spiritual Warfare

Matthew 6:9-13

389
WEEK 19
Spiritual Fruit

Galatians 5:22-23

409
WEEK 20
Biblical Justice & Giving

2 Corinthians 9:7

429
WEEK 21
Disciple Making

1 Thessalonians 2:8

INTRODUCTION

If anyone could create the perfect message and method capable of reaching across all cultures and withstanding the test of time, it would undoubtedly be the Author of time and creation Himself. Jesus did that by investing in His twelve disciples, especially His three closest disciples (Peter, James, and John). He had a big enough vision to think small. "Disciple-making disciples" is plan A, and there is no plan B! A certain level of spiritual growth only occurs when a more mature believer invests in a few younger disciples of Christ to help them grow spiritually. This threefold method of personal investment is how Jesus built His Church: gospel investment, life investment, and reproduction (1 Thessalonians 2:8; 2 Timothy 2:2).

You may be questioning the value of disciple-making. What can microgroup personal disciple-makers (groups of three to four) offer that cannot be found in a home Bible study or online studies? You may believe that you are too far along in your journey with Jesus for something seemingly so simple. In contrast, others will perceive that they are unworthy or incapable. In a culture infatuated with achievement, speed, and efficiency, it is no wonder that we struggle to understand the value of Jesus' method of disciple-making.

Today we travel from point A to point B as quickly as possible. Sadly, the modern church has applied this desire for speed to the application of spiritual growth and evangelism. As Jesus designed it, disciple-making is not boarding a plane already cruising at 600 mph at 30,000 feet above sea level. With the efficiency of flight, we gladly forego both scenery and experiences to get to our destination as quickly as possible. However, as Jesus demonstrated for us through His personal model of ministry, disciple-making is more a journey than a destination. Before the age of planes, trains, and automobiles, early travelers set out on a journey. The process and experiences of this adventure transformed and refined their character. The relationships formed between traveling acquaintances had the potential to become lifelong friendships. Disciple-making is a similar expedition. With compass and map in hand, our tiny group of Christ-followers departs hopeful but not fully aware of what is to come. A journey to summit a mountain by a small band of adventurers proves to be a solid metaphor for the Christian life. Accordingly, the Bible and the Holy Spirit serve as our compass—ever-pointing to the Truth of God. As a compass always points north, the Word of God and Spirit of God constantly point to the Truth of God.

There are countless ways to get to most destinations. For this reason, a biblical-based curriculum acts as a map—assisting you as you guide others along the disciple's path. This map will lend confidence to disciples who will lead others in the future. With each use, the disciplers will refine their skills. As a spiritual "tour guide," they will experience firsthand the rewards of knowing how to transfer vital spiritual knowledge, model personal devotion to Christ, train the next generation to be missionally-minded, and assist those who struggle with different sins and hang-ups—all while personally growing closer to Jesus.

Life-on-life, personal disciple-making is paramount to reaching the uppermost summits of the spiritual life. Though most assume the motivation to climb a mountain is solely to stand on the top, many climbers will tell you that the pure inspiration for such a task is the hope that the process will affect who you are. Welcome to the first step of your bid to reach the summit.

COMMON QUESTIONS:

Am I capable of doing this?

If you are a follower of Jesus, He has made you capable. Jesus does not call the equipped, He equips the called. Jesus designed the disciple-making environment for spiritual growth and equipping.

Will this material or process make me a disciple?

No, being a follower of Jesus makes you His disciple. This process will help you grow and will equip you to be intentional about His message and method to the benefit of both your life and, ultimately, the next generation of disciples. Like a carpenter's tool, it is up to you how you will use it.

How do I become a better disciple of Jesus?

The first followers of Jesus chose to accept His invitation; then they continued to follow Him as He challenged them to choose relationship over religion, love over legalism, and service over selfishness. Jesus has given us the same message of the gospel and the model of personal disciple-making. Trusting and obeying Christ—trusting and obeying the message and method of Christ—makes you a better disciple of Jesus.

How does the process of disciple-making work?

Following Jesus' model of personal disciple-making, the discipler of your group will act as your spiritual tour guide, not a travel agent. This is not a hierarchical model but a team approach to spiritual growth. "Together," your small group of three to four will grow in friendship and accountability as you study the Bible, pray, and share life. Your time together should be a season of accelerated growth as you challenge, encourage, and equip each other to grow into a deeper relationship with King Jesus and become more competent in service to His Kingdom priorities.

How well do I need to know the Bible?

There is no prerequisite of Bible knowledge to begin. In your disciple group, you will learn to read, study, memorize, and discuss God's Word. Some or all of this may feel foreign or difficult to you, which is okay. God's Word is unlike any other book. It is living and active (Hebrews 4:12), and the Author will speak to you through it (2 Timothy 3:16). It is fine to sit in the unknown and to be a little uncomfortable. God will reveal the truth and give you understanding in His time.

I've studied the Bible and taken part in other study groups. Do I need to be part of a disciple-group ("d-group")?

You might be an outstanding student of God's Word, but do you know how to nurture an environment where others can grow? Are you comfortable with the vulnerability and authenticity required to be held accountable and keep others accountable? Are you competent to use and train others through mutual accountability, Bible study methods, a disciple-making curriculum, spiritual disciplines, modeled evangelism, life-on-life friendships, and gospel fluency, all the while remaining dependent on the Holy Spirit? Even if you have participated in or even led countless Bible study groups in the past, you will be deeply challenged and encouraged through the disciple-making journey.

- **How is a disciple-group different from a small group or Sunday school class?**

    Jesus' investment in His first disciples was a long-term involvement on a very personal level. Your disciple group will require a higher level of commitment and will consist of a smaller group of people than the average small group or Sunday school class. This micro-group of three or four lends itself to more authentic friendships that become a fertile greenhouse environment for spiritual growth and Christ-centered ministry.

- **How do I use this curriculum?**

    This eight-week discipling on-ramp is a five-day per week regimen of teaching, devotional, and prayer time. If you do not already have a daily time of prayer and Bible study, we hope you will come to see the necessity of these spiritual disciplines in your walk with Jesus. At the end of each week, you will join your disciple group in to discuss the week's material, share memory verses, hold each other accountable, and train to lead others.

- **Is it possible to complete the curriculum in a single day?**

    By design, the daily format of this material encourages you to establish a consistent, personal time with the Lord each day. If you already practice healthy spiritual disciplines through Bible study, Scripture memorization, and prayer, then completing this content in one sitting is not detrimental. However, doing so will likely decrease your level of engagement and contribution with your group.

- **Do I need to pray the prayers listed each day?**

    The guided prayer section is intended to springboard you to a deeper and more meaningful conversation with the Lord. Consider the guided prayer section as an encouragement for those new to a personal relationship with God or those who struggle in their prayer life. Use this section to help you praise God for who He is, confess sin, and thank God for His provision.

- **How does a disciple-group work?**

    Disciple groups should meet weekly for about an hour and a half. This meeting can occur anywhere that is accessible and conducive to quality conversation—a home, coffee shop, restaurant, park, or church building are a few good examples. Your weekly meeting is a necessary appointment that you should prioritize, but your relationship with members of your group is not limited to this meeting. You are encouraged to do life with one another throughout this process—share a meal, communicate often, and find shared interests to participate in together. Do not underestimate the value of text messages and phone calls throughout the week.

DISCIPLE'S COMMITMENT

MUTUAL ACCOUNTABILITY

A healthy d-group has a culture of **accountability.** For this to happen, you must be transparent about your life. Be prepared to share your testimony, convictions, struggles, and praises with the members of your disciple group. The critical ingredients for biblical accountability in discipling relationships are confidentiality, authenticity, and obedience. Without the willingness to embrace this structure, accountability cannot happen.

I commit to being accountable. _____
signature

BIBLICAL TRUTH

The various concepts that shape your disciple group should come directly from the **Bible.** You are responsible for being in the Word daily and encouraging your fellow disciples to do the same. Some of the critical actions whereby the **Bible** is used in one's growth as a disciple are memorization, inductive study, and obedience. We memorize it, draw truth from it, and then apply it to our lives.

I commit to the Bible. _____
signature

REPRODUCIBLE TOOL

This book functions as a **tool** for you to use for yourself and for future generations of disciples. As a curriculum, it requires your attention leading up to your d-group meeting. It is helpful to work on it every day rather than cramming it in the day before your meeting. Its format is intended to train you to have daily Bible study, scripture memorization, devotional time, and prayer time. The other main expectation is that you prayerfully consider leading a disciple group yourself in the years to come. A good reproducible curriculum helps disciples make disciples.

I commit to use this tool. _____
signature

INTENTIONAL PRAYER

Prayer is an essential part of your relationship with the Lord. At the end of each session, you will find a prayer prompt. The hope is that you will not only pray through the written prompt but will use it to start an intentional time of prayer. Pray daily for the members of your disciple group. Pray for your circles of people—family, your local church body, friends, coworkers, and neighbors.

I commit to prayer. _____
signature

LIFE-ON-LIFE FRIENDSHIP

Disciple groups differ from other small groups and corporate worship. The life-on-life nature of a disciple group fosters **friendships** with a Kingdom-focused purpose. Through the journey of personal investment and sharing life struggles, you will develop deep friendships, which are not common outside of Christ-centered disciple-making. Use your time in this d-group to be intentional about building friendships for the sake of spiritual growth.

I commit to friendship. _____
signature

GOSPEL FLUENCY

Disicplers must be fluent in speaking about and living out **the gospel** in front of those they disciple. While you are aware that you should share the gospel with non-believers, it is also important to regularly discuss the good news of Jesus with your disciples. Make sure that those you are discipling not only hear you speak about the good news of Jesus but also witness you living it out. Prayerfully consider evangelistic projects or personal witnessing opportunities to share with your disciples over the next few months (missional events, mission trips, sharing Christ specifically with those being prayed for at the bottom of the accountability card, etc.).

I commit to sharing the gospel and living it out. _____
signature

PRACTICAL HELP FOR DISCIPLERS (LEADERS)

How do I choose who I should disciple?

- The first step is simple: Pray! Prayerfully consider who you should walk with through this discipling journey. Trust the Holy Spirit to provide, and be open and available to where He leads you. Good places to start looking may include a small group Bible study that you are already attending, your workplace, neighborhood, school, or gym. Men disciple men, and women disciple women. Married couples are an exception.

- When someone comes to mind through this prayer time, consider these five necessary characteristics that give evidence of another's salvation (using the acronym F-R-U-I-T). You cannot disciple an unbeliever. You share Christ with an unbeliever. So, you are looking for **Fundamentals** of spiritual conviction. Do they have a personal testimony of salvation through faith in Jesus? Second, true believers are defined by how they perceive the Scripture, the **Revelation** of God to us. Do they show any signs of spiritual hunger for the Word of God? You are also looking for someone **Unashamed** of the gospel. Do they display a simple unabashed appreciation for the truth of the gospel? Or do they shy away from talking about the saving work of Christ? Next is **Integrity**—a person with integrity will show a consistency between belief and behavior. Do their lips match their lives? Finally, look for **Tenderness**. Love characterizes all true believers, so you should see tenderness and compassion displayed throughout their lives.

- When the Holy Spirit provides a potential disciple, initiate a friendship. Clearly explain what the disciple-making journey looks like and what they can expect. Share the story of your spiritual journey and ask them to share their story likewise. If you feel led by God at the end of this initial meeting, invite them into a discipling relationship with you.

Where should we meet?

- Establishing a consistent meeting space and time is important. You want a place that is convenient and accessible for those in your group. The body of Christ is a diverse group of people. While one group is comfortable meeting in a busy restaurant, another group might find that atmosphere distracting. Sometimes you have to be creative with spaces to make your meeting possible. Where you meet is optional. If you are meeting during a lunch period, you might rotate through some of the nearest restaurants. If you have children accompanying, maybe you meet where they can be entertained, like a playground or indoor play area.

What is the schedule for a disciple group?

- Establish an attainable schedule for all involved, and prioritize your meetings. Commit to meeting with your group weekly for the next months but prayerfully consider staying together for subsequent training time for up to a year or more. Jesus spent eighteen months with His disciples training them to reproduce themselves. An average disciple group meeting will last about an hour and a half. Disruptions are inevitable. There will be times when your group cannot meet due to sickness, emergencies, or work conflicts. However, set the standard early that the meeting is a priority each week and you do not cancel unnecessarily.

How do I create an environment of authenticity?

- You have to be authentic. While there is only one model and mission for disciple-making, every disciple group will look different. Each will have its own character and personality. Be honest with yourself and with your group. Disciplers model authenticity and vulnerability to his or her group members. They are looking to you for an example to follow, but they need you to be authentic, not perfect.

How do I build a deep and lasting friendship?

- Friendship requires time and consistency. Prioritize these relationships by being available and look for opportunities outside of your meeting time to share life with them. Commit to walking alongside those you are discipling. Celebrate with them through every good thing they experience. When hardship comes, be there to love, serve, and encourage. Both fun and food facilitate deeper friendship. Frequent phone calls and text messages also add to the thoughtfulness required for better relationships.

How do I create a culture of accountability within our group?

- Take the first step in your group and open up to them about the things you personally struggle with in life. Be vulnerable and allow them to hold you accountable. Share your struggles and permit them to speak into your life. We encourage you to use the accountability questions provided to help facilitate this. Find out which questions are the best suited to your group by going through them the first few weeks. Evaluate where the most accountability is needed. At other times, just pick and choose the most relevant questions for the people of your group. Be sensitive to the needs of your group. Accountability needs may vary according to the changing in the group members. Be a good steward of the trust they have given you.

How do I encourage reading, meditating, studying, and memorizing Scripture?

- Once again, lead by example. Make sure you are abiding in the Word by reading, meditating, studying, and memorizing Scripture. As is often the case in one's spiritual journey, you cannot give away what you do not have. Share with them the high-points of what God is revealing to you through His Word, and ask them about their walk with God. Identify where they are struggling and help them overcome the obstacles. Equip them with tools to make them more confident in approaching God's Word, and pray that they would desire His Word daily.

What should we discuss during our disciple group?

- Start your disciple group by asking them how they are doing spiritually. Focus on daily life struggles and praises and then transition to a time of accountability. Pray for one another, and make a plan of action for accountability if needed. Avoid letting the entire group get derailed into one long counseling session, although some "counseling like" times might be necessary if your group members are going through especially hard times (job loss, sickness, divorce, etc). Spend the majority of your time working through the questions marked with this symbol. ▼ Give everyone time to share their comments and ask questions. Highlight anything that God has shown you throughout the week. Be prepared to spend extra time whenever special needs arise within your group. Ask the Holy Spirit for guidance throughout your time, and be sensitive to His promptings. Your meetings may look different week to week.

What is the big picture goal for this D-group?

- The goal of a disciple group is to equip followers of Christ to share the gospel and to disciple those who come to faith to lead them in spiritual growth to a place that can be replicated in others. This fulfills the Great Commission as we make Jesus known to all the nations by making disciples who make disciples.

THE TRUTH

DISCIPLER'S (LEADERS) COMMITMENT

MUTUAL ACCOUNTABILITY

A healthy d-group has a culture of **accountability.** For this to happen, you must be transparent about your life. Be prepared to model sharing your testimony of coming to faith in Christ, personal convictions, sin struggles, and joyful praises with the members of your disciple group. The critical ingredients for biblical accountability in discipling relationships are confidentiality, authenticity, and obedience. Without the willingness to embrace this process, accountability cannot happen. As a discipler, you prime the pump on accountability.

I commit to being accountable. _____
signature

BIBLICAL TRUTH

The various concepts that shape your disciple group should come directly from the **Bible**. You are responsible for being in the Word daily and encouraging your fellow disciples to do the same. The critical tasks you should passionately model for your disciples are memorization, inductive study, and obedience to the Word. Our disciples should not have to wonder whether we memorize it, draw truth from it, and apply it to our lives. As a discipler, you model what a life looks like that abides in the Word.

I commit to the Bible. _____
signature

REPRODUCIBLE TOOL

This book is a **tool** for you to use for yourself and for future generations of disciples. As a curriculum, it requires your attention during the week and leading up to your d-group meeting. It is helpful to work on it every day rather than cramming it all in the day before your meeting. This format is intended to encourage daily Bible study, Scripture memorization, devotional time, and prayer time.

I commit to use this tool. _____
signature

DISCIPLER'S (LEADERS) COMMITMENT

INTENTIONAL PRAYER

Prayer is an essential part of your relationship with the Lord and you should model this for your disciples. At the end of each session, you will find a prayer prompt. The hope is that your disciples will not only pray through the written prompt but that they will use it to start an intentional time of prayer. Pray daily for the members of your disciple group. Pray for your circles of people—family, your local church body, friends, coworkers, and neighbors. Intentionally display this for your disciples and celebrate with them any answers to prayer you see throughout the next weeks.

I commit to prayer. _____
signature

LIFE-ON-LIFE FRIENDSHIP

The life-on-life nature of a disciple group fosters **friendships** with a Kingdom-focused purpose. As the discipler, you should take the lead in developing the deep friendships necessary for Christ-centered disciple-making. Share your life struggles and victories first before you ask them to do the same. Use your time in this d-group to be intentional about building friendships for the sake of spiritual growth. Lead the way in finding time outside of the main group meeting to spend time together as friends (food, fun, family).

I commit to friendship. _____
signature

SPIRITUAL RELIANCE

God gave us His **Spirit** as our Helper, Convictor, and Comforter, and He is essential to disciple-making. Though you may not feel qualified for this work, you have the Bible and the Spirit, which is more than enough. God does not call the equipped, He equips the called, and He has called you. Trust the Holy Spirit during this disciple-making adventure.

I commit to relying on the Holy Spirit. _____
signature

DISCIPLER'S (LEADERS) COMMITMENT

GOSPEL FLUENCY

Disicplers must be fluent in speaking about and living out **the gospel** in front of those they disciple. While you are aware that you should share the gospel with non-believers, it is also important to regularly discuss the good news of Jesus with your disciples. Make sure that those you are discipling not only hear you speak about the good news of Jesus but also witness you living it out. Prayerfully consider evangelistic projects or personal witnessing opportunities to share with your disciples over the next few months (missional events, mission trips, sharing Christ specifically with those being prayed for at the bottom of the accountability card, etc.).

I commit to sharing the gospel and living it out. _____
signature

BELIEF IN CHRIST

020
WEEK 1
Knowing God

Exodus 3:13-14

039
WEEK 2
The Tri-unity of God

2 Corinthians 13:14,
Deuteronomy 29:29

057
WEEK 3
Made in God's Image

Genesis 1:26-27

075
WEEK 4
Sin

Romans 2:23
Psalm 51:5

093
WEEK 5
Salvation: Justification
& Redemption

Romans 3:24-25,
Ephesians 1:7

112
WEEK 6
Salvation: Reconciliation
& Propitiation

Romans 5:10,
1 John 4:10

131
WEEK 7
Salvation: Adoption

Romans 8:15-17

Week 01 • Day 01
KNOWING GOD

ESSENTIAL TRUTH

Although God cannot be fully known, He can be truly known in both His greatness and goodness. In His greatness, God reveals Himself as independent, unchangeable, eternal, all-powerful, all-knowing, everywhere present, and perfectly unified. These are attributes we cannot possess as finite creatures. In His goodness, God reveals Himself as the author and perfecter of wisdom, justice, mercy, holiness, goodness, graciousness, and love. These are attributes we can possess in measure. Inasmuch as God has made Himself known through all creation, knowing God requires special revelation from God.

1. After reading the Essential Truth, identify two phrases that stand out to you and write them below. Why are these phrases significant?

_____
_____
_____

2. Explain the difference between God's greatness and God's goodness.

_____
_____
_____

3. What are some ways that you have experienced the character of God?

___
___
___

EXERCISE memory verse

God said to Moses, "I AM WHO I AM"; and He said, "Thus you shall say to the sons of Israel, 'I AM has sent me to you.'"

Exodus 3:14

    Disciples of Jesus have the high and holy privilege of knowing God on a personal level. This week's memory verse comes from Exodus, which chronicles God's work to reveal Himself and rescue His people from slavery in Egypt. In the Old Testament, God revealed Himself to specific people such as Moses. Because of God's infinite distinctiveness from mankind, this is the only way anyone could have known Him. God must take the first step. God gave Moses a special revelation to lead His people out of bondage.

    Moses acknowledges his inabilities when God speaks to him through the burning bush. Moses asks, "Who am I that I should go to Pharaoh and bring the sons of Israel out of Egypt?" God responds, "I will be with you. Moses replied, "I will say to them, 'The God of your fathers has sent me to you.' Now they may say to me, 'What is His name?' What shall I say to them?'" God replies, "I AM WHO I AM" (Exodus 3:11-14). God's response affirms that He alone is all-powerful, all-knowing, and always present. Later in the week, we will discuss the implications of God calling Himself the great "I AM." To walk confidently, Moses needed to embrace both the revelation and the calling of God. God is the same yesterday, today, and forever (Hebrews 13:8). Similarly, you must walk confidently in God's revelation of Himself to you. You must also answer His calling to know Him personally and make Him known. What is impossible for us is possible with God (Luke 18:27; Mark 10:27).

> " Jesus Christ is the same yesterday and today and forever."
> *Hebrews 13:8*

EXAMPLE

The fictional characters of Mowgli and Tarzan depicted in children's stories are sadly based on real-life accounts. Apart from a compassionate and nurturing environment, these children did not develop the communication, posture, hygiene, or social skills that define civility.

Imagine an unkempt and aggressive young man or woman, more animal-like than human. Their frames would be rendered lean by famine and the harsh conditions of nature. With no way to communicate and no concept of family or community, what hope do they have in life? Though seemingly out of context to this study, this illustration is essential. Before Christ, you were a feral child.

God looked at your broken nature, aggression, and voraciousness and loved you. You growled and bit at Him out of fear. You took the blessings He offered and hid from Him. When you couldn't understand His Word or His ways, He pursued you. God has clothed you in newness. He has straightened your ways and righted your steps. Though He once seemed unknowable, He made Himself known to you. He has set a place for you at His table and loves you as His son or daughter.

THE TRUTH

MEDITATE Write out this week's verse below as you spend time committing them to memory.

ENGAGE

Praise God for being immutable (the same yesterday, today, and forever). Confess to Him how you tend to trust and rely on yourself instead of His promises. Thank Jesus Christ for being with you and taking the initiative to reveal Himself to you. Ask Him to reveal more of who He is to you this week.

Week 01 • Day 02
KNOWING GOD

EXERCISE

READ *Job 38:4-7, Exodus 3:1-6*

1. Early in the book that bears his name, Job curses the day of his birth and laments his life because of all his suffering (Job 3). Read Job 38:4-7 and note God's response about the nature of the universe's birth. How would this response bring clarity to Job's lamenting?

_____
_____
_____

2. Read Exodus 3:1-6 and write out below the exact wording of the "I AM" statement that God revealed to Moses through the burning bush

_____
_____
_____

Thanks to the Hubble Telescope, we know that our solar system is a tiny spec in a sea of galactic nebulas. If our little solar system defies our knowledge, how can we fully understand the One who spoke the universe into existence? Is it possible to know God?

Some think that God is so great that knowing Him is inconceivable. This belief would be true if knowing Him relied solely on human knowledge and study (Matthew 16:17; Isaiah 55:8-9). Job 38-41 expresses the magnitude and magnificence of God's incredible greatness. In today's Bible reading, God's expression of His power and perfection surpasses our ability to understand such truths. Where we struggle to comprehend a hundred years of history, God has always existed and will always be (Revelation 1:8). Humanity labors under the sun building for itself (Ecclesiastes 1:3-14). Yet, God spoke everything into existence (Romans 4:17). We are created in God's image (Genesis 1:26). Still, we do not possess God's power and greatness. Fully aware of our limitations, God gave us a glimpse of His greatness, divine nature, and power through His creation (Romans 1:20).

> Where were you when I laid the foundation of the earth?"
> *Job 38:4a*

The few who have entered into the presence of God have been overwhelmed by the experience (Isaiah 6:5; Job 40:3-5), and Moses was no exception. In Exodus 3:6, Moses became aware of God's absolute greatness and hid his face out of fear. Good theology reveals that we will never possess God's greatness nor fully understand it. We are not self-existent, unchangeable, infinite, all-powerful, all-knowing, or everywhere present. God is. Even though God cannot be fully known, He can be truly known. We know Him by faith in His gracious act of self-disclosure in Scripture, creation, and history.

- God is **Independent** (self-existent). God is not created and does not need us or any part of creation (Act 17:24-25; Isaiah 43:7; John 1:4).

- God is **Immutable** (unchangeable). God does not alter His being, attributes, purposes, or promises (Malachi 3:6; Psalm 33:11; Numbers 23:19; James 1:17; Hebrews 13:8).

- God is **Eternal** (infinite). God has no beginning, end, or succession of moments in His own being as He sees all time equally vividly, yet God sees events in time and acts in time (Revelation 1:8; Psalm 90:2; Job 36:26; John 1:1).

- God is **Omnipotent** (all-powerful). Within the context of His perfect nature, there is nothing God cannot do. God can do all His holy will desires (Genesis 18:14; Jeremiah 32:17; Ephesians 3:20; Matthew 19:26).

- God is **Omniscient** (all-knowing). God knows everything (1 John 3:20). He fully knows Himself and all actual and possible things (Job 37:16; Hebrews 4:23; Psalm 147:4-5; 1 Corinthians 2:10).

- God is **Omnipresent** (everywhere present). God is unlimited concerning space and time. God does not have size or spatial limitations and is always present in all space (Jeremiah 23:24; Psalm 139:7-10; Psalm 16:11; Amos 9:1-4).

- God is **Perfectly Unified**. God is unified in all His attributes. God is not divided into parts, yet we see different attributes of God emphasized at other times (1 John 1:5; 1 John 4:8; John 1:1; Deuteronomy 6:4).

God told Job that He set the foundation of the world in place at creation (Job 38:4). God spoke the rules of physics into the fabric of His work as He created matter from nothing (*ex nihilo*). With a singular exhale, God breathed human life into existence (Genesis 2:7). God is great (transcendent), but in His goodness (immanence), He reveals Himself to us (Romans 1:19-20; Hebrews 1:1-14).

1. Of the seven attributes of God listed above, which do you struggle with understanding the most? Read through the verses listed for that attribute and make some notes below to help you understand that specific characteristic of God better.

_____

_____

_____

2. How does the greatness of God encourage you to share the good news of Jesus and to disciple those who come to faith?

_____

_____

_____

3. The God that created the foundations of the world is the same God that created you. How does understanding God as Creator deepen your relationship with Him?

___

MEDITATE Fill in the blanks as you continue committing this week's verse to memory.

> God said to Moses, "I AM WHO I _____"; and He said, "Thus you shall say to the sons of _____, 'I AM has sent me to you.'"
>
> *Exodus 3:14*

ENGAGE

Praise God for being great—independent, unchangeable, eternal, all-powerful, all-knowing, everywhere present, and perfectly unified. Confess that your knowledge and understanding of His greatness is limited. Thank Him for *revealing* truth to you and for *giving* you understanding. Ask Him to continue to open your heart and mind to know more of who He is.

Week 01 • Day 03
KNOWING GOD

EXERCISE

READ   *Exodus 3:7-15 2:24-25*

1. List the three verbs describing what the Lord did in Exodus 3:7. Now go back and read Exodus 2:24-25 and list the four verbs used there as well. Based on studying these seven verbs, what do they reveal about God's character?

_____
_____
_____

2. In Exodus 3:11, Moses asks, "Who am I that I should go…?" In Exodus 4:10, he says, "I am not eloquent… I am slow of speech and of tongue." Note God's response to both questions in Exodus 3:12 and 4:11-12. What does God give Moses to equip him for the work He has called him to?

_____
_____
_____

Some might find it difficult to believe that such a great God would care about us. However, God's greatness (transcendence) is perfectly balanced with His goodness (immanence) to such an extent that God not only loves you (Romans 5:8) but knows every detail about you (Luke 12:7; Acts 17:24-28).

In His Omniscience (all knowing), God knew the affliction of His people. In His goodness and omnipotence (unlimited power), He prepared a way to deliver them. In His greatness, He protected a baby in a basket as it floated down the crocodile-filled waters of the Nile (Exodus 2:1-10). God knew that this particular baby would grow into a man standing before a burning bush.

In calling Moses to Himself, God does not offer him a divine resume. Moses did not need a divine resume; he needed God. In telling His name to Moses, God said, "I AM WHO I AM." Philosophically, God's name states that He absolutely Is. He is the very grounds of all existence. On a more personal level, God tells us He is always present. He is the ever-present One. He is always with us. God was present in the garden, and long after He heals the last broken heart, He will remain.

> So I have come down to deliver them from the power of the Egyptians, and to bring them up from that land to a good and spacious land, to a land flowing with milk and honey.
>
> *Exodus 3:8*

God's greatness is not an attribute that we can possess, but believers can embody aspects of God's goodness as we grow to be more like Him.

- God is **Wise.** God is full of wisdom (Romans 16:27; Job 9:4; Psalm 147:5).
- God is **Just.** God is right and perfect in all He does (Deuteronomy 32:4; Psalm 11:7; Job 36:6).
- God is **Merciful.** God is compassionate and forgiving (Romans 9:15-16; Psalm 103:8; Nehemiah 9:31; Jeremiah 3:12).
- God is **Holy**. God is both separate from anything unholy and perfect in all He is (Psalm 99:9; Isaiah 6:3; Leviticus 19:2).
- God is **Good.** God is kind and full of goodwill (Luke 18:19; Genesis 1:31; Nahum 1:7).
- God is **Gracious.** God is inclined to give undeserved favor (Genesis 2:15-17; Romans 6:23; Deuteronomy 7:6-8; Romans 3:24).
- God is **Love.** God loves us (1 John 4:8; John 17:24; Romans 5:8).

A view of God that places any of His attributes above another becomes bad theology. These attributes are true to God in a perfect, infinite, unified, and unchangeable way. We can be like Him in some respects, but never perfectly so. This is where the gospel becomes most clear. Through the life, death, and resurrection of Jesus, God fully demonstrated the perfect balance of His greatness and goodness.

1. Of the attributes of God listed above, which do you struggle with understanding the most? Read through the verses listed for those attributes and make notes below to grow your knowledge of that specific characteristic of God. ▼

_____
_____
_____

2. Which attribute gives you the most comfort? How does this characteristic allow you to trust and love God more fully?

_____
_____
_____

3. In what ways have you experienced God's goodness on a personal level?

_____
_____
_____

MEDITATE Fill in the blanks as you continue committing this week's verse to memory.

> I AM WHO I AM"; and He said, "Thus you shall say to the _____ of _____ , 'I AM has _____ me to you.'"
>
> Exodus 3:14

ENGAGE

Praise God for His good and perfect character. Ask Him to give you abundant wisdom, goodness, and love so that you may be more like Him. Confess that you are not deserving of His mercy and grace. Thank Him for rescuing you anyway.

Week 01 • Day 04
KNOWING GOD

EXAMINATION

READ
John 14:1-15

WATCH
Week 1 - Knowing God

To watch the video, scan the QR code below by opening your phone's camera and holding your device so that the QR code appears on the screen. Click the link associated with the QR code, and choose this week's video. https://qrco.de/be3SWs

EXERCISE

1. In His power, you take God seriously and in His goodness you receive the special, specific, and significant elements of His relationship with you. How have you experienced knowing God in a special, specific, and significant way?

___

___

___

2. God has called and equipped you through His greatness and goodness. In Jesus' commission to all believers to make disciples of all nations, He has promised to be with you. How does His goodness impact how you live and obey Him as a disciple?

_____
_____
_____

3. Identify the seven I AM statements of Jesus that Dr. Moody referenced in the video and note what each one identifies about God's character.

(a) John 6:35 - _____
(b) John 8:12 - _____
(c) John 10:7 - _____
(d) John 10: 11, 14 - _____
(e) John 11:25 - _____
(f) John 14:6 - _____
(g) John 15:1 - _____

READ *John 14:1-15*

The disciples had grown accustomed to following Jesus wherever He went. They had physically experienced His ministry, sat under His teaching, and enjoyed His friendship. Their hearts were understandably troubled when it came time for Jesus to leave them (John 14:1). Where was Jesus going? How would they find Him again? How would they find the Father without Jesus? Jesus clarifies for them that they know the Father because they know Him. Jesus and the Father are one God (John 10:30), and we come to know God the Father in a saving relationship through the life, death, and resurrection of Jesus Christ (John 14:6). As we seek to obey all that God has commanded us and make disciples of all nations (Matthew 28:19, Acts 1:8), we do so from a posture of faith. God is who He says He is—the great I AM. We trust Jesus as the only way to the Father, the absolute truth, and the life we don't deserve.

God is not some divine Santa Claus who solely exists to give gifts—no more than He is an angry curmudgeon waiting to punish you. A high view of theology teaches that God's power and love exceed our understanding. God loved you enough to allow Jesus to die so you could be restored to Him (John 3:16). Like Moses in the wilderness and Jesus' apostles in Israel, God is working in your life so that you will know Him and find He is strong enough to trust and near enough to touch (Acts 17:27).

MEDITATE   Below, attempt to write out this week's verse from memory.

ENGAGE

Praise God for being both great and good. Confess the ways you don't humble yourself to His greatness and the ways you don't treasure His goodness. Thank Him for His special, specific, and significant presence in your life. Ask Him to enable you to understand His power, authority, and intimacy in your life. Pray through specific ways to lean into and trust the character of God in your day-to-day life.

Week 01 • Day 05
KNOWING GOD

EXERCISE

READ   *Matthew 28:19-20*

Your call as a disciple-making disciple is not founded on your abilities or knowledge. It is built on the gospel of Jesus Christ. As a sinner separated from God, you were undeserving of His mercy and grace. Yet, in His goodness, He **rescued** you. He did not save you to fill your head with information or for you to sit in a pew. He has called you to be a **rescuer**. Like Moses, you may fabricate excuses about how you are ill-equipped for this work or why He should use someone else. This is the beauty of the last command found in the Great Commission: "Behold, I am with you always, even to the end of the age" (Matthew 28:20). You are equipped because He is with you. The independent, unchangeable, eternal, all-powerful, all-knowing, everywhere present, perfectly unified, wise, just, merciful, holy, good, gracious, and loving God is always with you.

1. Is the Great Commission only intended for Jesus' first disciples, or is it applicable to all His followers? Explain.

_____
_____
_____

2. As a disciple of Jesus, what is the source of your gifts and calling?

_____

_____

_____

3. As a disciple of Jesus, are you personally responsible for sharing the gospel and discipling those who come to faith? ▼

_____

_____

_____

EXAMPLE

Think back to the analogy of Mowgli and Tarzan. With best intentions, too many believers seemingly forget who they were before Christ. As wild children, it was impossible to understand God's Word and His character. Raised in the wilderness of a broken world, you were lost in the darkness.

God rescued you from fear, self-harm, and lack of purpose. He adopted you into His family. He forgave your ignorance and looked beyond your shortcomings. Through the life, death, and resurrection of Jesus, God saved you from the wilderness of your carnality. You have been rescued and sent out as a son or daughter to assist in the rescue of others. Look into the eyes of those who are still lost in the wilderness and do more than feel compassion. Introduce them to God.

MEDITATE   Practice reciting this week's verse from memory and be prepared to say them aloud to your d-group.

ENGAGE

Praise God for being Omnipresent (ever-present). Confess your struggles with trusting God's greatness and ability to be with you always. Thank Him for equipping you with His presence and providing everything you need to obey His call on your life.

ENCOURAGE

Use this checklist as a guide for your weekly d-group time. Refer to the discipler's guide at the front of the book for more encouragement and practical advice.

- Work through questions from the accountability page.
- Spend time praying specifics for one another.
- Take turns reciting the memory verses.
- Discuss answers to the questions throughout the week that are marked with this symbol. ▼

PRAYER REQUESTS

_____
_____
_____
_____
_____
_____
_____

ACCOUNTABILITY QUESTIONS

These questions are to be asked of one another in a spirit of accountability (Proverbs 27:17). They are intended to stimulate conversations of character and confession of sin in a safe environment that values honesty, vulnerability, confidentiality, and grace.

1. Have you spent quality time in your spiritual disciplines this week?

2. Have you taken advantage of opportunities to share your faith this week? Explain.

3. Have your words and actions been a good testimony this week to the gospel of Jesus?

4. Have your thoughts and speech been pure (cussing, criticism, negativity, etc.)?

5. Have you been sexually pure this week? Have you been exposed to sexually alluring material? (For those who are married: Have you prioritized quality romantic time with your spouse?)

6. Have you been a good steward of your finances? Have you lacked integrity in the handling of your finances?

7. Have you been honoring and generous in your meaningful relationships this week (Family, friends, etc.)?

8. Have you given in to any addictive behavior this past week? Explain.

9. Have you been completely honest with me?

I'm praying for the salvation of the following two people and prayerfully considering how to share Christ with them myself: _____

> "Therefore, confess your sins to one another, and pray for one another, so that you may be healed."
>
> *James 5:16a*

Week 02 • Day 01

THE TRI-UNITY OF GOD

ESSENTIAL TRUTH

God is one God, yet exists in three distinct persons who are in perfect unity: The Father (Creator), Jesus the Son (Redeemer), and the Holy Spirit (the Sanctifier). As a result of His triune nature, our own reality finds its foundation and expression in relational community. All relationships are consequently marked by selflessness and humble love.

1. Read the Essential Truth, identify two phrases that stand out to you, and write them below. Why are these phrases significant?

_____
_____
_____

2. In your own words, describe the three persons of God.

_____
_____
_____

3. Why is it important to study God's tri-unity?

_____
_____
_____

EXERCISE `memory verse`

> "The grace of the Lord Jesus Christ, and the love of God, and the fellowship of the Holy Spirit, be with you all."
>
> *2 Corinthians 13:14*

Throughout time, God's triune nature has confounded followers of Christ. Though some analogies can help us clarify slightly, there is nothing like God (Isaiah 64:4). To what can we compare Him (Isaiah 40:18; Deuteronomy 33:26)? The naturalist might attempt to explain the triune nature of God by using a three-leaf-clover. The baker may say sugar, flour, and butter make up the three ingredients of one recipe for shortbread. The physicist could attempt to define God's triune nature by the analogy of water as a solid, liquid, or gas. Analogies such as these can be helpful though they cannot fully explain God's triunity. It is essential to acknowledge that our ways are not His (Isaiah 55:8). Although we cannot fully know every intricacy of God, He has given us everything we need to know Him truly.

> "For My thoughts are not your thoughts, nor are your ways My ways," declares the LORD."
>
> *Isaiah 55:8*

EXAMPLE

Although newborn babies cannot well focus their eyes, they still gaze intently at their mother's face. Infants will smile at the sound of their mother's voice though they do not understand what she has said. Though babies have yet to master motor skills, they will grip their father's finger and lay their head on his chest. An infant doesn't need to know the intricacies of their family dynamics to know they are cared for in life.

In like manner, receiving God's love does not require us to understand every aspect of His nature. There is no other like God (1 Samuel. 2:2) to whom could we compare Him (Isaiah 40:18). The infant holding their father's finger does not understand what a bed is or that their father assembled it. Looking at their nursery, they can't comprehend construction or interior design. How could they know their mother lovingly hand-painted the scenes on their wall?

We are often like this infant as we attempt to understand God's tri-unity. The triune nature of God is unlike anything else. However, God gave us the family as a practical analogy. God designed the family to exist in unity and love for one another. Though our families' love and harmony may be imperfect, the relationship between God, Jesus, and the Holy Spirit is a perfect example for us to live by.

MEDITATE Write out this week's verse below as you spend time committing them to memory.

ENGAGE

Praise God for being the Father, the Son, and the Spirit. Confess that you do not fully understand His triune nature. Thank Him for providing everything that you need to love and obey Him. Ask Him to give you an understanding of His nature so you may fully love and trust Him. We pray to God the Father, through the Son, by the Spirit.

Week 02 • Day 02

THE TRI-UNITY OF GOD

EXERCISE

READ *John 17:1-26, Matthew 28:19*

1. How does Jesus' prayer in John 17 apply to His disciples today? Explain.

_____

_____

_____

2. Matthew 28:19 tells us to make disciples of all nations, baptizing them in the name (one, singular name) of the Father, the Son, and the Holy Spirit. How can one name include three different persons? ▼

_____

_____

_____

The human mind is not able to fully understand the tri-unity of God fully. The concept of someone simultaneously and eternally existing in three separate persons while simultaneously and eternally existing in one perfectly unified essence is not within human comprehension. However, Jesus reveals many essential truths that point us to a true understanding of God's tri-unity.

When asked to present evidence of the tri-unity of God in the text of Scripture, some may point to using plural pronouns in reference to God. For example, in Genesis 1:26a, *"Let us make man in our image"* (Genesis 1:26, 11:7; Isaiah 6:8).

The common Hebrew usage of the "plural of majesty," however, suggests that these examples should be used with caution.

Better textual evidence for God's tri-unity comes from passages like the Great Commission and the High Priestly Prayer of Jesus. In Matthew 28:19 (the Great Commission), God is referred to as three distinct persons—the Father, the Son, and the Holy Spirit (see also 2 Corinthians 13:14; John 15:26). In John 17 (The High Priestly Prayer), Jesus (the Son) is praying to God (the Father). The High Priestly Prayer is the longest-recorded prayer in all Scripture. Throughout this prayer, Jesus repeatedly reveals aspects of God's tri-unity. God sent Jesus and gave Him all authority (John 17:2, 3, 7, 8, 18). Jesus glorified the Father on earth by accomplishing the work that God the Father had given Him (John 17:4). The Father glorified Jesus with the glory they shared before the world's creation (John 17:5, 10, 22, 24). God and Jesus are one (John 17:11, 21, 22, 23). Jesus gave the disciples the Father's Word (John 17:14). God the Father loved Jesus, His Son, before the foundation of the world (John 17:23, 24, 26).

> "The grace of the Lord Jesus Christ, and the love of God, and the fellowship of the Holy Spirit, be with you all."
>
> *2 Corinthians 13:14*

Some tend to think of the Holy Spirit as a thing or a power, Scripture clearly and frequently affirms the Holy Spirit's personhood. As a distinct person, the Holy Spirit teaches (John 14:26), testifies (Romans 8:16), intercedes (Romans 8:16), knows (1 Corinthians 2:11), speaks (Acts 8:29), and is grieved (Ephesians 4:30). God the Father, Jesus the Son, and the Holy Spirit are three persons, and each person is fully God. God the Father is fully God (Genesis 1:1; Matthew 6:26, 30). God the Son is fully God (Philippians 2:5-11; Titus 2:13; John 1:1-3; 8:58; 20:28). God the Spirit is fully God (Acts 5:3-4; Psalm 139:7-8; 1 Corinthians 2:10-11).

THE TRUTH

1. Using Genesis 1:1, Matthew 6:26, and Matthew 6:30, list evidence below that the Father is fully God.

_____
_____
_____

2. Using Philippians 2:5-11, John 1:1-3, and John 20:28, list evidence below that the Son is fully God.

_____
_____
_____

3. Using Acts 5:3-4, Psalm 139:7-9, and 1 Corinthians 2:10-11, list evidence below that the Holy Spirit is fully God.

_____
_____
_____

MEDITATE Fill in the blanks as you continue committing this week's verse to memory.

"The _____ of the Lord Jesus Christ, and the love of God, and the _____ of the Holy Spirit, be with you all."

2 Corinthians 13:14

ENGAGE

Praise God for being all-knowing. Confess that you are not all-knowing and be honest about your struggle to understand the things of God. Thank Him for His revelation through the Spirit. Ask God to help you rely on the Spirit for truth as you study His Word. As He grows your understanding of His triune nature, ask Him to allow your heart to overflow with adoration toward His goodness.

Week 02 • Day 03

THE TRI-UNITY OF GOD

EXERCISE

READ *Deuteronomy 6:4-10, Matthew 3:13-17*

1. Deuteronomy 6:4 says, "the LORD is one!" The Israelites lived in a time when the people around them were polytheistic (believed in many gods). The concept of a singular God was counter-cultural. Why do you think this was important to know before hearing the commands that followed? Use 1 Corinthians 8:4-6 as a cross-reference.

_____
_____
_____

2. Read Matthew 3:13-17. In your own words, explain what happened to Jesus after His baptism in reference to the tri-unity of God. ▼

_____
_____
_____

Few Bible students will take issue with the tri-unity of God demonstrated in Matthew 3:13-17. The Holy Spirit set upon Jesus as a dove as the voice of God the Father resounded from the heavens. When Matthew 3 is contrasted against texts such as Deuteronomy 6:4, "The LORD is our God, the LORD is one," we find ourselves conflicted. It boggles the mind to think of God as three persons but also only as one God.

Last week, we read how God communicated His plan to provide for His people through a burning bush (Exodus 3:2-5). God would later lead them through the desert as a pillar of cloud by day and fire by night (Exodus 13:21-22). The existence of a pillar of cloud that was unaffected by thermal drafts or a fire that burned without fuel defied the laws of physics. In the attempt to grasp the triune nature of God, many feel like they have no other option but to deny God's existence or compromise sound doctrine. The correct response to such a mystery is to accept by faith that there is none like God (Deuteronomy 33:26).

From a human perspective, the tri-unity of God is either a contradiction, paradox, or mystery.

> - God is three persons.
> - Each person of God is fully God.
> - There is only one God.

Those who wish to define a comprehensive knowledge of God's tri-unity will often compromise at least one of the foundational truths above. Such compromises lead to 1) the denial of the full divinity of one or all the persons of the Trinity, 2) the denial of the perfect unity of God, or 3) the equally false conclusion that there is more than one God. From the perspective of a Christ follower, the tri-unity of God is a mystery that cannot be fully understood.

God the Father, God the Son, and God the Holy Spirit are equal in their attributes but distinct in their relationship to one another and to us. God is our creator, Jesus is our rescuer, and the Holy Spirit is our helper. Our salvation is secure because Father, Son, and Spirit are one. Each of them is worthy of our worship and affection.

> **"**
> After being baptized, Jesus came up immediately from the water; and behold, the heavens were opened, and he saw the Spirit of God descending as a dove and lighting on Him."
>
> *Matthew 3:16*

THE TRUTH

1. What does the perfect unity and love of the Father, Son, and the Spirit demonstrate for us as followers of Christ and disciple-makers?

_____
_____
_____

2. How have you personally experienced the reward of God the Father, Jesus, and the Holy Spirit?

_____
_____
_____

3. What questions or hang-ups do you have about the Tri-unity of God? List them below and ask God for clarity. Trust that He will provide understanding in His timing. ▼

_____
_____
_____

WEEK 2

MEDITATE — Fill in the blanks as you continue committing this week's verse to memory.

> "The _____ of the Lord Jesus Christ, and the _____ of God, and the _____ of the _____, be with you all."
>
> *2 Corinthians 13:14*

ENGAGE

Praise God for His good and perfect character. Confess that you are not deserving of His mercy and grace. Thank Him for rescuing you anyway. Ask Him to give you abundant wisdom, goodness, and love so that you may be more like Him.

THE TRUTH

Week 02 • Day 04
THE TRI-UNITY OF GOD

EXAMINATION

READ
Psalm 19:1-8

WATCH
Week 2 - The Tri-unity of God

To watch the video, scan the QR code below by opening your phone's camera and holding your device so that the QR code appears on the screen. Click the link associated with the QR code, and choose this week's video. https://qrco.de/be3SWs

1. What does it look like for you to accept that aspects of God will remain a mystery while continuing to pursue knowledge and understanding of who He is?

_____
_____
_____

2. In what practical ways can you pursue oneness within your local church? ⏵

_____
_____
_____

EXERCISE

READ *Psalm 19:1-8*

The unique intricacies of the universe bear witness to the God who created it. His perfection and harmony are witnessed throughout His creation. The sheer amount of data in your DNA and the invisible gravitational forces holding celestial bodies in orbit are but a few examples of God's power and perfection. Psalm 19 points to creation, declaring it the work of God's hands. As we grapple with understanding the complexity of God's character and nature, we trust Him for revelation. He has revealed Himself in His Word and in His creation. God provides the insights that believers need to trust and obey Him. For us, these insights do not include every answer to every question but are sufficient to know and love Him. All we know of God is known because He revealed it to us. "For since the creation of the world His invisible attributes, His eternal power and divine nature, have been clearly seen, being understood through what has been made, so that they are without excuse" (Romans 1:20). There's no excuse for non-belief in our lives. We believe in God's revelation about Himself through creation and His Word, and we are to pursue a life fully submitted to our great, good, and triune God.

MEDITATE Below, attempt to write out this week's verse from memory.

ENGAGE

Praise God for His character displayed through creation. Confess the ways that you overlook His presence and power in the world that He made. Thank Him for making Himself known to you.

Week 02 • Day 05

THE TRI-UNITY OF GOD

EXERCISE

READ *John 17:11*

God the Father, the Son, and the Holy Spirit existed in perfect unity before the world's creation. In John 17:11, Jesus asked the Father to keep His disciples in His name so they could share in His love. Maintaining unity with God and among believers is no easy task. First John 5:19 tells us, "We know that we are of God and that the whole world lies in the power of the evil one." Our adversary wants to cause disagreement between believers. We can see the effects of the enemy's attacks through the division and discord within some local church bodies.

Jesus encourages us in John 16:33 with these powerful words: "These things I have spoken to you, so that in Me you may have peace. In the world, you have tribulation, but take courage; I have overcome the world." We were created in the image of the triune God, and the unity that reflects His nature is essential in His church. We are diverse people with distinct functions but are all a part of the same body (1 Corinthians 12:12-13). When the church functions as Jesus designed, we witness a limited reflection of God's unity. An awareness of the efficiency and effectiveness of a diverse and unified church lends to the worship of God. The Church should strive to be of the same mind and judgment (1 Corinthians 1:10).

> "For even as the body is one and yet has many members of the body, though they are many, are one body, so also is Christ."
>
> *1 Corinthians 12:12*

EXAMPLE

Reading this, some will have struggled with the example on day one of this week, as they faced the hurt of an unhealthy or divided family. The enemy's attacks on the family have significantly injured our culture and congregations. Thankfully, we serve the God of resurrection. There is nothing He cannot heal.

Even if you do not have a single good family memory or moment to help you better understand the perfect unity and love of God's triune nature, you do have the Church. Like the biological family, the church family is not perfect. Too many followers of Christ acknowledge their failings yet still expect the local church to be flawless. Jesus tells us that the Church, as He designed it, should be defined by its unity and love for one another (John 13:35). As you study the Trinity, do not miss out on the lessons of unity, love, and service that God is modeling for us.

MEDITATE Practice reciting this week's verse from memory and be prepared to say them aloud to your d-group.

ENGAGE

Praise God for being unified with the Son and the Holy Spirit. Confess your struggle with being "of the same mind" as other believers. Thank God He allowed Jesus to enter our world and overcome the world. Ask Him to help you live in unity with other believers and to look to Jesus for conviction, example, and encouragement when you feel proud, divisive, or lonely.

THE TRUTH

ENCOURAGE
Accountability

Use this checklist as a guide for your weekly d-group time. Refer to the discipler's guide at the front of the book for more encouragement and practical advice.

- Work through questions from the accountability page.

- Spend time praying specifics for one another.

- Take turns reciting the memory verses.

- Discuss answers to the questions throughout the week that are marked with this symbol. ▼

PRAYER REQUESTS

_____
_____
_____
_____
_____
_____

ACCOUNTABILITY QUESTIONS

These questions are to be asked of one another in a spirit of accountability (Proverbs 27:17). They are intended to stimulate conversations of character and confession of sin in a safe environment that values honesty, vulnerability, confidentiality, and grace.

1. Have you spent quality time in your spiritual disciplines this week?
2. Have you taken advantage of opportunities to share your faith this week? Explain.
3. Have your words and actions been a good testimony this week to the gospel of Jesus?
4. Have your thoughts and speech been pure (cussing, criticism, negativity, etc.)?
5. Have you been sexually pure this week? Have you been exposed to sexually alluring material? (For those who are married: Have you prioritized quality romantic time with your spouse?)
6. Have you been a good steward of your finances? Have you lacked integrity in the handling of your finances?
7. Have you been honoring and generous in your meaningful relationships this week (Family, friends, etc.)?
8. Have you given in to any addictive behavior this past week? Explain.
9. Have you been completely honest with me?

I'm praying for the salvation of the following two people and prayerfully considering how to share Christ with them myself: _____

> "Therefore, confess your sins to one another, and pray for one another, so that you may be healed."
>
> *James 5:16a*

Week 03 • Day 01

MADE IN GOD'S IMAGE

ESSENTIAL TRUTH

Humans were specially created by God to bring Him glory as His image bearers. Functionally, this means that God's image is found in our relationships with each other and in our representation of God's kingdom. Essentially, this also means that God's image is bound to the complexity of the two unified parts of our nature, one material (body) and one immaterial (soul/spirit).

1. Read the Essential Truth, identify two phrases that stand out to you, and write them below. Why do you believe these phrases are significant?

_____
_____
_____

2. In your own words, describe what it means to be created in the image of God.

_____
_____
_____

3. Why is it important to identify and acknowledge that all people are created in the image of God?

_____
_____
_____

EXERCISE (memory verse)

> God created man in His own image, in the image of God He created him; male and female He created them."
>
> *Genesis 1:27*

God eternally exists in perfect relational harmony as God the Father, God the Son, and God the Spirit. God created humanity in His image and invites each of us into a similar relational harmony with Himself (John 17:11, 21). God is not dependent on humanity to be who He is. He created us to be dependent on Him. He created us to be in a relationship with Himself and to reflect His image in our other relationships, and to glorify Himself through everything we are and do. We find our identity and purpose as humans in representing God's kingdom interests (Genesis 1:26) and in our relationships with one another (Genesis 1:27).

All men and women are made in His image in this way (relationship and representation). With that said, God creates each of us with distinct characteristics, gifts, and roles—all of which are intended in holiness to reflect God's own diversity and complexity. God is not made in our image. We are made in His image. We are finite, but He is infinite. We are limited, but He is all-powerful. While we cannot reflect His greatness—His eternal, all-knowing, everywhere present, unchanging nature—we can reflect facets of His goodness. God is kind, gentle, wise, holy, and merciful. As His creation, we can represent Him in the world by reflecting these attributes in varying degrees (2 Corinthians 3:18).

> But we all, with unveiled face, beholding as in a mirror the glory of the Lord, are being transformed into the same image from glory to glory, just as from the Lord, the Spirit."
>
> *2 Corinthians 3:18*

EXAMPLE

Just at the break of dawn, golden rays of light peaked over the towering sheer granite walls of Yosemite. The green forests still in the shadows contrast against all the light touches. As the darkness gave way to sunrise, this famous scene's depth and detail were gradually revealed.

With the press of a button, a moment never to repeat is captured when the camera shutter opens and closes. The term photography is based on two Greek words, loosely defined as drawing or painting with light. Like the human eye, a camera captures light reflecting off objects. As such, the details and colors you would see in this magnificent sunrise are little more than a complex series of reflections.

As those specially created in God's image, we reflect the light of His image. Even those who are lost and far from God continue to reflect His image in some measure. As followers of Jesus, God is at work progressively restoring what sin distorted and defaced in our lives. With each pass of the sander and rotation of the polishing wheel, a disciple of Jesus steadily becomes a better reflection of God's image.

MEDITATE Write out this week's verse below as you spend time committing them to memory.

ENGAGE

Praise God for who He is – your Father and Creator. Confess how you struggle at times to remember, or even believe, that your identity is to be an image bearer of God. Thank Him for His love and kindness. Thank Him for bringing you into His perfect love and unity. Ask God to help you better understand who He created you to be.

Week 03 • Day 02

MADE IN GOD'S IMAGE

EXERCISE

READ *Genesis 1:24-31 and Psalm 8*

1. In Genesis 1:24-31, note the distinctions made in the text between the creation of living creatures (vv. 24-25) and the creation of human beings (vv. 26-30). What do you see as repeated or contrasted?

_____
_____
_____

2. What does Psalm 8 teach us about God's greatness and goodness? ⏷

_____
_____
_____

Humans have gazed at the heavens and questioned our value and purpose since the first sin in the Garden of Eden. The "atheist" says there is no god, identifying humanity as little more than an animal with only a self-defined purpose (Psalms 14:1). The typical "theist" will minimally affirm that "a god" or "gods" created humankind and that one's value cannot be ascertained with much certainty. Christ's followers maintain that God has created all humanity in His own image (Genesis 1:27; 1 Corinthians 11:7), and He offers both to rescue them by His grace alone (Ephesians 2:8-9; Romans 11:6) and progressively restore them to His image as they grow in Christlikeness (Philippians 1:6; 2 Corinthians 3:18; 1 Peter 1:16). The

Bible stands as the singular witness of God's great rescue plan to restore what sin has distorted (Colossians 3:10; Romans 12:2; Titus 3:5). Though God created us in His image, the presence of sin twisted that image. The birth, life, and death of Jesus were necessary to restore the image of God in those He rescues by His grace.

The restorative effects of Jesus' work of redemption and sanctification can be witnessed in the transformed lives of His followers (2 Corinthians 5:17). Every disciple of Jesus is in the process of sanctification. Unlike us, Jesus is the only person to represent the image of God fully and truly (Hebrew 1:3; John 5:19). Every human is still an image bearer of God and is worthy of honor and respect. Both the loving sacrifice of a parent and the artist's creativity display moderate expressions of God's universal image stamped on every human (Acts 17:28).

Today's reading in Genesis affirms the value of every conceived human life (Jeremiah 1:5). After creating the flora and fauna of the world, God acknowledged that "it was good" (Genesis 1:25b). After creating the first humans, He proclaimed His work was "very good" (Genesis 1:31a). This again affirms that every person has value because ALL are created in the image of God (Ephesians 2:10; Galatians 3:28).

Psalm 8 is a song of praise that begins and ends with "O LORD, our Lord, how majestic is your name in all the earth!" (Psalm 8:1,9). God's glory is on display throughout all of creation. We see the moon and stars, the oceans and mountains, and we remember the greatness of our Creator. How wonderful are His works! Then we look at humankind—the specific creation He allows to bear His image. The sin that has infiltrated our hearts and world is not a reflection of our Father. He is holy, undefiled, and separated from sinners (Hebrews 7:26). Instead of leaving us separated from Himself, God "cares" for us enough to provide a way of salvation and restoration (Psalm 8:4-5).

We should not become overwhelmed by the brokenness of the world. Instead, we should see those places of brokenness as opportunities to tell people the good news of what Jesus has done to restore their relationship to their Creator (James 3:7-9). As we grow in understanding through God's Word, we should be compelled to love people as He has loved us. God's universal stamp of His image and God's universal offer of salvation should influence us to see others and ourselves with great value (Romans 5:8; Luke 12:6-7).

THE TRUTH

1. How should the understanding that you were uniquely and exclusively created to bear God's image influence how you spend your life?

___

2. Is the title "image bearer" given to all people or only to believers? How does this universal reality affect the way that you treat non-believers?

___

3. Upon reception of God's universal gift of salvation, God begins the process of restoring His image in a believer—an image previously distorted by sin. In what ways have you seen God's image progressively restored in your life? ▼

___

MEDITATE   Fill in the blanks as you continue committing this week's verse to memory.

> God _____ man in His own image, in the image of God He created _____ ; male and female He created them."

Genesis 1:27

ENGAGE

Praise God for His majesty, supreme greatness, authority, and sovereignty. Confess how you might devalue others because you struggle to see God's image in them. Thank God for how He has begun to restore the parts of His image that sin previously distorted in you. Ask Him to open your eyes to the people around you in order that you may see them as His "image bearers" and treat them with honor and dignity. Trust God to help you see their places of brokenness as opportunities for you to tell them the good news of what Jesus has done to restore their relationship to their Creator.

Week 03 • Day 03

MADE IN GOD'S IMAGE

EXERCISE

READ *Galatians 3:26-29*

1. Through faith in Christ, we become sons of God (v. 26). What does it mean to "have clothed" ourselves with Christ (v. 27)? How is this one-time shift in identity at the point of salvation different from the progressive encouragements in Ephesians 4:22-24 and Colossians 3:9-10 to "put off the old" and "put on the new"?

_____
_____
_____

2. Read Romans 10:12-15. How does understanding that there is "no distinction" between people and that the same Lord is "Lord of all" (v. 12) affect how you respond to the remaining verses of that passage?

_____
_____
_____

Humanity is created in God's image, but we should not assume that God Himself is limited by physical form and environments (John 4:24). Being created in the image of God implies that our "best moments" can demonstrate aspects of God's goodness in all areas, material and nonmaterial (Romans 13:10; Romans 12:1-2). The desire for musicians to write music, carpenters to build, doctors to heal, and first responders to give aid are examples of God's image reasonably showing through His creation.

The knowledge that as a disciple of Jesus you are a son or daughter of God created in His image should inspire you to become a better representation of Him (2 Peter 3:18). Mirroring the goodness of God through daily life and speech is the reflection of God's "light" that is often referred to in Scripture (Matthew 5:14-16; Ephesians 5:8). Just as every disciple of Jesus is especially gifted and called to be an individual member of the body of Christ (1 Corinthians 12:12-31), every disciple of Jesus will reflect God's image in different ways.

As seen in today's reading, acknowledging that all humanity is created in the image of God is a biblical standard for the Church to oppose beliefs or behaviors that devalue human life (Galatians 3:28). Many of the great controversies of our day are informed by such a foundational truth. Human ethical errors in such areas as abortion, euthanasia, racism, gender fluidity, and sexual exploitation each revolve around lessening a person. In the case of abortion, one argument is that the baby (fetus) is not yet a person. The moral discussion on racism, sexual exploitation, and euthanasia revolves around devaluing the person's humanity. Believing that a person of a different gender, age, nationality, or physical appearance is a lesser person becomes the threshold for justifying exploitation. The sinful desire to be our own god requires the undervaluing of others (1 John 2:16).

1. Honestly evaluate your heart. Do you devalue any type of person? Explain.

_____

_____

_____

2. How does understanding God's image motivate you to change how you think or act towards people different from you?

_____

_____

_____

3. When you see the image of God in every person—regardless of age, gender, race, life choices, or circumstances—treat them with value and honor. How can this relational default perspective help you to obey the Great Commission (Matthew 28:19-20)?

_____

_____

_____

MEDITATE Fill in the blanks as you continue committing this week's verse to memory.

"God _____ man in His own _____, in the image of God He created him; male and female He _____ them."

Genesis 1:27

ENGAGE

Praise God for being Creator. Confess your missed opportunities to honor Him in how you perceive and treat others. Thank God for making Himself known through everything He created, for choosing to give humanity His image, and for creating you to be you. Ask Him to provide you with a proper understanding of who He is, who you are, and who He is creating you to be. Pray for the passion to love Him and His people from the overflow of that knowledge.

Week 03 • Day 04

MADE IN GOD'S IMAGE

EXAMINATION

READ
Psalm 8

WATCH
Week 3 - Made in God's Image

To watch the video, scan the QR code below by opening your phone's camera and holding your device so that the QR code appears on the screen. Click the link associated with the QR code, and choose this week's video. https://qrco.de/be3SWs

1. Like the Rembrandt painting, sin muddies the image of God in us. But, despite our sinful nature, God sees the masterpiece in us first. How does this understanding of all humans as God's masterpieces affect the way that you think about and treat yourself and others?

_____
_____
_____

2. How is God working in your heart and mind today to transform you into the image of His Son? ▼

_____
_____
_____

3. To be made in the image of God means that we are enabled to love God and love people. In what specific ways do you need to turn from sin and look to Jesus' example for how you are to love God and others? ▼

_____
_____
_____

EXERCISE

READ *Psalm 8*

God in His greatness, created the world and everything in it, and it all reflects His magnificence. In His goodness, He cares intimately about His creation. He is not just mindful of mankind, but He cares for them. He has crowned people with glory and honor and has given them authority over the rest of His creation. We marvel at the character of God that we see in how He creates, loves, and values people made in His image. As we sing this Psalm, praising God for who He is, we understand more of who we are. We see the place of privilege that God has gifted to people, and how that gives us identity, value, and purpose. We look around and see that our family, neighbors, co-workers, and all people everywhere are gifted with this identity. With each person being made in the image of a great and good God, they are worthy of our value, love, and care.

WEEK 3

MEDITATE — Write out this week's verse below as you spend time committing them to memory.

ENGAGE

Praise God for His majestic name made known to all the earth (Psalm 8:1). Confess the ways that you do not reflect the value placed on your identity and the identity of others. Thank God for giving you an identity, a position, and a purpose. Ask Him to help you honor Him with your life and reflect His goodness towards the people around you.

Week 03 • Day 05

MADE IN GOD'S IMAGE

EXERCISE

READ *Psalm 139:14*

Aware of our struggles and shortcomings, it is easy to see the negatives in ourselves. Most of us relate well to Paul's conflict with his sinful nature in Romans 7, where he states, "the good that I want, I do not do, but I practice the very evil that I do not want" (Romans 7:19). Concentrating solely on the sins and struggles of life, you will undoubtedly become discouraged. Some disregard God's calling because they do not believe He can use them. Within the belief that they are unworthy of His love, some will cease to acknowledge the truth of His Word. In understanding that you are an "image bearer," your eyes shift from yourself to your Creator.

EXAMPLE

Photography allows us to capture images of life seemingly frozen in time. Through this medium, we can view the emotion and magnitude of a moment that we often overlook. There is an undeniable expression of love in the gaze of parents holding their newborn child for the first time. Words cannot convey a father's joy as he walks his daughter down the aisle toward her groom. Where words are lacking, a picture can capture the gambit of complex emotions.

These moments range from the wide eyes of a child excited by the grandeur of Christmas morning. Such images demonstrate that we are made in the image of God. These brief moments are a reminder that God is the absolute definition of good. In our lives, these moments of purity are sadly fleeting. In contrast, God's unchanging and eternal character is defined by this and so much more.

MEDITATE Practice reciting this week's verse from memory and be prepared to say them aloud to your d-group.

ENGAGE

Praise God for being unified with the Son and the Holy Spirit. Confess your struggle with being "of the same mind" as other believers. Thank God He allowed Jesus to enter our world and overcome the world. Ask Him to help you live in unity with other believers and to look to Jesus for conviction, example, and encouragement when you feel proud, divisive, or lonely.

THE TRUTH

ENCOURAGE
Accountability

Use this checklist as a guide for your weekly d-group time. Refer to the discipler's note at the front of the book for more encouragement and practical advice.

- Work through questions from the accountability page.
- Spend time praying specifics for one another.
- Take turns reciting memory verses.
- Discuss answers to the questions throughout the week that are marked with this symbol. ▼

PRAYER REQUESTS

_____
_____
_____
_____
_____
_____
_____

ACCOUNTABILITY QUESTIONS

These questions are to be asked of one another in a spirit of accountability (Proverbs 27:17). They are intended to stimulate conversations of character and confession of sin in a safe environment that values honesty, vulnerability, confidentiality, and grace.

1. Have you spent quality time in your spiritual disciplines this week?

2. Have you taken advantage of opportunities to share your faith this week? Explain.

3. Have your words and actions been a good testimony this week to the gospel of Jesus?

4. Have your thoughts and speech been pure (cussing, criticism, negativity, etc.)?

5. Have you been sexually pure this week? Have you been exposed to sexually alluring material? (For those who are married: Have you prioritized quality romantic time with your spouse?)

6. Have you been a good steward of your finances? Have you lacked integrity in the handling of your finances?

7. Have you been honoring and generous in your meaningful relationships this week (Family, friends, etc.)?

8. Have you given in to any addictive behavior this past week? Explain.

9. Have you been completely honest with me?

I'm praying for the salvation of the following two people and prayerfully considering how to share Christ with them myself: _____

> "Therefore, confess your sins to one another, and pray for one another, so that you may be healed."
>
> *James 5:16a*

Week 04 • Day 01
SIN

ESSENTIAL TRUTH

Even though humans are created in God's image, that image has been distorted by the guilt and corruption of sin (sin nature). The various sins (plural) of humanity expressed in actions, thoughts, and attitudes come from this rebellious human sin (singular) nature. In Christ, believers have full forgiveness from the penalty of sin, progressive release from the power of sin, and eventual removal from the presence of sin in heaven.

1. Read the Essential Truth, identify two phrases that stand out to you, and write them below. Why do you believe these phrases are significant?

_____
_____
_____

2. In your own words, give a personal definition of the word "sin."

_____
_____
_____

3. Why is it important to understand what sin is, how sin affects us, and the consequences of sin?

_____
_____
_____

3. Why is it important to understand what sin is, how sin affects us, and the consequences of sin? ▾

_____
_____
_____

EXERCISE `memory verse`

> "For all have sinned and fall short of the glory of God."
>
> *Romans 3:23*

Understanding and acknowledging sin is essential for both salvation and sanctification. Without acknowledging sin, we cannot understand the penalty of our transgressions and the high cost of redemption. If we do not grasp how sin continues to infiltrate our hearts and minds, we will not trust God for the progressive release from its power and the eventual removal of its presence. First John 1:8-10 states, "If we say that we have no sin, we are deceiving ourselves and the truth is not in us. If we confess our sins, He is faithful and just to forgive us our sins and to cleanse us from all unrighteousness. If we say that we have not sinned, we make Him a liar and His Word is not in us." Everyone is affected by sin and requires redemption and reconciliation. The saving grace of Jesus is our only hope.

EXAMPLE

The sad story of those who would later be known as Radium Girls occurred in the early 19th century. Radium Girls were women who were employed by watch manufacturers and spent countless hours using radium to paint the meticulous details and hands of luxury wristwatches. Radium was a seemingly miraculous, self-illuminating paint that incredibly allowed watch faces to glow. The practice of using radium in wristwatches went on for several decades.

Eventually it was discovered that the amazing glow of radium was caused by radiation. Thousands of Radium Girls spent years exposed to the invisible and toxic properties of radium, leading to radiation poisoning. Assured by their employers that radium was safe, some workers regularly painted their nails and even their teeth with this deadly compound.

Only later in life did the deforming and destructive effects of this low-dose, gradual radiation poisoning become apparent. In many ways, the effects of sin in our lives and those around us are like those of radium. The world has assured us that sin is harmless, yet this assurance is a lie. Like radium, the toxicity of sin is not always visible at first. The poison of sin has affected each of us to the point of deformity (poor image bearer of God) and gradual death (wages of sin).

MEDITATE Write out this week's verse below as you spend time committing them to memory.

ENGAGE

Praise God for His right precepts and pure commandments (Psalm 19:8). Confess your brokenness and sinfulness apart from Christ. Thank Him for loving you, even when you were dead in your transgressions (Ephesians 2:4-5). Express your faith in God that He can set you free from the sins that most easily entangle your heart. Ask God to enlighten your eyes and give your heart joy through His Word.

Week 04 • Day 02

SIN

EXERCISE

READ *Genesis 2:16-18; 3:1-13*

1. In your own words, what is the command from God in Genesis 2:16-18 and the lie from the serpent in 3:4-5?

_____
_____
_____

2. According to Genesis 3:6, what were the three motives of Eve that led her to disobey God? ⌄

_____
_____
_____

Fundamentally, sin directly disagrees with God's perfect nature. God can neither sin nor be tempted by evil (James 1:13) because He is perfect in His absolute goodness and holiness (James 1:17; Deuteronomy 32:4; Habakkuk 1:13). Although God created everything (John 1:3; Colossians 1:16), sin is not a created thing. Rather sin is any thought, action, or attitude directly opposing God's perfect nature. Ephesians 1:11 says God "works all things according to the counsel of His will." Thus, God did not create sin. The option to defy God only exists because He gave His creation an alternative to worship something or someone other than Himself (Romans 1:18-23; 3:10-18).

In His infinite wisdom and knowledge, God did not create us to be enslaved people or robots. He created us to be with Him forever as lovers of God. In Genesis 2, God set the stage for the "Great Romance" by creating a garden environment that fulfilled Adam's physical needs. God gave Adam the single command to not eat from the tree of the knowledge of good and evil (Genesis 2:17). God also gave Adam and Eve the freedom to choose to obey or disobey His command. Eating from the forbidden tree expressed their defiance, and they willfully chose the temptation of being like a god over the gift of being with God.

In Genesis 3:5, the serpent tempted Adam and Eve to exercise their choice to turn from God and control their lives as if they themselves were gods. Satan knew what he was doing because sin was present in the angelic world before the disobedience of Adam and Eve (Isaiah 14:12-15; Luke 10:18). Today's reading in Genesis 3 outlines the progression of sin still present in our lives. The same action verbs play out in our lives as we sin daily. Eve saw, desired, took, ate, and then shared. Rarely is a sin committed alone, and all sin harms us and those around us. In choosing to disobey God, Adam and Eve chose to sin. Sin entered creation through one man, forever corrupting all humanity with both the guilt of sin and an inherited sinful nature (Romans 5:12-21; Ephesians 2:3; Psalms 51:1-5).

1. Before you had a saving relationship with Jesus, how did you exercise your freedom to obey or disobey God's commandments? How has that changed as a follower of Jesus?

_____

_____

_____

2. Based on the motives that led Eve to disobey God, how are you tempted similarly in your daily life?

_____
_____
_____

3. In what ways have you experienced the effects of those around you who are walking in sin? How might your sin have affected others through different seasons of your life?

_____
_____
_____

MEDITATE Fill in the blanks as you continue committing this week's verse to memory.

" For all have _____ and fall short of the glory of God."

Romans 3:23

ENGAGE

Praise God for being holy and righteous (Psalm 11:7; 99:5). Confess the specific sin struggles of your thoughts, actions, and attitudes toward Him. Thank Him for using His Word and the Holy Spirit to convict you of sin and allow you to become more like Him. Ask Him to make you holy as He is holy *(1 Peter 1:15-16)*.

Week 04 • Day 03

SIN

EXERCISE

READ *Genesis 3:20-4:8*

1. Restate in your own words the warning that the Lord gave Cain regarding sin in Genesis 4:7.

_____

_____

_____

2. Cain did not rule over his sin but killed his brother instead (Genesis 4:8). Working through Genesis 4:1-8, note the specific circumstances that tempted Cain and how he responded to them.

_____

_____

_____

The Word of God is the foundation for understanding sin. We are commanded to have no other gods (Exodus 20:3). This command appears simple until we realize how easily we turn even good things into idols. The Ten Commandments also tell us that murder is a sin (Exodus 20:13), but Jesus rightly proclaims that murder begins in the heart as anger (Matthew 5:21). Sin starts in the heart. This is true in the story of Eve's sin in the garden and David's sin with Bathsheba. Eve desired the fruit, and David desired Bathsheba (Genesis 3:6; 2 Samuel 11:2). They saw, desired, took, and partook.

Even though all sin is destructive, God is the creator and sustainer of all good things (Psalm 104). God is the source of all life and goodness (James 1:17). But when we choose to sin, we choose death and evil (3 John 1:11). In this sense, the choosing of sin then proves to be quite poisonous. Think of sin as a drop of cyanide in a bottle of water. Even the smallest drop of poison pollutes the entire vessel. No matter how hard we try to eliminate the poison, we cannot make the water pure again. Similarly, we cannot get rid of sin ourselves. We cannot hide or justify our sin. Consequently, like Adam and Eve, we can do little more than cover ourselves with fig leaves (Genesis 3:7).

Here is the summary: everyone has been corrupted by the guilt of sin, and everyone sins (Romans 3:23; 5:12). We all have sinned (past tense), and we all fall short of God's standards (present tense). As a result, the proper punishment for our sin is death—eternal separation from God (Romans 6:23; 2 Thessalonians 1:9). When we use phrases such as "little white lies" or "I'm just human," we demonstrate just how common sin is in our daily lives. The size of the sin proves not as important as the wounded party of the sin. Which of the following proves to be the greater violation: striking a friend, a police officer, or the ruler of a nation?

> For all have sinned and fall short of the glory of God."
>
> *Romans 3:23*

The punishment must consider the elevated status of the violated party. Believing in God's divine righteousness, all sin deserves divine punishment. The rescue plan takes this dynamic into account as well. The full atonement for a single sin would still require the sinless birth, life, ministry, death, and resurrection of Jesus Christ (1 Corinthians 15:3-4). Every sin equates to death and eternal separation from God, but every sin can be forgiven through Jesus (Romans 5:20; 1 John 1:9). Of course, the rescue plan of Jesus goes far beyond mere forgiveness of our "sins" to the washing of our "sin"—our sin nature. Jesus also has the power to clean the poison out of our bottles. This is not just grace—this is amazing grace.

1. How have you seen sin progress in your life?

_____

_____

2. If Cain had obeyed the Lord's warning in Genesis 4:7, how would verse 8 have been different? How does knowing the power of sin affect your attitude and how you think and act in difficult circumstances?

_____
_____
_____

3. Is there something you need to confess to the Lord now so that it does not become more destructive in your life or the lives around you? Where do you need repentance (change of thinking and action) today? ▼

_____
_____
_____

MEDITATE   Fill in the blanks as you continue committing this week's verse to memory.

" For all have _____ and fall short of the _____ of God."

Romans 2:23

ENGAGE

Praise God for being the author and perfecter of our faith (Hebrews 12:2). Search your heart for any sin that is poisoning you and making you sick. Agree with God about those sins that "easily entangle" your heart (Hebrews 12:1) and confess them to Him. Thank Jesus for His perfect example of endurance. Ask the Holy Spirit to continually use the Word of God to teach, reprove, correct, and train you (2 Timothy 3:16) so that you may run your race with endurance and keep your eyes fixed on Jesus (Hebrews 12:1-2).

Week 04 • Day 04
SIN

EXAMINATION

READ
Psalm 51:1-6

WATCH
Week 4 - Sin

To watch the video, scan the QR code below by opening your phone's camera and holding your device so that the QR code appears on the screen. Click the link associated with the QR code, and choose this week's video. https://qrco.de/be3SWs

1. Now that you know what sin is, what do you do? How do you sin less in life?

_____
_____
_____

2. Like the boy in C.S. Lewis's allegorical story, do you find yourself holding onto sinful parts of your life and personality for fear of losing yourself? What may happen if you allow God to transform those elements of your life?

_____
_____
_____

3. What does it look like to walk with a younger believer and encourage them in their victory over sin?

_____
_____
_____

EXERCISE

READ   *Psalm 51:1-6*

    We often look to the Psalms to understand how to process and communicate our complex emotions and situations with God. We can find rich insight into speaking to God through prayer in the Psalms and can model our prayer lives after those of the Psalmists. In Psalm 51, David confesses his sin to the Lord and cries out for mercy. David was a man that loved the Lord and did what was right in His eyes, but he had sinned against Bathsheba and Uriah. In his sin, he understood his offenses to be against the Lord. His sin had hurt people, but ultimately, it damaged his relationship with the Lord. He now begged God for cleansing, mercy, and wisdom. Our sin hurts people, damages relationships, changes circumstances, and in all things we have sinned against the Lord. In prayer, we confess our sin to Him consistently. Like David, we ask for mercy, cleansing, and wisdom. God has made a way to provide these things to us through Jesus. So, we look for sin in our lives, confess it, turn from it, and trust God in his steadfast love and abundant mercy.

MEDITATE   Below, attempt to write out this week's verse from memory.

ENGAGE

Praise God for His steadfast love and abundant mercy (Psalm 51:1). Confess the ways that you have sinned against people and ultimately sinned against God (Psalm 51:3-4a). Thank God that He is justified in His words and blameless in His judgments (Psalm 51:4b). Ask Him to help you delight in truth as He does, and to give you wisdom (Psalm 51:6).

Week 04 • Day 05
SIN

EXERCISE

READ *1 John 1:7-9*

The Greek word in the Bible for "confess" means "to agree with God"—to say the same thing about your sin that He does. Confession of sin involves acknowledging our sinful condition and need for forgiveness. First John 1:7 says, "If we walk in the light as He Himself is in the light, we have fellowship with one another, and the blood of Jesus His Son cleanses us from all sin." Do not be deceived into believing that you are without sin. God gives us all we need for life and godliness, but you must first agree that you need Him. Without Him, you cannot have life or godliness. Confess your sin to Him who has called you by His glory and excellence for His glory and goodness (2 Peter 1:3). Never forget, God is "faithful and righteous to forgive us our sins and to cleanse us from all unrighteousness" (1 John 1:9).

EXAMPLE

Like the previous example of Radium Girls, many historic artists were gradually poisoned by toxins utilized as paint pigments. Cobalt blue and white lead are two common examples of paint colors created by the oxidation properties of toxic heavy metals. The symptoms of such exposure included tooth loss, digestive issues, hair loss, and excruciating stomach pains. These symptoms explain the origins of the idiom that "art is pain."

Unlike the Radium Girls, many of these artists were aware that they were progressively poisoning themselves. The drive to craft their generation's most prevalent painting caused many to ignore the risks. Sadly, some will try to justify sin as an unfortunate part of their job or as a short-term necessity. Like the artists using paints they know are toxic, too many within the church perceive sin as a necessary evil. The longing for success or a relationship at any cost destroys more than we realize. Sin is toxic to the point of death, and without the saving grace of Christ, it is toxic to the point of eternal death.

MEDITATE   Below, attempt to write out this week's verse from memory.

ENGAGE

Praise God for His righteousness and kindness (Psalm 145:17). Confess how you often dismiss sin without repenting. Thank God that He chose to forgive and cleanse you of all unrighteousness (1 John 1:9).

THE TRUTH

ENCOURAGE
Accountability

Use this checklist as a guide for your weekly d-group time. Refer to the discipler's guide at the front of the book for more encouragement and practical advice.

- Work through questions from the accountability page.
- Spend time praying specifics for one another.
- Take turns reciting the memory verses.
- Discuss answers to the questions throughout the week that are marked with this symbol. ⊙

PRAYER REQUESTS

_____
_____
_____
_____
_____
_____
_____

ACCOUNTABILITY QUESTIONS

These questions are to be asked of one another in a spirit of accountability (Proverbs 27:17). They are intended to stimulate conversations of character and confession of sin in a safe environment that values honesty, vulnerability, confidentiality, and grace.

1. Have you spent quality time in your spiritual disciplines this week?

2. Have you taken advantage of opportunities to share your faith this week? Explain.

3. Have your words and actions been a good testimony this week to the gospel of Jesus?

4. Have your thoughts and speech been pure (cussing, criticism, negativity, etc.)?

5. Have you been sexually pure this week? Have you been exposed to sexually alluring material? (For those who are married: Have you prioritized quality romantic time with your spouse?)

6. Have you been a good steward of your finances? Have you lacked integrity in the handling of your finances?

7. Have you been honoring and generous in your meaningful relationships this week (Family, friends, etc.)?

8. Have you given in to any addictive behavior this past week? Explain.

9. Have you been completely honest with me?

I'm praying for the salvation of the following two people and prayerfully considering how to share Christ with them myself: _____

> "Therefore, confess your sins to one another, and
> pray for one another, so that you may be healed."
>
> *James 5:16a*

Week 05 • Day 01

SALVATION: JUSTIFICATION & REDEMPTION

ESSENTIAL TRUTH

The Bible paints five different pictures of the saving work of Jesus Christ on our behalf (**justification, reconciliation, redemption, propitiation,** and **adoption**).

Biblical **justification** (a legal term) is the gift of God by which sinners are declared righteous before God by no work of their own. This instantaneous legal act of God occurs by grace through faith.

Jesus paid an extremely high **redemption** price (a market term) to set sinners free from their sin. The currency of Jesus Christ's shed blood publicly demonstrated that God is both just and loving.

1. Read the Essential Truth, identify two phrases that stand out to you, and write them below. Why do you believe these phrases are significant?

_____
_____
_____

2. In your own words, give a personal definition of the words "justification" and "redemption."

_____
_____
_____

WEEK 5

3. Why is it important to study and understand your salvation?

_____

_____

_____

EXERCISE memory verse

> "Being justified as a gift by His grace through the redemption which is in Christ Jesus."
>
> *Romans 3:24*

What we believe about our salvation influences every aspect of our lives. Other world religions, like Buddhism, Islam, and Hinduism, share a works-based view of salvation. Those on such a path are left alone to work towards self-deliverance by denying themselves while doing good work and gaining merit. Christianity is entirely different. Christ-followers talk about salvation in the past tense ("I have been justified," "I have been redeemed"). Disciples of Jesus know that there is nothing they can do to earn salvation (Ephesians 2:8). The work of salvation is accomplished fully, finally, and forever by Jesus.

Salvation is a gift received by faith in the work started by Jesus on the cross and completed with His resurrection. Studying these five pictures of salvation over the next three weeks will help support a more biblical view of salvation. The vibrant presentation of salvation in Scripture allows disciple-making disciples numerous access points to view their own deliverance story. As believers, we have an assurance that the work of salvation is finished and personal. Because of Christ and what He's done, we approach life from a position of rest—not work. The follower of Christ fights from victory, not for victory.

EXAMPLE

Imagine you standing before a judge, aware of your guilt and the high cost of the crimes committed. Undeniable testimonies and witness accounts filled the previous days. With each piece of tangible evidence, you gradually became indisputably guilty. The court had listened as the failings of your character were revealed from a witness stand that played host to every person you ever wronged. As each of these accounts disclosed the personal pain and damage your choices inflicted, you began to grasp the severity of your actions. Given the overwhelming evidence, no jury or judge could possibly find you innocent.

It is only within this ominous legal atmosphere that we can begin to understand the depth of biblical justification. Standing before God, the reality of our sin is known in a way we cannot comprehend. Though our guilt is absolute, the saving grace of Jesus allows His disciples to be declared righteous forensically (legally). This righteousness is due to the great work of Jesus through His perfect life, ministry, death, and resurrection (2 Corinthians 5:21).

MEDITATE Write out this week's verse below as you spend time committing them to memory.

ENGAGE

Praise God for being the One who is able. Confess and turn from the tireless labor of attempting to earn God's favor and rest in the hope we have in Christ. Thank God for His work that has saved you fully, finally, and forever. Ask God to shape your thoughts and understanding toward biblical salvation in the next few weeks. Pray that understanding who He is and what He's done reshapes how you think, feel, and act.

THE TRUTH

Week 05 • Day 02

SALVATION: JUSTIFICATION & REDEMPTION

EXERCISE

READ *Romans 3:21-26*

1. Justification as a forensic term (court) means to be declared "not guilty" before God. Who needs justification and why (vv. 22-23)? How does one receive it, and what happens to the record of their sin (vv. 22, 25)?

_____
_____
_____

2. Justification is offered to those who have faith in Jesus. Use verse 24 to finish the phrases below.

   ⓐ As: _____
   ⓑ By: _____
   ⓒ Through: _____

3. What do you learn of God's character in verse 26? Use cross references—Romans 3:30 and 8:3—to support your conclusion.

_____
_____
_____

WEEK 5

It does not require a degree in electrical engineering to turn on a light switch. Though most will never consider the physics involved, understanding the risk of electrocution is essential. Similarly, salvation in Christ does not require a complete understanding of the doctrine of salvation (soteriology; Romans 10:9-13). However, a misunderstanding or false teaching related to salvation can be detrimental (1 Timothy 6:3). In the next three weeks, we will focus on better understanding **the gift** of salvation.

Every definition of salvation implies the need to be saved or delivered from something. Contrary to biblical Christianity, most world religions and secular beliefs hinge on works (good deeds) done to gain God's favor. These errant beliefs argue that someone's good only needs to outweigh their bad. Today's reading in Paul's letter to the Church in Rome reminds us that everyone has sinned and stands condemned before God (Romans 3:23; Ecclesiastes 7:20). Think back to last week's study about sin. The Bible makes it adamantly clear that every person desperately needs salvation (2 Thessalonians 1:8; 1 Timothy 2:4). It also declares that Christ is the only one who has fully, finally, and forever provided salvation to all who believe. Because of the universal predicament of human sinfulness, salvation cannot be a reward for the good things condemned humans do. That is not how justice works. It has to be given as a gift and received as a gift.

Romans 3:21-26 explains how God grants righteousness through Jesus Christ as a free gift. Sadly, many followers of Christ do not sufficiently understand how God has secured their salvation on their behalf (Ephesians 2:8-9; Romans 6:14). Throughout the early chapters of Romans, Paul consistently reminds his Jewish and Gentile audience about the doctrine of condemnation, summarized so well in Romans 3:23, "All have sinned and fall short of God's glory." Yet, Romans 3:24 is a radical reversal from that of condemnation to justification. This great "turnaround" is at the core of salvation. Humans desperately need salvation apart from themselves, and Jesus has provided it as a completely free gift. Every human ever born stands before God, the perfect judge, and is rightfully condemned to eternal death for their sin (Romans 3:23; Matthew 25:41). But–believers in Jesus Christ are given a radical reversal of fortunes when they are declared "justified" by God (Galatians 2:16; Titus 3:7). Jesus, the sinless one, was condemned so sinners could be justified. Owning your condemnation (bad news) is a prerequisite to receiving the free gift of justification (good news). We are justified by grace (gift) through faith. Faith is what you do when there is nothing else you can do, and nothing else you have to do.

In this way, justification is more than being merely pardoned or shown mercy. The usage of this court term is a "declaration of righteousness." No behavior, sacrament, religious ritual, or combination of good deeds could make you worthy of Christ's justification (Galatians 3:11). God does not shift from condemnation to declaring you justified (righteous) because of your works! It is all about Jesus' works in His substitutionary life and death. God declares believers justified because of the righteousness of Jesus Himself. The "alien" righteousness of Jesus covers them (Romans 5:1). God looks at the sinner and now sees the Savior. Without a biblical understanding of justification, followers of Christ will spend their lives attempting to earn heaven. Or worse, they will assume they have obtained righteousness through their merit or a combination of their works and Christ's works. The gift of Christ's righteousness becomes the security for believers to rest in Christ's completed work on their behalf and the motivation to follow God daily.

1. God's Word is clear: justification is freely given and cannot be earned. Evaluate your actions and motives and see if there is anywhere that you are trying to earn God's favor or make yourself worthy of receiving salvation.

2. Had God only pardoned your sin and not covered you in Jesus' righteousness, would you still be able to have a relationship with Him? Why or why not?

3. If good works do not contribute to your salvation, what is their place in the life of a follower of Christ?

THE TRUTH

MEDITATE — Fill in the blanks as you continue committing this week's verse to memory.

> "Being _____ as a gift by His grace through the _____ which is in Christ Jesus."
>
> *Romans 3:24*

ENGAGE

Praise God for being the perfect Judge. Celebrate Romans 8:1, "There is now no condemnation for those who are in Christ Jesus." Confess you guilt before Him. Thank Jesus for taking on Himself the punishment you deserve so that you may be declared innocent before God with the perfect "foreign" righteousness of Jesus Himself. Ask God to keep this truth at the forefront of your mind so that you may live a life of security in your relationship with God.

Week 05 • Day 03

SALVATION: JUSTIFICATION & REDEMPTION

EXERCISE

READ *Romans 3:24-31 / Ephesians 1:7-11*

1. Use Romans 3:23-24 and Colossians 1:13-14 to define redemption.

_____

_____

_____

2. In the Old Testament, we see God's redemption when He leads Israel out of captivity into the promised land (Exodus 6:6). Compare and contrast Israel's redemption to the redemption of all people through Jesus.

_____

_____

_____

God cannot simply ignore sin (Romans 3:10). Any judge who sympathetically acquits a confirmed career criminal of a lifetime of charges would be rightfully called "unjust." In the first week of this guidebook, we studied the perfections of God. God is not only perfectly gracious, loving, and merciful, but He is also perfectly wise, holy, and just. Overlooking your sin might seem gracious, loving, and merciful, yet doing so opposes God's perfect wisdom, holiness, and justice. Biblical justification cannot excuse or overlook the wages of sin (Romans 6:23). A verdict must be made, and a punishment given for God's righteous justice to be satisfied. God, therefore, made "Him who knew no sin to be sin on our behalf, so that we might become the righteousness of God in Him" (2 Corinthians 5:21). Justification in Christ is free for believers (Ephesians 2:8-9), but it was not free for God (Romans 5:8).

If justification is a "court" term, redemption is a "market" term. Numerous Greek terms in the Bible are translated by the English word redemption. One prominent Greek word translated as redemption in the New Testament is *agoratzo*, which means "to purchase in a market." Another Greek word is *apolutrosis*, which means "to release by payment of ransom." These terms express the idea of redemption as paying a "purchase price" or the "ransoming" of an enslaved person and setting them free. Whereas biblical justification is God declaring a believer to have been given the gift of Christ's righteousness, the redemption (cost) of that gift is Jesus Himself (Ephesians 1:7). Today's reading in Ephesians could be viewed as a "bill of sale." The price is "His blood" for forgiving "our trespasses." Understanding the cost of your salvation refines one's theology quite drastically. Which is more loving: God overlooking your sin or God paying the full ransom for your sin to save you (Colossians 2:13-14)?

In John 8:34, Jesus says "everyone who commits sin is the slave of sin." Heaven will be filled with those who, by no work of their own, are set free from the enslavement of sin. Justification is free to you because Jesus paid for the high price of your redemption. Think of the thief on the cross next to Jesus (Luke 23:40-43). This man admitted that he deserved the cross he was nailed to and had nothing to offer. Jesus said, "Today you shall be with me in Paradise." Paul puts it all together in one verse in Romans 3. We are rescued by God by "being **justified** (covered by Jesus' righteousness) as a **gift** (free) by His **grace** (unmerited favor) through the **redemption** (ransom paid) which is in Christ Jesus" (Romans 3:24). Be still and take ownership of this beautiful truth.

In summary, justification means you are free from the legal guilt of your sins. This gift is extended through the life, death, and resurrection of Jesus Christ. Disciples of Jesus have been declared (past tense) "innocent" of their sins because of the substitutionary death of Jesus and declared "righteous" because of the substitutionary life of Jesus. The redemption of a believer explains the process by which they are purchased from their slavery to sin at the cost of Christ's suffering, death, and resurrection. Romans 6:23 says, "For the wages of sin is death, but the free gift of God is eternal life in Christ Jesus our Lord." His death paid for sin in full and redeemed us for a relationship with God through the life of Jesus. In acknowledging Jesus' high price for salvation, we feel the weight of "the riches of His grace which He lavished on us" (Ephesians 1:7-8).

THE TRUTH

1. How does knowing that God paid a high price for your low living make you feel? How can having a "cheap" view of God's grace affect one's behavior? ▼

2. What was the cost of your salvation? ▼

3. How does the truth of your redemption influence how you live?

THE TRUTH

MEDITATE Fill in the blanks as you continue committing this week's verse to memory.

"Being _____ as a gift by His _____ through the _____ which is in Christ Jesus."

Romans 3:24

ENGAGE

Praise God for being perfectly just and perfectly loving. Confess how your life does not reflect the high price of your redemption. Thank Him for the riches of His grace that He has lavished on you. Ask God to allow this truth to overflow onto the people around you. Trust Him to use you to share His redemption gift with those around you so they may know God and be built up in the truth.

Week 05 • Day 04

SALVATION: JUSTIFICATION & REDEMPTION

EXAMINATION

READ
Psalm 111:6-9

WATCH
Week 5 - Salvation: Justification & Redemption

To watch the video, scan the QR code below by opening your phone's camera and holding your device so that the QR code appears on the screen. Click the link associated with the QR code, and choose this week's video. https://qrco.de/be3SWs

1. In what ways are you still trying to "pull yourself up by your bootstraps" and earn your salvation?

___

2. How does the double exchange—Jesus removing the penalty for your sin and giving you His righteousness—affect how you live?

___

3. Remember your own salvation story. Specifically, how did receiving salvation through faith in Jesus change your life?

_____
_____
_____

EXERCISE

READ *Psalm 111:6-9*

Throughout God's Word, we see justice and redemption for the people of God. In the Old Testament, when Israel disobeyed God, He punished sin and provided a way for the people to return to Him. Over and over, throughout history, God pursued His people so that they may have a relationship with Him. In the New Testament, God provides Jesus as the ultimate fulfillment of His justification and redemption. All people need the sacrifice of Jesus. Mankind has proven itself to be disobedient and unfaithful throughout all of history. God has proven Himself to be faithful to redeem His people. Through faith in Jesus, we can receive salvation and enter into a relationship with God. We praise God that the works of His hands are true and just (Psalm 111:7). His words are sure and endure forever and ever (Psalm 111:7-8). He has redeemed His people into His forever covenant. "Holy and awesome is His name" (Psalm 111:9).

> "He has sent redemption to His people; He has ordained His covenant forever; Holy and awesome is His name."
>
> *Psalm 111:9*

MEDITATE

Below, attempt to write out this week's verse from memory.

ENGAGE

Praise God for being true and just in all that He does (Psalm 111:7). Confess the ways you try to rely on yourself for the things that only God can do. Thank Him for providing salvation to disobedient and undeserving people. Ask Him to fill your heart and mind with the truth of who He is and all that He's done so that it may overflow in all that you think, say, and do.

Week 05 • Day 05
SALVATION: JUSTIFICATION & REDEMPTION

EXERCISE

READ *1 Peter 2:23-24*

God's love and justice come together perfectly in the work of justification and redemption. First Peter 2:21 says that Jesus Christ, in His suffering, left us an example so that we may follow in His footsteps. When He faced hardship and adversity, He "continued entrusting Himself to Him who judges justly" (1 Peter 2:23). God has proven Himself perfectly just and perfectly loving through redemption and justification so that we can trust Him within adversity. When overwhelmed by brokenness, you can be sure that God will deal with every wrong deed justly. First Peter 2:24 calls us to die to sin and live to righteousness, not to earn salvation, but because we have already been "healed." This healing leads us to live a changed life where we turn from sin and commit ourselves to live in a manner that reflects Christ's righteousness.

EXAMPLE

Although the specific details are lost to history, many credit A.J. Gordon with a story often used to help explain redemption. Gordon, a popular 18th-century pastor, is said to have seen a young boy with several birds in an old cage. When asked about his plans for the birds, the young boy said he intended to play with them for a bit and later feed them to his cat. As the story goes, seeing the cruelty of this boy motivated Gordon to purchase the birds for a high price and release them.

Though the story helps explain redemption, there are significant differences between the liberation of a few birds and the redemption of the Church. As a cruel little boy snared the birds, our enemy ensnared each of us with sin. The wages of this sin would act as the rusty cage, cruelly shaken by our adversary. But the cost of your redemption was not a currency given from a wallet. The cost of your redemption was paid from the flesh of Jesus as He hung on the cross. Though your redemption was free to you, it cost God greatly. In a sense, the receipt of your salvation was signed and paid for by the blood of Jesus.

MEDITATE   Practice reciting this week's verse from memory and be prepared to say them aloud to your d-group.

ENGAGE

Praise God for being holy and righteous. Confess the ways you struggle with times of personal suffering and how you desire, at times, to take justice into your own hands when mistreated. Thank Jesus for His perfect example of trusting God continually and for His perfect righteousness in the face of suffering. Ask God to help you die to sin, live to righteousness daily, and always trust the One who judges perfectly.

WEEK 5

ENCOURAGE
Accountability

Use this checklist as a guide for your weekly d-group time. Refer to the discipler's note at the front of the book for more encouragement and practical advice.

- Work through questions from the accountability page.

- Spend time praying specifics for one another.

- Take turns reciting the memory verse.

- Discuss answers to the questions throughout the week that are marked with this symbol. ⬇

PRAYER REQUESTS

_____
_____
_____
_____
_____
_____
_____

ACCOUNTABILITY QUESTIONS

These questions are to be asked of one another in a spirit of accountability (Proverbs 27:17). They are intended to stimulate conversations of character and confession of sin in a safe environment that values honesty, vulnerability, confidentiality, and grace.

1. Have you spent quality time in your spiritual disciplines this week?

2. Have you taken advantage of opportunities to share your faith this week? Explain.

3. Have your words and actions been a good testimony this week to the gospel of Jesus?

4. Have your thoughts and speech been pure (cussing, criticism, negativity, etc.)?

5. Have you been sexually pure this week? Have you been exposed to sexually alluring material? (For those who are married: Have you prioritized quality romantic time with your spouse?)

6. Have you been a good steward of your finances? Have you lacked integrity in the handling of your finances?

7. Have you been honoring and generous in your meaningful relationships this week (Family, friends, etc.)?

8. Have you given in to any addictive behavior this past week? Explain.

9. Have you been completely honest with me?

I'm praying for the salvation of the following two people and prayerfully considering how to share Christ with them myself: _____

> "Therefore, confess your sins to one another, and pray for one another, so that you may be healed."
>
> *James 5:16a*

Week 06 • Day 01

SALVATION: RECONCILIATION & PROPITIATION

ESSENTIAL TRUTH

The Bible paints five different pictures of the saving work of Jesus Christ on our behalf (**justification, reconciliation, redemption, propitiation,** and **adoption**).

Reconciliation (a relational term) describes the change from hostility to nearness brought by the gift of salvation. God reconciles people to Himself through Jesus Christ by way of a double exchange: our sin to Christ's account through Christ's death and Christ's righteousness to our account through Christ's life.

Propitiation (a temple term) is the appeasement of God's wrath that could only be accomplished in the death of Christ on the cross. The cross publicly displayed the satisfaction of God's wrath against sin and the reconciliation of sinful man to a holy and just God.

1. Read the Essential Truth, identify two phrases that stand out to you, and write them below. Why do you believe these phrases are significant?

___

2. In your own words, give a personal definition of reconciliation and propitiation.

___

3. What is the difference between reconciliation and propitiation?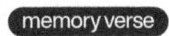

_____
_____
_____

EXAMPLE

At 8:46 a.m., a Boeing 757 carrying 44 passengers impacted the North Tower of the World Trade Center. Three days after what would become known as 9/11, Mark Stroman went on a shooting spree targeting anyone whom he believed to be of Arabic descent. One of his victims was a young man by the name of Rais Bhuiyan. Though Rais survived being shot in the face, some years later the tables were turned as Mark Stroman was given the death penalty. Instead of focusing on Storman's hate and the resulting years of recovery, Rais chose to campaign for Storman's rehabilitation. With a single trigger pull, Mark Stroman cost Rais his vision in one eye, the financial burden of several surgical procedures, and untold emotional and mental trauma. There is nothing Stroman could do to right (reconcile) the wrongs he had committed. It was Rais who chose to clear the ledger and forgive Stroman. Similarly, we cannot reconcile the multitudes of wrongs we have committed against God and remove the resulting hostility without the reconciling work of Jesus Christ.

EXERCISE `memory verse`

> For if while we were enemies we were reconciled to God through the death of His Son, much more, having been reconciled, we shall be saved by His life.
>
> *Romans 5:10*

Reconciliation is a "relational" term that implies the restoring of a relationship from one of strife and discord to one of harmony and unity. In this way, reconciliation is the removal of hostility between enemies. We were once "helpless," "ungodly," "sinners," and "enemies" of God (Romans 5:6-10), completely separated from Him. Such hostility requires reconciliation to be initiated by God Himself. Left to our means, we would remain alienated from God. Romans 8:3 clarifies that such a resolution could not be accomplished by the Law or through the work of humans. Only God could do what was required to reconcile sinful humanity to a loving God. He did that by "sending His own Son in the likeness of sinful flesh, and, as an offering for sin, He condemned sin in the flesh" (Romans 8:3-4). The language of reconciliation powerfully presents salvation as the divine gift of a intimate and eternal relationship with our Father. By God's doing, not ours, we are placed "IN Christ Jesus, who became to us wisdom from God, and righteousness and sanctification, and redemption, so that, just as it is written, 'LET HIM WHO BOASTS, BOAST IN THE LORD'" (1 Corinthians 1:30-31).

The biblical teaching of reconciliation is often associated with the imagery of balancing accounts (Romans 5:10-21). Within this extended picture, sins are seen as debts, and righteousness is seen as a contribution. A disciple of Jesus receives reconciliation to God by way of the double exchange (or double imputation): our sins to Christ's account through the death of Christ and Christ's righteousness to our account through the life of Jesus. Second Corinthians 5:21 says, "He made Him who knew no sin to be sin on our behalf so that we might become the righteousness of God in Him." In this way, the double exchange removes the hostility between God and disciples of Jesus.

MEDITATE Write out this week's verse below as you spend time committing them to memory.

ENGAGE

Praise God for being the God of peace. Celebrate that your sins were transferred to Christ's account through Jesus' death and that Christ's righteousness was transferred to your account through Jesus' life. Confess aspects of your past hostility with God that Jesus Christ has removed by His grace alone. Thank Him for reconciling your relationship so that you may know Him, love Him, and serve Him forever. Ask God to remove any feelings of self-sufficiency or boastfulness from you so that you may declare His glory and works with humility and thankfulness. Ask Him to use you to reveal the good news of salvation to all those around you.

Week 06 • Day 02

SALVATION: RECONCILIATION & PROPITIATION

EXERCISE

READ *Romans 5:1-11 / 2 Corinthians 5:18-21*

1. Highlight the main points of Romans 5:10 by answering the following quick questions:

   (a) Who were we before reconciliation?

   (b) Who were we reconciled to?

   (c) What were we reconciled through?

   (d) Having been reconciled, how are we saved?

2. Romans 5:1-11 gives us three reasons to rejoice ("exult" in the NASB). What are they?

3. Second Corinthians 5:18 states that as reconciled people, we are given the ministry of reconciliation. What is the corresponding title given to us in 5:20? Based on that title, what would be a possible mission statement of our ministry of reconciliation?

_____
_____
_____

This week continues our three-week examination of the doctrine of salvation (aka. "*soteriology*," from the Greek word for salvation, *soter*). Salvation is God's rescue of us from our condemnation. However, peeling back the layers of biblical salvation reveals so much more than a simple statement of deliverance from condemnation. A deeper understanding of your salvation in every way enhances your view of the gospel. Biblical justification demonstrates God's goodness by declaring sinful people innocent and imparting Christ's righteousness to them. Biblical redemption from sin points to God purchasing sinners from enslavement at the high cost of Jesus and enhances our concept of the extravagance of God's love.

In Romans 5:1-11, Paul utilizes multiple forms of the Greek word *katallage*, which is often translated as "reconciliation." The English-speaking mind most often correlates the term "reconciliation" with the concept of a reconciled or restored relationship. The Apostle Paul's writings extend the relational bases of reconciliation to include a banking analogy of financial accounts. The accrual of large financial debts helps to illustrate the relational rift between sinful humanity and God. The forgiveness of our debt of sin through the cross and the subsequent riches of Christ's righteousness, "imputed" to our account through His perfect life, explain how God "reconciles" us to Himself through Jesus (2 Corinthians 5:18; Romans 5:8-19).

Advancing the scriptural analogy into your story, it is as if you worked your entire life earning a wage for sin (Romans 6:23). At the point of your salvation experience, Jesus Christ offered to pay your sin debt and load up your heavenly account with the wealth of His own righteousness... and you said "yes" to this incredible transaction. Jesus not only took the debt of our sin upon Himself (1 Peter 2:24), He credited us with His own righteousness. This great exchange of our sin for His perfect rightness with God is what we called earlier the "double exchange." In the Lord's prayer of

Matthew 6, Jesus uses this same banking analogy of sin and tells His followers to pray to their heavenly Father to "forgive us our debts" (Matthew 6:12a).

Let's put it all together. Through His perfect life and sacrifice, Jesus pays our debt, imparts His righteousness, and restores our relationship with God (2 Corinthians 5:18). This act of grace is made even more amazing by the knowledge that He did this while we were "helpless," "ungodly," "sinners," and "enemies" of God (Romans 5:6-10; James 4:4). Take a moment and marvel again at the great reversal of fortunes found in 2 Corinthians 5:18-21. Because we are reconciled to God through Jesus, He has deemed each of His disciples to serve as His ambassador to a hostile and spiritually bankrupt world. We represent His kingdom interests in this foreign world through the ministry of reconciliation. Simply put, disciples of Jesus are rescued and charged to assist in the rescue of others. As "rescuers," we die to sin and live to righteousness—not to earn salvation or to prove our worth, but because our ambassadorship reflects the character and expectation of our Father (1 Peter 2:24).

1. How should the good news of Jesus paying our sin debt completely and then imparting His righteousness to us affect how we interact with Him through His Word and in prayer?

_____
_____
_____

2. How are you called to live as an effective ambassador for Christ?

_____
_____
_____

THE TRUTH

MEDITATE Fill in the blanks as you continue committing this week's verse to memory.

> "For if while we were _____ we were reconciled to God through the death of His Son, much more, having been _____, we shall be saved by His life."
>
> *Romans 5:10*

ENGAGE

Praise God for being righteous in all His ways. Confess any sin pattern in your life and acknowledge once again that Christ died to set you free from sin. Thank God for the work of Jesus' life and death as your payment for sin and your new righteous identity. Ask God to help you live as an ambassador for Christ and not as a slave to sin.

Week 06 • Day 03

SALVATION: RECONCILIATION & PROPITIATION

EXERCISE

READ   *Romans 3:10-26 / Romans 1:16-23*

1. Biblical propitiation is the satisfaction of the wrath of God against sin. According to Romans 3:10-20, why might God be "wrathful" toward humans?

2. Explain propitiation in your own words Use Romans 3:23-26 and the Essential Truth from Day 1 of this week to form your definition.

3. What attributes of God do you see when studying propitiation?

It is unlikely you have heard the word propitiation outside of a sermon or a Bible study. To be sure, the Bible often uses the concept of propitiation to illustrate God's work in salvation. Propitiation is the fourth biblical image in our series that helps refine our understanding of what it means to be rescued by Jesus. First, we looked at **justification** as a "legal" concept embodying imagery of being found innocent before a righteous judge (Romans 5:8-10). Second we spent time examining **redemption** as a "market" term, which led us to picture the high price paid to emancipate an enslaved person from the shackles of sin and death (Ephesians 1:7). Third, we studied salvation as seen through the lens of reconciliation—a "relational" concept highlighting the change from hostility to nearness that salvation in Jesus Christ brings. The exchange of sin debts for righteousness credits in God's heavenly ledger book results in the perfect restoration of relationship between God and man (Colossians 1:20). Now, we will advance our understanding of salvation by thinking about the concept of **propitiation**, a "temple" term pointing toward the appeasement of God's wrath (Romans 3:25).

Understanding biblical propitiation requires an acknowledgment that sin makes God viscerally angry. Our sin requires more than "expiation," a violation that expects a mere payment. On the contrary, our sin before a holy God has an emotional element that needs satisfying. Some Christian thinkers have incorrectly concluded that God is incapable of anger or wrath (Exodus 16:7; Romans 2:5). This inaccurate theology is partly due to a misunderstanding of the biblical propitiation made through Jesus Christ. A disciple of Christ may also struggle to see God as angry because that is not their experience with God. They have only known the peace of God. Of course, this peace is only experienced because Jesus has taken the anger leveled against them and placed it on Himself.

Jesus provided substitutionary satisfaction of the wrath of God on the cross. The trials, torture, and crucifixion of Jesus Christ, as described in John 19, illustrate the visceral nature of God's wrath poured out on Jesus as our substitute. Jesus stood before courts that would have easily found us guilty. He took the insults, punches, and beatings we deserved. The extent of biblical satisfaction was the poured-out blood of Jesus, the perfect sacrifice (Hebrews 9:14). He was the lamb without blemish sacrificed on our behalf to satisfy the anger of God against human sin (1 Peter 1:19). Of the twenty-two sermons recorded within the Book of Acts each one points to the death, burial, and resurrection of Jesus Christ. The early Church understood that being covered by Jesus' blood was central to the gospel (Hebrews 9:12-14).

Why such anger from God? Sin is lawlessness (1 John 3:4), lust (Colossians 3:5), greed (Matthew 6:24), ruin, and destruction (1 Timothy 6:9). Matthew 15:19 tells us that "out of the heart come evil thoughts, murder, adultery, sexual immorality, theft, false witness, slander." Sin does more than hurt the sinner. Sin harms the innocent, assaults the weak, and abuses the pure. How could a loving, righteous God look at human history and not be angry? A study of salvation in the Bible shows that Jesus took our legal guilt, paid the price of our enslavement, fulfilled our debt, reconciled our relationship and appeased the righteous anger of God. No wonder the seemingly simple phrase "Jesus loves me, this I know" is one of the most beautiful and eternal truths.

1. Knowing about God's attributes differs significantly from knowing "Him" as Savior and Lord. What truths have you learned this week that will lead your heart and mind to honor God and personally thank Him?

___

2. How does understanding God's wrath towards sin influence how you think, speak, and act today?

___

THE TRUTH

MEDITATE — Fill in the blanks as you continue committing this week's verse to memory.

> "For if while we were _____ we were _____ to God through the death of His Son, much more, having been _____ , we shall be _____ by His life."
> *Romans 5:10*

ENGAGE

Praise God for being holy. Confess how you sometimes live as though you are still a slave to sin. Thank God for removing the hostility between you and Him by pouring out His wrath on Jesus instead of on you. Ask Him to help you understand the depth of who He is and what He has done for you. Pray that He convicts you and equips you to pursue a life of holiness and intimacy with Him.

Week 06 • Day 04

SALVATION: RECONCILIATION & PROPITIATION

EXAMINATION

READ
Galatians 2:15-20

WATCH
Week 6 - Salvation: Reconciliation & Propitiation

To watch the video, scan the QR code below by opening your phone's camera and holding your device so that the QR code appears on the screen. Click the link associated with the QR code, and choose this week's video. https://qrco.de/be3SWs

1. When you think of the good news of Christ on your behalf, how do you describe it?

_____
_____
_____

2. In Romans 3:25-26, we see that believers are saved from God, by God. In your own words, explain what that means. ▼

_____
_____

3. How would you teach the double exchange to a disciple?

_____
_____
_____

EXERCISE

READ *Galatians 2:15-20*

    Salvation through Jesus Christ saves you from God's righteous wrath for the purpose of His loving relationship. The price Jesus paid removed the penalty for sin and imparted Christ's righteousness in its place. When you receive salvation, you are crucified with Christ. You no longer live as a slave to sin. Instead, you live in the power of the One who has defeated sin. Christ gifts His disciples with righteousness and enables them to walk in a manner worthy of that gift. Your life is no longer characterized by sinful depravity. That person was crucified with Christ. You now live by faith in Jesus, who loved and gave Himself up for you. This new identity changes who you are and how you live. Although you are not yet entirely freed from the effects of sin in this world, you are promised complete victory in Heaven. The world's burdens are ever-present, but believers are invited into the yoke of Christ (Matthew 11:28-30). Christ's burden is light and easy because His work of salvation has been completed. As we take on this yoke, we work and endure within the broken world from a place of rest and hope.

> "Come to Me, all who are weary and heavy-laden, and I will give you rest."
>
> *Matthew 11:28*

MEDITATE   Below, attempt to write out this week's verse from memory.

ENGAGE

Praise God for defeating sin through the life, death, and resurrection of Jesus Christ. Confess how you live as one who has not been crucified with Christ. Thank Him for providing a way to appease His wrath towards you and reconcile your life. Ask Him to help you embrace the yoke of Christ and enjoy the rest and hope that has been offered to you.

Week 06 • Day 05

SALVATION: RECONCILIATION & PROPITIATION

EXERCISE

READ *Hebrews 9:11-15*

Sin has always incurred debt and has always required a blood offering. The New Testament book of Hebrews points us to the Old Testament books of Exodus and Leviticus—passages demonstrating specific requirements to fulfill sin offerings. Sin must be dealt with for us to enter the presence of God. The Old Covenant under Moses required a continual process of providing sin offerings that the High Priests had to practice in order to enter the Tabernacle and then the temple. This old arrangement allowed the High Priest to enter the presence of God once a year. Here, we see Jesus as the better and "perfect" fulfillment of the debt of sin. His blood was the "once and for all" payment for sin. No other sacrifice has ever been sufficient, and no other sacrifice will ever be required. Jesus, the ultimate High Priest, has entered the Most Holy Place once and for all. We now have a better and "permanent" experience of the presence of God in our lives. We no longer must go to a temple or tabernacle to experience God's presence. Through the substitutionary life and death of our High Priest Jesus Christ, God has made us "temples of the Holy Spirit" (1 Corinthians 6:19). God takes away the first temple "in order to establish the second. By this will we have been sanctified through the offering of the body of Jesus Christ once for all" (Hebrews 10:9-10).

EXAMPLE

Propitiation, though an unfamiliar term, is likely a familiar concept. Those who have lived through the pain of addictions and abuse in their families are all too aware of the agony and difficulty of watching those they love hurt themselves and others.

Suppose such harmful behaviors cause simple and sinful people to accumulate justified anger. How much more significant and justified is God's righteous anger as the children He loves are harmed, extorted, or abused? The required appeasement of justified frustration and anger in our damaged relationships pale when compared to God's required propitiation. An essential aspect of Jesus' saving work in our lives is deliverance from God's wrath.

MEDITATE Practice reciting this week's verse from memory and be prepared to say them aloud to your d-group.

ENGAGE

Praise God for His kindness. Confess how you take your salvation for granted and do not acknowledge the high price Jesus paid to rescue you. Thank Jesus for His perfect sacrifice, for paying that debt that you owed, and for satisfying the wrath that you deserve. Ask God to give you an unrelenting desire to share this truth with everyone around you and that they would be saved by confessing their sin and trusting in Jesus as their Savior.

ENCOURAGE
Accountability

Use this checklist as a guide for your weekly d-group time. Refer to the discipler's guide at the front of the book for more encouragement and practical advice.

- Work through questions from the accountability page.

- Spend time praying specifics for one another.

- Take turns reciting memory verses.

- Discuss answers to the questions throughout the week that are marked with this symbol ⊙

PRAYER REQUESTS

_____
_____
_____
_____
_____
_____
_____

ACCOUNTABILITY QUESTIONS

These questions are to be asked of one another in a spirit of accountability (Proverbs 27:17). They are intended to stimulate conversations of character and confession of sin in a safe environment that values honesty, vulnerability, confidentiality, and grace.

1. Have you spent quality time in your spiritual disciplines this week?
2. Have you taken advantage of opportunities to share your faith this week? Explain.
3. Have your words and actions been a good testimony this week to the gospel of Jesus?
4. Have your thoughts and speech been pure (cussing, criticism, negativity, etc.)?
5. Have you been sexually pure this week? Have you been exposed to sexually alluring material? (For those who are married: Have you prioritized quality romantic time with your spouse?)
6. Have you been a good steward of your finances? Have you lacked integrity in the handling of your finances?
7. Have you been honoring and generous in your meaningful relationships this week (Family, friends, etc.)?
8. Have you given in to any addictive behavior this past week? Explain.
9. Have you been completely honest with me?

I'm praying for the salvation of the following two people and prayerfully considering how to share Christ with them myself: _____

> "Therefore, confess your sins to one another, and pray for one another, so that you may be healed."
> James 5:16a

Week 07 • Day 01

SALVATION: ADOPTION

ESSENTIAL TRUTH

The Bible paints five different pictures of the saving work of Jesus Christ on our behalf (**justification, reconciliation, redemption, propitiation,** and **adoption**).

Adoption (a domestic term) into the family of God is the highest privilege of the completed work of Christ on our behalf. Followers of Christ are forever a part of God's family and will eternally enjoy the full standing of a child of God: intimacy, identity, and inheritance.

1. Read the Essential Truth, identify two phrases that stand out to you, and write them below. Why do you believe these phrases are significant?

___

___

___

2. In your own words, give a personal definition of biblical adoption.

___

___

___

3. Make a few observations below as you compare and contrast adoption into a nuclear family in your culture and spiritual adoption into God's family ⌄

_____
_____
_____

EXERCISE `memory verses`

> "For you have not received a spirit of slavery leading to fear again, but you have received a spirit of adoption as sons by which we cry out, 'Abba! Father!' The Spirit Himself testifies with our spirit that we are children of God"
>
> *Romans 8:15-17*

The biblical formula of salvation—"by grace through faith" in Christ—is beautifully exquisite. If you are in Christ, you have been declared justified and righteous before God because you have received the gift of Jesus Christ. Biblical faith is what you do when there is nothing left to do—when there is nothing you can do. Christ has already paid the high price for our redemption—His shed blood on the cross. There is no other way to be set free from sin. God reconciled all believers to Himself by crediting our sins to Christ's account and by crediting Christ's righteousness to our account. This gift of reconciliation removed the hostility between God and us. God's wrath towards sin was appeased through Christ's death on the cross as a perfect act of propitiation. Because of all these elements of our salvation, we are granted the highest privilege to be adopted into the family of God. As children adopted into the family of God, we enjoy close **intimacy** with our Father, special **identity** as His sons and daughters, and the promise of eternal **inheritance** as co-heirs with Christ. We were once slaves to sin and fear, but that is no longer our reality. The Holy Spirit was given to us as the assurance of our salvation and the testimony of our standing as children of God. You are now free to walk in the fullness of who you are and to whom you belong.

EXAMPLE

Cinema and literature set the stage for a myriad of stories and narratives based on the adversity orphans face. These literary productions include famous works such as *Oliver Twist, Great Expectations, Jane Eyre,* Superman, and even the Harry Potter franchise. Across time and cultures, audiences have continued to sympathize with and rally behind the protagonists in these works. Perhaps our engagement with these characters springs from a deep awareness that we were once orphans. Every disciple of Jesus was once a spiritual street urchin. Like Moses, you floated on the hazardous waters of the Nile. Thankfully, you were adopted into a family far greater than Pharaoh's. You were adopted into the family of God.

MEDITATE   Write out this week's verses below as you spend time committing them to memory.

ENGAGE

Praise God for choosing you to be His child and for being such a good Father. Confess how you sometimes continue to live as if you are a slave to sin or fear. Thank Him for bringing you into His family and making you a fellow heir with Christ. Ask Him to help you walk in obedience as a child of God in every area of your life.

Week 07 • Day 02

SALVATION: ADOPTION

EXERCISED

READ *Hebrews 2:9-13 / Romans 8:14-17*

1. Restate Hebrews 2:11 in your own words.

_____
_____
_____

2. Hebrews 2:12 quotes Psalm 22, which is a Psalm that is full of prophetic references to the crucifixion of Jesus. How does the sufferings of Christ on the cross facilitate the "bringing many sons to glory (2:10)?"

_____
_____
_____

3. According to Romans 8:15-16, how would you describe the reversal of fortunes of a child adopted into the family of God? ▼

_____
_____
_____

The natural desire to be part of a community or family was present before the introduction of sin in the Garden of Eden. Eve was created because it was "not good for man to be alone" (Genesis 2:18). God created humanity with an innate desire for relationships and belonging. Jesus collected a small group of close friends to share His life and ministry (John 15:15). Later, Jesus' first disciples would surround themselves with a community of brothers and sisters in Christ.

God created all things and all people for His glory, but He has created a special relationship with those He adopts for all eternity (Isaiah 43:7; Romans 11:36). The progressive narrative of the Bible consistently demonstrates God's perfect love and nature. The story reaches its apex at the cross of Christ and the resulting salvation of those who accept the invitation to join God's family (John 1:12). The gift of a new **identity** as a son or daughter of God brings great significance and community. In a world that treats relationships like a commodity, it can be challenging to grasp the incredible truth of our identity as children of God.

Today's reading from Paul's letter to the Romans reminds the Church that their inheritance is not one of slavery or fear but adoption as sons (Romans 8:15). Paul could have chosen to substitute the Greek word for "children" in the place of the word for "sons," but Paul is trying to make a point. While such a word choice would be well received in our modern egalitarian culture, such wording in Greek and Hebrew cultures would have implied a lack of inheritance. Our adoption "as sons" means we stand to inherit. Whether male or female, our adoption explicitly means we are co-heirs with Christ Himself. The word "sons" is intentionally used because all followers of Christ enjoy the legacy and **inheritance** of their adoption.

Upon salvation, our position in the world changes—we are no longer slaves but sons. However, our lives, attitudes, and actions do not always reflect that position. We are prone to forgetfulness and fear. Instead of living in the security and hope of children of God, we turn back to the "weak and worthless elemental things, to which [we] desire to be enslaved all over again" (Galatians 4:9). God did not rescue us from slavery to sin only to have us turn back to the things of the world in the highs and lows of life. We are to cling to Him as a child does his father and look to Him for provision.

The phrase "Abba Father" in Romans 8:15 is loaded with imagery of a young child lovingly calling their father "daddy," a term of great endearment (Galatians 4:6). Part of a believer's adoption through Christ is the gift of fearless **intimacy** with God.

God communicated with priests and prophets in the Old Testament (Hebrews 1:1; Luke 1:70), but none would have dared approach Him as a child would their daddy (Isaiah 6:5; Hebrews 12:21). It is only within the intimate relationship enjoyed by a child of God through New Covenant promises that we can fearlessly approach Him in the same way a young child would crawl into their father's lap.

One of the most profound realities of salvation is the freedom to talk to God in a way that the high priest of Israel could never have imagined. A disciple of Jesus is not required to burn offerings, make sacrifices, and depend upon a priest to approach God because Jesus is the perfect Prophet, Priest, and King. God adopts us into a new and better way of approaching Him, a way greater than any Old Testament believer could have imagined (Hebrews 10:19-25). We are to spend intimate time with Him through reading and studying His Word and through continuous prayer. We are to remember His faithfulness, trust His provision, and rest securely in His perfect love. We are His children, and He is our loving and perfect Father.

1. How have you seen your adoption into God's family and the placement of the Holy Spirit within you transform your day-to-day life?

_____

_____

_____

2. Consider the realities of your present relationship with God. Confess an area that you are not walking in a "spirit" of adoption (Romans 8:15). Are you walking with your Father in identity, intimacy, and inheritance? ▼

_____

_____

_____

THE TRUTH

MEDITATE — Fill in the blanks as you continue committing this week's verses to memory.

> For you have not received a spirit of _____ leading to fear again, but you have received a spirit of adoption as sons by which we cry out, 'Abba! _____!' The Spirit Himself testifies with our spirit that we are _____ of God"
>
> *Romans 8:15-16*

ENGAGE

Praise God for being faithful. Confess how you are not faithful to Him. Thank God for loving you enough to provide a way into His family and for pursuing you and drawing you to Himself. Ask God to help you comprehend the privilege of being a child of God and to walk fully in that identity. Ask the Holy Spirit to testify to your spirit once again that you are a child of God, and then rest in who He says you are!

Week 07 • Day 03

SALVATION: ADOPTION

EXERCISE

READ *John 1:9-14, Romans 8:1-39*

1. Who can become a child of God? Reference John 1:11-13 and John 3:16 specifically.

___

2. Rewrite John 1:14 in your own words, highlighting what it reveals about Jesus.

___

3. The word "Spirit" occurs fifteen times in Romans 8. Within the larger context of Romans 8, how is verses 15 through 19 the climax of the chapter? How does "suffering" as the people of God factor into this climax of identity as His children?

___

As previously discussed, justification is a "legal" word for lawful innocence (Romans 5:8-10). Redemption is a "market" term for the purchasing and setting free of an enslaved person (Ephesians 1:7). Reconciliation is a "banking" word demonstrating the exchange of debt for credits (Colossians 1:20). Propitiation is a "temple" term for the appeasement of God's wrath (Romans 3:25). The word adoption comes from the "domestic" setting of the family (Romans 8:14-15). Adoption through Christ represents the complete and eternal introduction to the family of God.

A better understanding of salvation affirms that the title of "son" or "daughter" of God is not a metaphor. God's Word assures disciples of Jesus that they are formally adopted into His eternal family (Romans 8:16). This family is comprised of all types of people from all races and all nations (Galatians 3:28). The basic human need for belonging and relationships is fulfilled through intimacy with God and His extended children who are new brothers and sisters in Christ (Ephesians 2:19).

The Holy Spirit of God testifies to the complete adoption of each believer (Romans 8:16). Spiritual adoption is the foundation of a believer's value and identity. As many within the modern Church seem to struggle with defining their purpose, children of God should not hesitate from looking to their Father God and engaging in the family business (Matthew 6:33, 9:37). Jesus was singularly focused on the Father's business (John 5:19) and told His first disciples, "Follow Me, and I will make you fishers of men" (Matthew 4:19). Jesus had the heart of the Father and came to seek and save the lost (Luke 19:10). The identity of the Church is affirmed by the Spirit of God and lived out through the ministry of personal disciple-making (Matthew 28:19-20).

In addition to fearless **intimacy** with God and **identity**, adoption through Christ includes an eternal **inheritance**. As "sons," we are "heirs of God and co-heirs with Jesus" (Romans 8:17). We discussed earlier how the specifically chosen word "sons" makes it explicit that we all stand to inherit something. In a society that equates inheritance with financial gain, it would benefit us to reference Revelation 21. If the streets of Heaven are pure gold, being a co-heir with Jesus is more than monetary riches. Revelation 21:3-4 stands as one of the best examples of what the disciple of Jesus will inherit. John says, "I heard a loud voice from the throne, saying, 'Behold, the tabernacle of God is among men, and He will dwell among them, and they shall be His people, and God Himself will be among them, and He will wipe away every tear from their eyes; and there will no longer be any death; there will no longer be any mourning, or crying, or pain; the first things have passed away.'" What treasure is more valuable than being with God?

1. Spend some time reflecting on your adoption into the family of God. Has your life come to look more like your Father? More like Jesus? Do you live with your eyes fixed on what you stand to inherit in Heaven? Explain.

_____
_____
_____

2. Do you tend to value fellow disciples of Jesus differently based on social standards like economic status, ethnicity, or human effort, or do you seek unity and relationship with your brothers and sisters in Christ? Explain.

_____
_____
_____

MEDITATE   Fill in the blanks as you continue committing this week's verses to memory.

❝

For you have not received a spirit of _____ leading to fear again, but you have received a spirit of _____ as sons by which we cry out, 'Abba! _____!' The Spirit Himself _____ with our spirit that we are _____ of God"

Romans 8:15-17

ENGAGE

Praise God for being the loving Father that He is. Confess how you sometimes do not value intimacy with Him, nor do you longingly anticipate the things to come. Thank Him for your promised inheritance. Ask Him to help you live in a way that reflects His character, anticipates the hope to come, and invites others into the family.

Week 07 • Day 04
SALVATION: ADOPTION

EXAMINATION

READ
1 John 3:1-3

WATCH
Week 7 - Salvation: Adoption

To watch the video, scan the QR code below by opening your phone's camera and holding your device so that the QR code appears on the screen. Click the link associated with the QR code, and choose this week's video. https://qrco.de/be3SWs

1. When have you experienced the need for belonging and the need for community in your life?

___

2. Which of the five elements of salvation that we've studied the past few weeks hit you the hardest? ⊙

___

3. Believers are forever a part of God's family and will eternally enjoy the full standing of a child of God. Describe your intimacy, identity, and inheritance as a child of God.

_____
_____
_____

EXERCISE

READ *1 John 3:1-3*

Is there a greater love than the one God bestowed on believers in calling us His children? The entire Bible is the story of God creating a family. From creation to redemption, God is preparing a way to bring His image bearers into a harmonious relationship with Himself. The completed work of Christ on our behalf is our highest privilege as believers. This work allows God to adopt us into His family and gives us intimacy, identity, and inheritance. Our deepest desires of belonging and community are fulfilled in the intimate relationship with our Father and the family He's placed us within. We are given the identity of sons and enabled to do the work that He's prepared for us. We look forward with longing and hope of an eternal inheritance. One day we will enjoy the fullness of this relationship without sin or hindrance. Until we receive our inheritance, we embrace and enjoy the family that He's provided for us in brothers and sisters in Christ. God's desire for a relationship with humanity is pure, and believers become pure as they trust Him with faith and model themselves after Jesus. When we love, serve, and do life with the body of believers that God has placed around us, we get to enjoy the belonging and community we were created for. We love our brothers and sisters as God, our Father, first loved us (1 John 4:19).

MEDITATE   Below, attempt to write out this week's verses from memory.

ENGAGE

Praise God for being a perfect Father. Confess the ways you seek to fulfill the need for belonging and community in unhealthy ways. Thank God for providing a family for you to do life with now and for the salvation that brought you into a relationship with the Father, Son, and Spirit. Ask God to help you grow in your relationship with Him and with your brothers and sisters in Christ.

Week 07 • Day 05

SALVATION: ADOPTION

EXERCISE

READ *Ephesians 4:1-6*

These past three weeks studying salvation, you have witnessed the faithfulness of God towards His unfaithful children. God has given you more than you deserve and more than you can understand. We are declared righteous, freed from our sins, covered in Christ's righteousness, and forever made a part of the family of God. The passage today from Paul's letter to the Ephesians calls us to live like it is true. We are commanded to live a life worthy of this great calling—a calling that we did not earn nor deserve. Consequently, our lives are characterized by humility, gentleness, patience, and long-suffering.

We are called to pursue unity within the family of God. We know that God does not call people into his family based on economic status, ethnicity, or human effort, so we can expect the family of God to be a very diverse group of humble people—people who have been graciously loved by God and have no idea why. We all have different backgrounds, cultures, preferences, ideas, and gifts. Our nature and culture might want to use these things to divide us. These differences, however, are meant to help us make a unique contribution to the family of God. The "donation" of your life matters most, not the "duration." Be intentional with how you live to pursue unity within your faith family. That is just what Paul is calling us to do here. We are one body with one Father. We are united through salvation but must intentionally pursue unity with our brothers and sisters in Christ.

EXAMPLE

Maybe you or someone you know has been impacted by adoption. A baby, child, or teen may be brought into a new family because of hardships that prevented their parents from parenting. In most scenarios in our lives, we look to our own experience and understanding to compute the truths of God and how they apply to our lives. All experiences are limited in their ability to offer insight into spiritual things, so we break down the differences to help us understand how God is greater than anything we can imagine. God is not like us, and spiritual adoption is not the same experience as earthly adoption. Adoptive parents are parents who love the children that are entrusted to them. While a parent's love for their child does not differ based on how that child entered their family, it is always an imperfect love. God can use all circumstances for good, but earthly adoption doesn't solve the big problem of hurt and the deep need within every person's heart. When God brings people into His family through adoption, it is very different. It is a rescue act. It provides help, love, and presence amid the broken world, and hope for complete redemption and a perfect relationship for the future. Calling Him Father is a transformative gift in the life of a believer. It is a new identity, a new hope, and a new future. Spiritual adoption is the greatest need and the greatest gift for every single person.

MEDITATE   Practice reciting this week's verses from memory and be prepared to say them aloud to your d-group.

ENGAGE

Praise God for being Father to a diverse group of people. Confess the ways that you allow things to divide your relationships with other brothers and sisters of the faith. Thank God for bringing many different personalities and gifts into the faith family. Ask Him to help you value all believers as brothers and sisters in Christ. Ask the Holy Spirit to reveal to you ways to build others up, encourage them in the faith, and empower them to walk in their specific gifts.

ENCOURAGE
Accountability

Use this checklist as a guide for your weekly d-group time. Refer to the discipler's guide at the front of the book for more encouragement and practical advice.

- Work through questions from the accountability card.
- Spend time praying specifics for one another.
- Take turns reciting memory verses.
- Discuss answers to the questions throughout the week that are marked with this symbol ▼

PRAYER REQUEST

_____
_____
_____
_____
_____
_____

ACCOUNTABILITY QUESTIONS

These questions are to be asked of one another in a spirit of accountability (Proverbs 27:17). They are intended to stimulate conversations of character and confession of sin in a safe environment that values honesty, vulnerability, confidentiality, and grace.

1. Have you spent quality time in your spiritual disciplines this week?

2. Have you taken advantage of opportunities to share your faith this week? Explain.

3. Have your words and actions been a good testimony this week to the gospel of Jesus?

4. Have your thoughts and speech been pure (cussing, criticism, negativity, etc.)?

5. Have you been sexually pure this week? Have you been exposed to sexually alluring material? (For those who are married: Have you prioritized quality romantic time with your spouse?)

6. Have you been a good steward of your finances? Have you lacked integrity in the handling of your finances?

7. Have you been honoring and generous in your meaningful relationships this week (Family, friends, etc.)?

8. Have you given in to any addictive behavior this past week? Explain.

9. Have you been completely honest with me?

I'm praying for the salvation of the following two people and prayerfully considering how to share Christ with them myself: _____

> "Therefore, confess your sins to one another, and pray for one another, so that you may be healed."
>
> *James 5:16a*

THE TRUTH

BEHAVIORS IN CHRIST

152
WEEK 8
Spiritual Life &
Spiritual Disciplines

Hebrews 12:1-2

171
WEEK 9
Bible Reading &
Memorization

2 Timothy 3:16-17

190
WEEK 10
Bible Study &
Meditation

Hebrews 4:12

213
WEEK 11
Prayer

Matthew 6:9-13

235
WEEK 12
Worship

Revelation 4:11,
Romans 12:1

256
WEEK 13
Witness

Acts 1:8,
Romans 6:23

281
WEEK 14
Trust and Obedience

Proverbs 3:5-6

THE TRUTH

Week 08 • Day 01

SPIRITUAL LIFE AND SPIRITUAL DISCIPLINES

ESSENTIAL TRUTH

Since the life of faith is more like a marathon than a sprint, we cannot just try to run it; we must train to run it! Disciples of Jesus, therefore, intentionally and consistently train with other disciples of Jesus in the competency of spiritual disciplines like Bible study, prayer, and fasting. These holy habits are behaviors that boost our spiritual growth, encouraging a disciple to "die to self" and "live for Christ."

1. Read the Essential Truth, identify two phrases that stand out, and write them below. Why do you believe these phrases are significant?

_____
_____
_____

2. Is there a spiritual discipline that feels easier to you? Which spiritual discipline do you need to develop?

_____
_____
_____

3. Why do you think spiritual disciplines are essential in the lives of those who follow Jesus? ▼

_____

_____

_____

EXERCISE memory verses

 Therefore, since we have so great a cloud of witnesses surrounding us, let us also lay aside every encumbrance and the sin which so easily entangles us, and let us run with endurance the race that is set before us, fixing our eyes on Jesus, the author and perfecter of faith, who for the joy set before Him endured the cross, despising the shame, and has sat down at the right hand of the throne of God."

Hebrews 12:1-2

Have you ever considered how similar your life as a disciple of Jesus is to that of a "race?" Other believers before us have run the race of faith and bear witness to its importance and intensity. The writer of Hebrews gives a list of biblical pioneers in Hebrews 11 who constitute this "great cloud of witnesses." For this reason, Hebrews 11 is often called the "Hall of Faith," where men and women like Abel, Enoch, Noah, Abraham, Sarah, and Moses were commended for faithfully running the race "set before" them. Followers of Christ are called to turn away from the things that slow them down and run the race "set before" them with endurance. Throughout this race, the disciples of Jesus are told to "fix their eyes" on Jesus. Jesus started and flawlessly finished this race and is both the "source" (energy/strength) and the "course" (example/standard) of your spiritual life. Jesus endured the cross and despised the shame of it all with His eyes fixed on the exhilarating finish line set before Him. He knew what the outcome would be. As a disciple of Jesus, you will endure hardships.

The race set before you—living as a disciple of Jesus in a broken world—requires energy and endurance. You might be tempted to quit the race, but you must keep running.

For this reason, God's Word tells us the finish line is Christ Himself. We do not run merely to run—we run to finish the race. Spiritual disciplines help you keep your eyes fixed on Jesus and your desires set on the hope of what will come as you move forward. We hear from God through His Word, speak to Him through prayer, and grow in relationship with Him. All good relationships require good communication, and your relationship with God is no different. As your heart and mind are filled with the truths of God's Word, apply them through obedience, and God will cause you to become more Christ-like. As you run toward the finish line, God sets your race "before" others to reveal His truth to those around you, especially those around you in a small disciple group.

EXAMPLE

At first glance, Americans seem obsessed with personal fitness. Fad fitness programs, diets, and supplements are a sixty-billion-dollar industry. It is surprising how poorly American health ranks compared to other countries. The problem is that many engage in fitness, looking for quick physical change, with little concern for their overall health and longevity. Appearance alone rarely encourages lasting lifestyle choices.

Choosing healthy habits is never easy, but doing so is the beginning of breaking the cycle of poor health. Spiritual health and maturity are similar in that many look for shortcuts and the guarantee of quick results. Still, few put in the consistency over time required to achieve their desired results. Equally, many are worried about how they appear to others instead of focusing on growing in Christ and serving His kingdom interests. Spiritual disciplines are consistent, healthy choices that help a disciple of Jesus grow closer to God and better serve Him. Following Jesus is not a New Year's resolution abandoned on the gym floor. Following Jesus is a daily commitment to a lifetime of growth in sanctification and service.

THE TRUTH

MEDITATE — Write out this week's verses below as you spend time committing them to memory.

MORE — If you'd like to increase your time in Scripture, commit to this optional weekly Bible reading plan.
Read (or listen via an audio Bible)

- ☐ (Day 1) John 1
- ☐ (Day 2) John 2
- ☐ (Day 3) John 3
- ☐ (Day 4) John 4
- ☐ (Day 5) John 5

ENGAGE

Praise God for being the joy set before you. Confess the obstacles in your life and how easily you are entangled in sin. Thank Him for the examples of faith in Scripture and the originator and perfecter of the faith—Jesus. Ask Him to give you endurance and hope in every season of your race so that you may run faithfully.

Week 08 • Day 02
SPIRITUAL LIFE AND SPIRITUAL DISCIPLINES

EXERCISE

READ *Hebrews 12:1-3 + 2 Corinthians 11:24-27*
☐ Want More? Read John 2

1. Depending on your translation, Hebrews 12:1-2 has 6 verbs. **Highlight** them by listing them below. You can even use an actual highlighter to make note of them in your copy of Scripture. Yes, it is very appropriate to mark up your Bible.

Two imperative verbs—what believers are being commanded to do:

One progressive verb—what a believer is to do continually:

Three past tense verbs—what Jesus has already accomplished:

2. Read the verses before and after 2 Corinthians 11:24–27. **Explain** why Paul is listing the many struggles that he endured. ▼

_____
_____
_____

Scripture provides countless examples of God's goodness and provision (Deuteronomy 3:24, Joshua 10:13, Matthew 14:13-21). God miraculously met the needs of His people as He led them out of slavery to a promised land (Exodus). Generations later, God marvelously shook the earth to liberate Paul and Silas from prison (Acts 16:16-40). Perhaps no other early disciple of Jesus lived a more magnificent life than Paul. Paul endured great suffering and was afforded even greater success in serving Christ's great Kingdom (2 Corinthians 11).

It is easy to understand why we often focus on the wondrous mountaintops of God's provision and the extreme commitment of those who climb toward His calling. However, when seeking a metaphor to communicate the Christ-centered life, Paul does not employ the imagery of a mountain climber or a powerlifter. He instead utilizes the imagery of a marathon runner (Hebrews 12:1-2; 1 Corinthians 9:24-27; 2 Timothy 4:7; Philippians 3:14). Although the lives of those who follow Christ will contain mountaintop moments, these experiences are rarely the defining attributes of their faith.

> I press on toward the goal for the prize of the upward call of God in Christ Jesus."
>
> *Phillippians 3:14*

The continued use of the illustration of a marathon throughout Paul's writings demonstrates how the Christ-centered life is to be defined by running with a faithful community, running free of those things that slow us down, and running with both a gospel focus and Kingdom endurance (1 Corinthians 9:27). Today's examination of Hebrews 12:1 first reminds us that we should not run this race alone (Ecclesiastes 4:9-12; Galatians 6:2). God has placed around us a "great cloud of witnesses" (Hebrews 12:1). A believer is never alone. Every disciple of Jesus has equal access to the Spirit of God, the Word of God, and the people of God. In a community of Christ followers, we have a people with which to train, replacing harmful habits with healthy behaviors. Such a "cloud of witnesses" develops an environment of accountability and encouragement. This is one of many reasons why disciples of Jesus are commanded to embrace the provision of Jesus' Church and seek to be in vital partnership with a local body of believers (Acts 20:28; Philippians 1:5; Hebrews 10:25).

Hebrews 12:1 also encourages us to "lay aside every encumbrance and the sin that so easily entangles us." This stands as a striking appeal to live out your spiritual life within the freedom of Christ—a freedom that fundamentally requires training in the discipline of "letting things go." Traditionally called the discipline of "fasting," the ability to say "no" to certain things proves much broader and more holistic than just food and drink. Although not commanded in scripture, the Bible highlights fasting as beneficial. The early Church in Acts fasted before making important decisions (Acts 13:2; 14:23). Scripture often interlinks fasting and prayer as an opportunity to focus entirely on God. Paul says it plainly, "It is for freedom that Christ has set you free" (Galatians 5:1). Jesus fully liberated His disciples from the shackles of sin (Romans 6:6) and chains of living for lesser things (Matthew 6:33; Colossian 3:2). Sadly, many followers succumb to the lies of the enemy (2 Corinthians 11:3) and continue to place their wrists into bonds that no longer lock (John 8:36). Those who do so are not realizing that the starting shot of a believer's marathon rings out from the victory of Jesus. The race is already won. Consequently, the disciple of Jesus does not race to win. We run with endurance "the race set before us," a race that Jesus has already won on behalf of others. The "joy set before" us then is sharing in Jesus' kingdom advancement—seeing others come under the reign of Christ and the freedom it brings. We run so others might hear the gospel and be won to Christ and His Kingdom.

1. Acknowledge this timeless truth about good relationships as God has designed them. Why do good relationships require discipline and endurance? List some of the habits of all good relationships.

___

2. Can you think of a disciple of Jesus in your Christian community who exemplifies the diligence and discipline of good relationships? What does endurance look like in their life? What "habit-forming" or "habit-destroying" disciplines do you see in their life? ▼

___

THE TRUTH

3. Respond to this truth. What specific actions of obedience are God calling you to now? Write down at least one "habit-forming" discipline (Bible study, prayer, etc.) and one "habit-destroying" discipline (fasting, accountability, boundaries, etc.) you would like to focus on during this season of your spiritual journey.

_____

_____

_____

MEDITATE   Fill in the blanks as you continue committing this week's verses to memory.

> "Therefore, since we have so great a cloud of _____ surrounding us, let us also lay aside every encumbrance and the sin which so easily _____ us, and let us run with _____ the race that is set before us, fixing our eyes on Jesus, the author and perfecter of faith, who for the joy set before Him _____ the cross, despising the shame, and has sat down at the right hand of the throne of God."

Hebrews 12:1-2

ENGAGE

Praise God for being with us. Confess how you grow tired, lonely, or frustrated spiritually. Thank Him for being consistently faithful, even when you are not. Ask Him to light the fire of discipline in your heart so that you may pursue intimate time with Him and intentional work for Him.

Week 08 • Day 03

SPIRITUAL LIFE AND SPIRITUAL DISCIPLINES

EXERCISE

READ *Hebrews 12:1-3 / 2 Timothy 4:7-8*

☐ Want More? Read John 3

1. Considering these two passages, what is the joy set before you, or what do you have to look forward to when your race is finished?

_____

_____

_____

2. First Corinthians 9:25 gives some additional insight into our future reward. How is the believer's final reward different from an athlete's reward?

_____

_____

_____

The first disciples of Jesus and the early Church ran the marathon of their faith with seemingly supernatural conviction and consistency (1 Corinthians 15:58; Titus 2:7-8). In the service of Christ, Paul faced shipwreck, hunger, persecution, and countless perils. The early church endured immense persecution (John 15:10; Acts 8:1; 2 Timothy 3:12). In the name of Jesus, many lost their businesses, their homes, their citizenship, and even their lives. Standing before the impending darkness of such difficulty, these ordinary men and women of faith held a steadfast focus on Jesus. They "accepted joyfully the seizure" of their property, knowing that they have for themselves "a better possession and a lasting one" (Hebrews 10:34). Paul, fully aware he would soon be executed, wrote to Timothy from a solitary prison cell. Although he had been abandoned by those who claimed to be friends, Paul assured Timothy that Jesus remains with him even in prison (2 Timothy 4:16-18). The presence and pleasure of Jesus Christ is indeed a better and lasting possession.

Such spiritual maturity rarely develops outside of the marathon of continually pursuing Christ. Hebrews 12:2 instructs the disciples of Jesus to "fix their eyes on Jesus, the author, and perfecter of faith." A life defined by holy habits is lived with a fixed focus on Jesus. A believer who has filled their heart with the Word of God (Psalms 119:11) has little room for the trappings of a broken world (Luke 16:13). Likewise, a disciple dedicated to prayer for their enemies (Matthew 5:44) will grow to love even those who persecute them (Luke 6:27-28). As "the author and perfecter of faith," Jesus completed the same race we are being asked to run. He has designed a perfect marathon for each of His disciples. In such a marathon, spiritual growth is a byproduct of each continual step with Jesus. By taking intentional steps of faith, we begin "to walk by faith" (2 Corinthians 5:7), embarking on a faith journey.

A life characterized by the marathon of running for Christ is a life defined by faithfulness, freedom, focus, and finishing well. Such a marathon celebrates Jesus' great work through the hands and feet of those who follow Him (Romans 10:15). Jesus was aware of the cross and spent His ministry driven from village to village and person to person. With focus and intent, Jesus fully invested Himself in the lives of those around Him. Hebrews 12:3 reminds us to consider the "hostility" that Jesus Himself endured during His earthly race so that we will "not grow weary and lose heart" during our endurance race of faith.

As Paul gets closer to finishing His spiritual marathon, he takes time to reflect on his journey at the end of his life. Second Timothy is the last known letter written by Paul before his martyrdom. Examining his life in Second Timothy 4:7-9, Paul is sure he had run well. Sadly, many within the church cannot evaluate their life with such boldness and assurance. A life lived compared to others is a life lived focused on the marathon of others. A life fixed on personal gain, comfort, or fleeting goals is lived for the moment, but Paul's assurance comes from knowing that he kept his focus on Jesus and ran with the endurance to finish well, considering God's kingdom agenda.

1. If today was the end of your life, would you have the assurance of a well-run race? Explain.

_____
_____
_____

2. What distracts you from focusing on Jesus? What is going on in your heart and mind that needs to be set aside so you can focus on Jesus entirely?

_____
_____
_____

3. Which spiritual discipline are you feeling compelled to pursue more consistently?

_____
_____
_____

THE TRUTH

MEDITATE — Fill in the blanks as you continue committing this week's verses to memory.

> "Therefore, since we have so great a cloud of _____ surrounding us, let us also lay aside every _____ and the sin which so easily _____ us, and let us run with _____ the race that is set before us, fixing our eyes on Jesus, the author and _____ of faith, who for the joy set before Him _____ the cross, despising the _____, and has sat down at the right hand of the throne of God"
>
> Hebrews 12:1-2

ENGAGE

Praise God for being present in His Word and when we speak to Him through prayer. Confess how you undervalue these two main spiritual disciplines. Thank Him for meeting you right where you are, being with you when your mind is distracted, and not leaving you. Ask God to help you be present with Him in prayer and Bible study as a response to His consistent presence in these places and times.

Week 08 • Day 04
SPIRITUAL LIFE AND SPIRITUAL DISCIPLINES

EXAMINATION

READ
John 14:1-15   ☐ Want More? Read John 4

WATCH
Week 8 - Spiritual Life and Spiritual Disciplines

To watch the video, scan the QR code below by opening your phone's camera and holding your device so that the QR code appears on the screen. Click the link associated with the QR code, and choose this week's video. https://qrco.de/be3SWs

1. Wrestling, warfare, building construction, farming, and marathons are all used to display the work of the spiritual life throughout Scripture. Which analogy is most relatable to you and why?

2. Hebrews 12:1-2 displays the value of training to develop the inner being. The question is not if you are running, but how? Describe your training and any changes that you feel called to make.

_____
_____
_____

3. Prayer is conforming and communal. Through your time in prayer, are you becoming more like God in your thinking and actions (being conformed to Christ)? Are you enjoying quality with God through prayer (community with God)?

_____
_____
_____

EXERCISE

READ *Proverbs 27:17*

Spiritual disciplines are not developed in isolation. When a piece of iron needs sharpening, it is paired with another piece of iron. One is consistently rubbed against the other with appropriate pressure, generating heat and friction between the two. This process will eventually refine the dull iron, making it sharper and more effective for its job. When you are tempted to compare your commitment, consistency, and depth within the spiritual disciplines with that of another believer, remember that character does not grow in isolation. Likely, the person you observe has walked in pressure, consistency, and accountability with another. Spiritual disciplines that display a deep and intimate relationship with the Lord have been cultivated within a faithful and consistent community. You have been given the gift of community and accountability within this disciple group. Don't miss your chance to be refined and sharpened to live an obedient, disciple-making life. Commit yourselves to the spiritual disciplines alongside your brothers and sisters. Spiritual growth is not accidental. We learn how to submit ourselves to the authority of God, and through His power, we are transformed.

> But He said to them, "I have food to eat that you do not know about."
>
> *John 4:32*

MEDITATE Below, attempt to write out this week's verses from memory.

ENGAGE

Praise God for being relational with you. Confess the ways you want to hide in isolation until you feel worthy of committing or investing in community. Thank Him for giving you the Church as a helper, specifically the people in your d-group as spiritual running partners. Ask Him to allow your group to grow in accountability and consistency so that you will each be sharpened by the other and equipped for the work you are called to.

Week 08 • Day 05
SPIRITUAL LIFE AND SPIRITUAL DISCIPLINES

EXERCISE

READ *James 1:9-12*
☐ Want More? Read John 5

Jesus has promised and secured eternal life for us with Himself forever in Heaven. A disciple of Jesus looks forward with hope, knowing that the victory has been won and their future is secured. We do not have to wait for Heaven to experience God because Jesus has provided a way for us to have a relationship with Him today. How do we experience God personally? We experience God through His Word, through prayer, and through practicing self-denial (fasting). His Word is living and active, and we hear Him through it. We speak to Him through prayer, and He is with us. He hears us and knows our hearts and circumstances. When we trust and obey God in these three fundamental ways, we live the "spiritual life." Denying self and living for Christ creates the ordained rhythm of success and significance we cannot get any other way. Oppressed by the weight of the broken world, we need Him. We have the vast and holy privilege of living with the full assurance of "Immanuel"—God with us (Matthew 1:23; 20:28). But we all neglect spiritual disciplines. Too often, time with God is seen as an easily compromised luxury. Spiritual disciplines in the life of a disciple of Christ provide essential nutrients for those who would otherwise be starving.

Lasting growth in Christ will not develop from a self-help movement, intellectual study, or scientific exploration. The assurances and intimacy we experience when we walk with God will only develop with a consistent dedication to spiritual disciplines. The more we spend time with God in prayer and Bible study, the more we want to know about Him. The more we know about Him, the more we want to let go of other things to spend time with Him.

EXAMPLE

During the 1968 Summer Olympics, John Stephen Akawari of Tanzania gained global notoriety. Early in the race, John suffered an injury that resulted in a badly bruised leg and dislocated knee. Through grueling pain, John refused to quit, choosing instead to hobble and limp through what remained of the 26.2-mile Olympic marathon. When interviewed, John said, "My country did not send me 5,000 miles to start a race; they sent me 5,000 miles to finish a race." What a great attitude! The race Jesus has called you to is not a simple event you experience from the sidelines, nor a short-term commitment. The race you run as a disciple of Jesus is a lifetime endurance endeavor. Jesus did not grant us His goodness and Spirit to start this race. He gave us His goodness and Spirit to finish it.

MEDITATE   Practice reciting this week's verses from memory and be prepared to say them aloud to your d-group.

THE TRUTH

ENGAGE

Praise God for being your Father. Confess the ways that you neglect your relationship with Him. Thank Him for his consistent presence, power, and relationship in your life. Ask Him to convict you of sin and to give you a clear focus on Him. Ask Him to draw you to His Word and to prayer. Tell Him you want to be authentic in your relationship with Him. As you commit yourself daily to the spiritual disciplines, trust Him to be with you and provide for your needs.

ENCOURAGE

Use this checklist as a guide for your weekly d-group time. Refer to the discipler's guide at the front of the book for more encouragement and practical advice.

- Work through questions from the accountability page.

- Spend time praying specifics for one another.

- Take turns reciting the memory verses.

- Discuss answers to the questions throughout the week that are marked with this symbol. ⊙

PRAYER REQUESTS

ACCOUNTABILITY QUESTIONS

These questions are to be asked of one another in a spirit of accountability (Proverbs 27:17). They are intended to stimulate conversations of character and confession of sin in a safe environment that values honesty, vulnerability, confidentiality, and grace.

1. Have you spent quality time in your spiritual disciplines this week?
2. Have you taken advantage of opportunities to share your faith this week? Explain.
3. Have your words and actions been a good testimony this week to the gospel of Jesus?
4. Have your thoughts and speech been pure (cussing, criticism, negativity, etc.)?
5. Have you been sexually pure this week? Have you been exposed to sexually alluring material? (For those who are married: Have you prioritized quality romantic time with your spouse?)
6. Have you been a good steward of your finances? Have you lacked integrity in the handling of your finances?
7. Have you been honoring and generous in your meaningful relationships this week (Family, friends, etc.)?
8. Have you given in to any addictive behavior this past week? Explain.
9. Have you been completely honest with me?

I'm praying for the salvation of the following two people and prayerfully considering how to share Christ with them myself: _____

> "Therefore, confess your sins to one another, and pray for one another, so that you may be healed."
>
> *James 5:16a*

Week 09 • Day 01
BIBLE READING AND MEMORIZATION

ESSENTIAL TRUTH

The Word of God is to the soul what food is to the body. Disciples of Jesus, in a very real way, live by the Book, trusting and obeying God as they trust and obey Scripture. A disciple of Jesus pulls away daily from the busyness of life to spend personal time with Jesus Christ by reading, studying, and memorizing the Word of God.

1. Read the Essential Truth, identify two phrases that stand out to you, and write them below. Why do you believe these phrases are significant?

_____
_____
_____

2. How would you describe your current Bible reading and memorization habits? Are these habits enabling you to trust and obey God?

_____
_____

3. Is your Bible reading and memorization inconsistent or nonexistent, or do you consistently pull away from the busyness of life to spend personal time with Jesus Christ?

_____
_____
_____

EXERCISE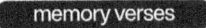

> All Scripture is inspired by God and profitable for teaching, for reproof, for correction, for training in righteousness; so that the man of God may be adequate, equipped for every good work."
>
> *2 Timothy 3:16-17*

The Bible is a collection of 66 books, written over 1,500 years by 40 authors on 3 continents, in 3 different languages. Remarkably, the individuals God inspired to record His Word (2 Peter 1:21) were kings, servants, philosophers, fishermen, poets, doctors, military leaders, herdsmen, and even a first-century IRS agent. With the diversity of 40 different authors writing from all walks of life over 1,500 years, the Bible speaks with supernatural unity. It is the unified story of how God worked throughout history to restore His relationship with humanity. Scripture is without error and perfectly unified, which is only possible because the Bible has one master architect. The Bible is God's Word to humanity. The Bible's supernatural "dual" authorship makes it just as relevant today as it was for the original audience thousands of years ago. The Living Word of God contains timeless answers for raising kids, improving your marriage, managing your emotions, handling money, breaking bad habits, finding fulfillment, experiencing God's forgiveness, and receiving eternal life. Scripture is essential to your life. With that in mind, many followers of Christ find Bible reading plans helpful to track progress and work strategically.

EXAMPLE

New vehicles arrive with a manual written explicitly for each make and model. This manual explains the operation and care of one of life's most expensive and complex purchases. However, this book generally remains in the glovebox. Ask any dealership service advisor and you are guaranteed to hear stories of drivers who could hardly reach the steering wheel and pedals, unaware that the power seats could move forward with the push of a button. One larger family even discovered a year later that their family vehicle had an entire back seat that only needed to be folded out.

The Word of God is far more than an operations guide or owner's manual for daily life. Unfortunately, many followers of Christ treat the Bible like the owner's manual for their car—putting it away where they can find it in emergencies. A follower of Jesus cannot afford to drive through life, only looking to God's Word as a last resort. Without consistent study and application of Scripture, how can you possibly understand God and His statutes?

WEEK 09

MEDITATE — Write out this week's verses below as you spend time committing them to memory.

MORE — If you'd like to increase your time in Scripture, commit to this optional weekly Bible reading plan.
Read (or listen via an audio Bible)

- ☐ (Day 1) John 6
- ☐ (Day 2) John 7
- ☐ (Day 3) John 8
- ☐ (Day 4) John 9
- ☐ (Day 5) John 10

ENGAGE

Praise God for giving us the Bible—His inspired, infallible, inerrant Word. Confess how you underestimate the power of God's Word in your life. Thank God for the ability to hear Him through His Word and for its ability to penetrate your heart and mind. Ask Him to help you commit to reading, memorizing, and studying the Bible so that you can be prepared and equipped for the work He's called you to.

THE TRUTH

Week 09 • Day 02
BIBLE READING AND MEMORIZATION

EXERCISE

READ   *Psalm 119:33-40*

☐ Want More? Read John 7

1. According to 2 Timothy 3:16, why should you spend time in God's Word? How do you see this affirmed in Psalm 119:33-40?

_____
_____
_____

2. Reference Psalm 119:33-40. For each verse of this text, **Highlight** the request the Psalmist made to the Lord and his desire that led to the request.

1. Ps. 119:33	Teach me the way of your statutes	I shall observe them to the end
2. Ps. 119:34		
3. Ps. 119:35		
4. Ps. 119:36		
5. Ps. 119:37		
6. Ps. 119:38		
7. Ps. 119:39		
8. Ps. 119:40		

Psalm 119 is the longest chapter in the Bible, encompassing worship, prayer, and poetry. The overarching format of Psalm 119 is an acrostic of the Hebrew alphabet, emphasizing an apparent order of thoughts. Though the author of Psalms 119 is unknown, we can take comfort in knowing he endured significant difficulties while consistently extolling the practical value of God's Word. This book utilizes a series of terms to describe God's Word—law, testimony, precept, statute, commandment, ways, judgment, word, and promise—many of which are in today's reading.

In Psalm 119:33-40, the Psalmist asks the Lord to teach him (v. 33), to give him understanding (v. 34), to help him obey (v. 35), to incline his heart (v. 36), to help him keep his eyes fixed (v. 37), and to establish the Word in his heart and mind (v. 38). The Psalmist demonstrates his longing to obey God's Word with all his heart and for all of his days (v. 33-34). He desires to look to Scripture (v. 35) and not to things that are selfishly dishonest (v.36) or fleeting (v. 37). He wants the Word of God to produce an appropriate fear of the Lord (v. 38). He knows the Word of the Lord is good (v. 39). He longs for God's Word (v. 40).

Many religious texts speak about morality and right living through differing aspects of a work-based system. Books such as the Quran, Vedas, and the Book of Mormon encourage doing good works to please an unreachable god. The Bible alone teaches that salvation is a free gift from God that cannot be earned and must be given. Whereas other religious texts can be condensed to a list of rules and regulations, the Bible centers on the restoration of our relationship with God and what He has already accomplished to secure for us a right standing with Himself through the life, death, and resurrection of Jesus. In this way, the Bible is a love letter and much more.

The Word of God is the baseline for godly living. It is the standard by which you can understand God's character and His calling on your life. The Bible is how followers of Christ can know the gospel (Romans 10:13-17) and how they maintain their spiritual life (Matthew 4:4). The Bible provides the only infallible foundation for truth. This truth is expressed through the lives of different languages, cultures, demographics, economics, governments, and occupations. The sixty-six books of the Bible have withstood the test of time as the sole pillar of absolute truth. To such an extent, the apostle John used references to the person of Jesus and to the Word of God interchangeably in the first chapter of his gospel (John 1:1) .

In a society saturated with information, there is no shortage of sermons, books, podcasts, media, and apps. You may ask why a follower of Jesus should spend time in God's Word—and even memorizing it—when others who claim to be experts have formatted the information. There are many good reasons. Most importantly, God commands it (Joshua 1:8), success demands it (Psalm 1:1-3), and relationships require it (2 Timothy 3:16). A person who spends time reading, studying, and memorizing the Bible will be able to discern rightly what is said about God. They can live victoriously because they know what God expects from them (Psalm 119:11). A student of Scripture can both defend their faith (1 Peter 3:15; 2 Corinthians 10:5; 2 Timothy 2:15) and tell others the truth (2 Timothy 4:2-4). There is no substitute for the Word of God in the life of a disciple of Jesus—an accessible Word from God that is read, studied, memorized, and obeyed.

1. Acknowledge one of the timeless truths that you have learned about God's Word today. Which of the following list of truths seem most meaningful to you at this point in your life: Scripture is inspired, without error, clear, available, sufficient, relevant, living, and trustworthy.

___

___

___

2. Respond to the value you place on Scripture. Where do you go first for answers, information, and encouragement (list three below). If it is sermons, books, blog posts, social media—why do you think that is your first stop? ▼

___

___

___

3. As a disciple of Jesus, do you believe your time spent in the Word of God is adequate for trusting and obeying Him and teaching others to do the same? ▼

_____
_____
_____

MEDITATE Fill in the blanks as you continue committing this week's verses to memory.

> "All Scripture is inspired by God and profitable for _____, for _____, for _____, for training in righteousness; so that the man of God may be adequate, equipped for every good work."
>
> *2 Timothy 3:16-17*

ENGAGE

Praise God for His faithfulness through all generations (Psalm 119:90). Confess how you seek understanding outside God's Word. Thank God for His continual pursuit of you and His faithfulness and loving kindness towards you. Ask Him to give you the desire to spend time in His Word. Pray that He will make your time spent in His Word as sweet like honey (Psalm 119:103), a lamp for your path (Psalm 119:105), and the joy of your heart (Psalm 119:111).

Week 09 • Day 03
BIBLE READING AND MEMORIZATION

EXERCISE

READ   *John 8:28-36*

☐ Want More? Read John 8

1. In today's verses, Jesus said to the Jews who had believed him, "the truth will make you free" (John 8:32). They questioned their need for freedom since they had never been enslaved to anyone (John 8:33). **Highlight** how Jesus defines their slavery and need for freedom in verses 34-36? ⓥ

_____
_____
_____

2. Jesus said, "If you continue in My word, then you are truly disciples of Mine" (John 8:31-32). Other versions use the word abide or hold to. Read John 15:4-9 and **Acknowledge** the timeless truth of what it means to abide in Christ and His Word. ⓥ

_____
_____
_____

Referring to yesterday's discussion of Psalm 119, the Psalmist says in verse 131, "I open my mouth and pant, longing for your command." The English word pant translates from the word sha'aph, which expresses the imagery of gasping for air. A disciple of Jesus requires the Word of God, as much as they need to breathe. Like breathing, a believer cannot go without studying the Bible. Although the Word of God is essential for the disciple of Christ, it is equally foreign and often offensive for those who do not know God. Unbelievers can study the Bible academically and intellectually, but apart from salvation in Christ and the Holy Spirit, they cannot fully understand it (1 Corinthians 2:14).

In today's chapter from the Gospel of John, Jesus sets a qualifier for being His disciple. The qualifier He set is to abide or remain in His Word. The term abide in the original Greek text means "to live in something continually." Another way to say it would be "continually being at home." The word disciple in Greek is often taught to mean follower, but the word disciple also means student. A student of the Word spends time in Scripture regularly with a desire to learn, understand, and apply. As disciples, when you let the Word richly dwell within you (Colossians 3:16), it will mark you. The Word of God is intended to complete a believer (2 Timothy 3:16). Countless masses have professed to be Christians throughout history, but Jesus tells us those who follow Him will abide in His Word.

Believers are challenged to read God's Word with careful observation and to meditate on its truths day and night (Deuteronomy 17:19; Psalm 1:2). Plan a time and place to spend in God's Word each day. It is unlikely that someone has to remind you about your scheduled vacation. You scheduled it because it is important to you. Similarly, schedule your time in the Word and show up. A simple study method includes four parts: **Highlight** what the text is saying and how it is communicated, **Explain** what it meant to the original audience, **Acknowledge** the timeless theological truths presented, and **Respond** personally to those truths in a specific and measurable way. Begin a discipline of Bible memorization. Memorizing is hard work, but the Word of God will be in your heart and mind during times of crisis, ministry, and daily life. "Hiding God's Word in your heart" by committing scripture to memory will transform how you think and act (Psalm 119:11).

In John 8:32, Jesus assures those Jews who believe in Him that abiding in His Word will allow them to know the truth, and the truth will set them free. Many people present in the crowd that day did not believe and could not fully understand that Jesus was not referring to physical bondage. He was teaching about enslavement to sin. Trusting and obeying the Word of God liberates His followers from the chains of worry, addiction, and self-destruction. The Bible requires your attention and obedience so that you might walk in a manner worthy of your calling as a disciple of Jesus (Ephesians 4:1).

1. Evaluating your thoughts and actions daily, how might someone **respond** to the question of what marks or defines you? ▼

_____
_____
_____

2. How does your time spent in the Bible reflect your identity as a disciple—a student of the Word who regularly spends time in Scripture with the desire to learn, understand, and apply? Prayerfully respond to God and write down how you hope to grow in this area? ▼

_____
_____
_____

3. Consider an example from your life when your time in God's Word overflowed into your prayer life and relationships. What was your part, and what was God's part, in you being a "doer of the Word?"

_____
_____
_____

MEDITATE — Fill in the blanks as you continue committing this week's verses to memory.

> "All Scripture is inspired by God and profitable for _____, for _____, for _____, for training in _____; so that the man of God may be _____, equipped for every good _____."
>
> *2 Timothy 3:16-17*

ENGAGE

Praise God for His living and active Word (Hebrews 4:12). Confess how you are marked by other forms of input instead of God's Word. Thank Him for providing His Word to shape you into the image of Jesus and enable you to do the work He has called you to. Ask Him for conviction to grow consistently as a student of the Word by committing to reading, studying, and memorizing Scripture.

Week 09 • Day 04
BIBLE READING AND MEMORIZATION

EXAMINATION

READ
Joshua 1:6-9 ☐ Want More? Read John 9

WATCH
Week 9 - Bible Reading and Memorization

To watch the video, scan the QR code below by opening your phone's camera and holding your device so that the QR code appears on the screen. Click the link associated with the QR code, and choose this week's video. https://qrco.de/be3SWs

1. How does the truth of God's Word being God-breathed impact how you read its contents? ⊙

_____
_____
_____

2. God's Word is reliable and sufficient for all of life's troubles and questions. Describe how you acknowledge the sufficiency of Scripture and how you approach it as a learner, dependent on its truth for every circumstance.

_____
_____
_____

3. Why should you read the Bible? List all of the answers you can come up with and use Psalm 119 to add to your list.

_____
_____
_____

EXERCISE

READ *Joshua 1:6-9*

Our culture has been trained to consume bite-sized pieces of information and quickly move on to the next. Because we've adapted to this information consumption, most people struggle to focus their attention. Fewer books are being read, and fewer topics are being deeply researched as people can resort to visually engaging videos with easy-to-consume information. How a follower of Christ is commanded to abide in the Word is counter-cultural. The Bible is intended to be read, re-read, and studied deeply to understand its original intention. It is designed to be memorized so the believer may meditate on its contents day and night. It is a living document, different from any other book that we may have in our possession. It is God-breathed; therefore, we read, study, memorize, and repeat because it is His daily Word. We come to know Him, love Him, trust Him, obey Him, and teach others to do the same through our consistent time in His Word.

> This book of the law shall not depart from your mouth, but you shall meditate on it day and night, so that you may be careful to do according to all that is written in it; for then you will make your way prosperous, and then you will have success."
>
> *Joshua 1:8*

MEDITATE Below, attempt to write out this week's verses from memory.

ENGAGE

Praise God for His Word in our lives. Confess how you resort to short summaries of the truth instead of consistently residing in the contents of Scripture. Thank God for being relational with us and allowing us to hear from Him day and night. Ask Him to increase your focus and attention abilities so you may consistently plant yourself in His Word and be careful to do all that is written in it.

Week 09 • Day 05

BIBLE READING AND MEMORIZATION

EXERCISE

READ *Colossians 3:1-17*
☐ Want More? Read John 10

Colossians 3:5 identifies a life separated from Christ: immoral, impure, evil, greedy, and idolatrous. This characterizes both the life we were born into and the natural bent of our world. However, when a person is raised up with Christ and rescued from this sin, they put aside the anger, wrath, malice, slander, and abusive speech (Colossians 3:8). The seek to quickly "fast" from these toxic actions and attitudes. They do not merely "try" to get rid of these behaviors, they "train" to get rid of these unholy habits and replace them with holy ones. A disciple of Jesus trains to set their minds on the things above. The believer—one who is chosen, holy, and beloved—trains to learn to walk in compassion, kindness, humility, gentleness, patience, forgiveness, and peace (Colossians 3:12-15). This fruit reveals itself in our lives when we allow the Word of Christ through spiritual disciplines to dwell richly within us (Colossians 3:16). When we abide in the Word, we receive wisdom, teaching, correction, training, and endless reasons to "sing with thankfulness in our hearts to God" (Colossians 3:16). The transformation that happens in our hearts through abiding in the Word, overflows into our lives. When the Word of God dwells richly within us, we will "do all in the name of the Lord Jesus, giving thanks through Him to God the Father" (Colossians 3:17).

EXAMPLE

David Livingstone, the famous 19th-century explorer and physician, was rumored to have started his famous exploration of the African continent with a library of over 70 books. The sheer weight of these books pitted against the harsh African terrain left Livingstone no option but to diminish his library gradually until one book remained—his Bible. If behavior indicates belief, Livingston believed the Bible was more important than maps, navigation, and survival techniques. History plays host to the stories of those who hid sections of Scripture in secret places and smuggled Bible pages. Aware of the importance of God's Word, John Wyclif, Eric Liddell, Bob Fu, and countless unknowns took significant risks to hold the pages of Scripture or to get others to hold them. Containing aspects of history, anthropology, psychology, physics, and theology, the Bible is the most complex and intricate love letter ever written.

MEDITATE Practice reciting this week's verses from memory and be prepared to say them aloud to your d-group.

ENGAGE

Praise God for His desire and ability to be with us. Confess how you sometimes look to others and/or yourself for help before coming to God. Thank Him for providing everything that you need through Himself and His Word. Ask Him to make Himself known to you in new and powerful ways through His Word, to reveal more of your sin so that you may turn from it and become more like Jesus. Ask Him to allow His Word to infiltrate your thoughts, words, and actions.

ENCOURAGE

Use this checklist as a guide for your weekly d-group time. Refer to the discipler's guide at the back of the book for more encouragement and practical advice.

- Work through questions from the accountability page.

- Spend time praying specifics for one another.

- Take turns reciting the memory verses.

- Discuss answers to the questions throughout the week that are marked with this symbol. ▼

PRAYER REQUESTS

ACCOUNTABILITY QUESTIONS

These questions are to be asked of one another in a spirit of accountability (Proverbs 27:17). They are intended to stimulate conversations of character and confession of sin in a safe environment that values honesty, vulnerability, confidentiality, and grace.

1. Have you spent quality time in your spiritual disciplines this week?

2. Have you taken advantage of opportunities to share your faith this week? Explain.

3. Have your words and actions been a good testimony this week to the gospel of Jesus?

4. Have your thoughts and speech been pure (cussing, criticism, negativity, etc.)?

5. Have you been sexually pure this week? Have you been exposed to sexually alluring material? (For those who are married: Have you prioritized quality romantic time with your spouse?)

6. Have you been a good steward of your finances? Have you lacked integrity in the handling of your finances?

7. Have you been honoring and generous in your meaningful relationships this week (Family, friends, etc.)?

8. Have you given in to any addictive behavior this past week? Explain.

9. Have you been completely honest with me?

I'm praying for the salvation of the following two people and prayerfully considering how to share Christ with them myself: _____

> "Therefore, confess your sins to one another, and pray for one another, so that you may be healed."
> *James 5:16a*

Week 10 • Day 01

BIBLE STUDY AND MEDITATION

ESSENTIAL TRUTH

The critical task of personal Bible study is to HEAR from God, ensuring that we are pulling the correct meaning "out of" Scripture and not putting meaning "into" Scripture. This is called inductive Bible study, and it has four steps: observation (Highlight what is says), interpretation (Explain what it means to them), implication (Acknowledge the timeless theological truth), and application (Respond with specific action). Once we have confidence that we know the Bible's originally intended meaning, hearing from God personally drives us to both meditate on it and obey it passionately.

1. Read the Essential Truth, identify two phrases that stand out, and write them below. Why do you believe these phrases are significant?

_____
_____
_____

2. How would you describe your method of Bible Study?

_____
_____
_____

3. Why do you think Bible study and meditating on God's Word are both essential? ⊙

_____
_____
_____

EXERCISE `memory verse`

> "For the Word of God is alive and active. Sharper than any double-edged sword, it penetrates even to dividing soul and spirit, joints and marrow; it judges the thoughts and attitudes of the heart."
>
> *Hebrews 4:12*

Bible study and meditation are supporting spiritual disciplines. God gave us the Bible so we could know Him better. Disciple of Jesus profits more from their time in the Word when they let more of it into their hearts and minds. The right question is not "How many times have you been through the Bible?" but "How many times has the Bible been through you" Unfortunately, the contemporary church is often infatuated with slick processes that promise spiritual growth but lack deep and intentional engagement in Scripture. A disciple of Jesus will not significantly mature apart from personal time in God's Word. Like milk for newborn babies, the Word of God grants nourishment and supports growth (1 Peter 2:2). It is through the study and application of Scripture that a Christ follower learns to distinguish between good and evil, right and wrong, and spiritual health assumes we are living by the Book (Hebrews 5:11-14). God uses Scripture as the key tool to transform you progressively into the likeness of Jesus as the truths of Scripture are ingested (taken in), digested (studied and acknowledged), and metabolized (lived out).

The writer of Hebrews wants the reader to acknowledge that the Word of God is unlike any other text of literature. Though the Bible is a book, no other book is alive and active like the Bible. In John 6:63, Jesus claims, "It is the Spirit who gives life; the flesh provides no benefit; the Words that I have spoken to you are spirit, and are life." Jesus emphasizes that His words are the source of true life, purpose, and provision. The apostle John begins his biography of Jesus' life (the Gospel of John) by equating the person of Jesus with the phrase "the Word" of God, further enforcing the importance of God's Word. John declares, "In the beginning was the Word, and the Word was with God, and the Word was God. He was in the beginning with God" (John 1:1-2). To study the Bible is to examine the person of Christ. To spend time with the Bible is to spend time with Christ.

EXAMPLE

In 1845, Sir John Franklin departed England with two ships and 129 men. Franklin, a British Royal Navy officer, sought to explore and map a safe route through the Northwest Passage. As accomplished mariners and navigators, Sir Franklin and his crew confidently embarked. Franklin had personally engineered significant modifications to both vessels while strategically planning for all known contingencies. This well-supplied expedition was outfitted with modern canned rations, nautical clocks, compasses, and charters. Though well-prepared, Franklin could not foresee the then cutting-edge canned foods causing lead poisoning—no more than he forecasted the adverse effects of extreme cold on the nautical clocks required to plot an accurate longitude. He did not know what he did not know. Like many within the modern Church, Sir Franklin had overestimated himself and placed too much faith in "cutting-edge" technologies. Too many believers run to the Bible only after finding themselves wrecked upon the ice. Desperate and no longer in their right minds, they forget that in the Bible, God has given them an infallible map. This map, combined with the skills to understand it, the guidance of the Holy Spirit, and the support of the local church, establishes God's secure turn-by-turn directions.

THE TRUTH

MEDITATE — Write out this week's verse below as you spend time committing them to memory.

MORE — If you'd like to increase your time in Scripture, commit to this optional weekly Bible reading plan.
Read (or listen via an audio Bible)

- ☐ (Day 1) John 11
- ☐ (Day 2) John 12
- ☐ (Day 3) John 13
- ☐ (Day 4) John 14
- ☐ (Day 5) John 15

ENGAGE

Praise God for His living and active presence in and through His Word. Confess the excuses you make to avoid studying and meditating on Scripture. Thank Him for pursuing a relationship with you and transforming your life. Ask God to give you a desire "to live by the Book." Pray that you experience Scripture as more precious than gold, sweeter than honey, and the great reward in obedience (Psalm 19:10-11).

Week 10 • Day 02

BIBLE STUDY AND MEDITATION

EXERCISE

READ *John 12:27-37*

☐ Want More? Read John 12

1. Does the book of John include everything that Jesus did in the presence of His disciples? Do you think the Bible contains an answer to every question?

___
___

2. What is the intention of the information that was included in the Gospel of John?

___
___

After reading a Bible passage, the correct question should be, "What does this verse(s) mean?" However, many tend to lean towards another question: "What does this mean to me?" Doing so reverses the order of proper Bible study. The danger of such a self-focused question is that the Bible's original audience generally lived in very different contexts. Each person processes information through the unique "optics" of their experiences, circumstances, and presuppositions. If a verse or passage is directly interpreted through the subjective optics of individual life experiences, the reader risks developing a bias or even inaccurate understanding. Sometimes, God directs a passage of Scripture to all believers of all time, but more often than not, we are not the original audience of Scripture. The contemporary student of Scripture is separated by thousands of years, thousands of miles, and completely unknown cultural contexts. This is where good Bible interpretation does its most important work: "What did this verse(s) mean to the original audience?" We face this "original audience" hurdle whenever we open the Word of God.

First Step Obstervation: The first step of good Bible study is not interpretation but **observation.** Before asking, "What does it mean?" we must ask, "What do I see?" To help with this distinction, imagine going on a mission trip to another country. After your airplane lands, you arrive at the family's door you plan on visiting. Observe their home: **"What do I see?"** As you walk through their home, that is the primary question you ask to understand their distinct culture and minister to them appropriately. Otherwise, you will not understand and make cultural and relational mistakes. You observe how they interact. Are they shaking hands, holding hands, or kissing cheeks (Do you see how that could be an important observation?). How do they eat? Do they use their hands, chopsticks, or forks?

When we approach a text of Scripture, ask the same questions. **"What do I see?"** This demands that we examine the text thoughtfully, repeatedly, patiently, meditatively, and purposefully. Doing so allows us to pull the correct meaning out of Scripture instead of blanketing an assumed meaning over Scripture. Said most practically, we **Highlight** what stands out most. We identify the primary content of the passage. **Highlight** repeated or unique phrases, words, or ideas. We look for conjunctions and note. Note what they are connecting. We should pay special attention to verbs and pronouns and recognize their function. The more you look, the more you will see.

Second Step Interpretation: The second step of a good Bible study method is **interpretation.** Looking at the words or phrases you highlighted during the observation step, the student of the Bible begins to make connections and draw conclusions. Using the mission trip analogy, understand their home: **What does it mean**? If you see two men holding hands in some cultures, it is a sign of friendship, while in other cultures, it means something completely different. What does it mean when you see that your host home family does not use any utensils and only eats with the right hand? In some cultures, the left hand is considered unclean. Interpretation shifts the process from content to context. What is the primary context of the passage? For this reason, a good student of Scripture cautiously attempts to **Explain** in one to three sentences the meaning of a passage within the context of its surrounding verses. If you spend enough time in observation, interpretation becomes easier. If this step proves to be too difficult, seek help from a trusted study Bible or Bible commentary.

Third Step Implication: The third step of a proper Bible study method is **implication**. Implication is the 30,000-foot view where we develop most of our theology. Discover how the text travels. In the mission trip analogy, imagine you are on an airplane flying home after a trip to a foreign country. Bring it back home: **"How does it relate?"** After you have left that country, ask yourself what you learned in that culture that applies to your culture. For instance, after leaving a country in Asia—where people are known for great hospitality—what did you learn about a better way to do hospitality? We do not live in the Old Testament or New Testament cultures. The Bible text you are studying has to travel almost like traveling over a bridge or a flight over the ocean. As you think through the implications of a particular Bible text, **Acknowledge** the timeless theological truths you have learned. What is the primary connection of the passage? How does this connect to life in any century, much less the 21st century? What have you learned about God, humanity, God's kingdom, or God's kingdom plan?

Forth Step Application: The fourth and final step of a competent Bible study method is **application**. In light of the mission trip illustration, see yourself arriving at your home and applying the text to where you live, how you live, and who you live with as a Christ follower. Apply it in your home: **What do I do?** Prayerfully discover how the text transforms your life. Most of the time, this is where we start; how does this apply to my life? If we do this, we often miss the real point of the passage. Only after adequately understanding a Bible text's true meaning can we rightly ask the passage's primary purpose. Having clearly heard from God through this text of Scripture, how should we act? At this step, you write down how you will **Respond** with a specific action to this Word from God.

THE TRUTH

Practice the **H.E.A.R.** method of inductive Bible study on John 12:27-37 (a text from today's Bible reading). Write at least one sentence for each letter below. Consult the notes from a study Bible if you need help.

1. *Observation:* As you read through John 12:27-37, **Highlight** the occurrence of the word "this." Here is a hint: The New American Standard Bible has seven occurrences of the word "this" (and the plural "these" is also mentioned in v. 36). Make a list below.

_____
_____
_____

2. *Interpretation:* In one to two sentences, **Explain** what Jesus is trying to "communicate" to the crowd. Use a study Bible for help if you have one.

_____
_____
_____

3. *Implication:* **Acknowledge** what this passage confirms about the nature of God's salvation plan through the death of Christ on our behalf (12:33)? What does John 12:44-50 add to our understanding of God's plan (note the word "sayings")?

_____
_____
_____

4. *Application:* **Respond** to the text personally and share one action that you think God wants you to take after studying this text?

_____
_____
_____

WEEK 10

MEDITATE Fill in the blanks as you continue committing this week's verse to memory.

" For the _____ of God is alive and active. Sharper than any double-edged sword, it _____ even to dividing soul and spirit, joints and marrow; it _____ the thoughts and attitudes of the heart "

Hebrews 4:12

ENGAGE

Praise God for being active in us through the Holy Spirit. Confess your bad attitudes toward God's Word (laziness, carelessness, skepticism, etc.). Thank Him for allowing His Word to endure throughout the generations so you may believe and have life in His name (John 20:31). Ask God to help you slow down and be intentional with your Bible study and meditation. Pray that He will allow you to look and listen when observing the Scriptures.

Week 10 • Day 03
BIBLE STUDY AND MEDITATION

EXERCISE

READ *John 13:12-22*

☐ Want More? Read John 13

1. Highlight—Read through John 13:12-22 with a highlighter, making special note of the phrase "Truly, truly, I say to you" (three times). Make a list of the verse numbers below, putting into your own words what Jesus is saying to His twelve followers.

_____
_____
_____

2. Explain—See if you can express what Jesus is trying to communicate to the twelve in one to two sentences. Use a study Bible for help if you have one.

_____
_____
_____

THE TRUTH

3. Acknowledge– What timeless truth(s) do we learn from this text about the kind of service Jesus wants from His disciples?

_____
_____
_____

4. Respond– What is one action that you think God wants you to take after studying this text? ▼

_____
_____
_____

At this point, we need to let you off the hook by conceding that people find themselves at different stages when studying the Bible. Is this the first time you have had someone train you to study your Bible using a proper methodology? Was last week the first time you worked through a Bible reading plan? Or are you a veteran student of the Bible looking to hone your interpretation skills? This week's methodology might feel overwhelming depending on where you find yourself along the disciple's path (new believer, older believer). Let us take a few moments to be honest about the various levels of personal Bible study and available tools.

LEVELS OF BIBLE STUDY

Level One: If you are new to your Christian walk, we highly suggest you start reading your Bible using a Bible reading plan. Many printed Bibles and Bible apps are arranged with this in mind. Check out *The One Year Bible*, the *Chronological One Year Bible*, and the YouVersion Bible App, just to name a few. Again, if you have never read through the Bible from beginning to end, this is where we would suggest you spend your time this next year. Bible reading plans are the best use of your time early on in your spiritual journey.

Level Two: If you have some experience and success with Bible reading plans, the next place we would encourage you to look to advance your personal time studying the Bible would be to spend time on a particular Bible book. Purchase a Study Bible and read through both the text of Scripture and its relative study notes. Another option for this level of study is using Bible study manuals and workbooks that include background information and study questions for you to work through in your personal study time. These can be very helpful if you struggle to maintain a disciplined study schedule. A third option for those wanting to go further with Bible knowledge would be to purchase a Bible Commentary book orseries like the Bible Knowledge Commentary (2 Volumes) or the Bible Exposition Commentary series (many volumes).

Level Three: Once you have experience in both Bible reading plans and introductory study aids, the next level of involvement would be to work through various Bible books "chapter by chapter" and "paragraph by paragraph" using an inductive Bible study method like we the H.E.A.R. method; **Highlight**/Observation, **Explain**/Interpretation, **Acknowledge**/Implication, **Respond**/Application). More detailed Bible commentaries and robust Bible study computer software like the Logos Bible Study platform prove quite helpful at this level of Bible study.

Level Four: Being able to interpret a passage of Scripture confidently sets the disciple of Christ on a lifetime journey of trusting and obeying God through His written Word. Just as a marathoner (26.2 miles) starts their training by learning to run 5Ks (3.1 miles) and an ultramarathoner (100 miles) trains by running marathons (26.2 miles), students of the Bible can reach higher levels of Bible study discipline that would be unthinkable by those on the "couch to 5k" level of spiritual exercise. All levels of Bible study are legitimate as long as you continue to push forward in your journey of faith. Fourth-level Bible study habits include memorizing entire books or chapters of Scripture (James, Philippians, 1 John 1, Romans 8, Psalm 23, etc.) and preparing Bible studies for others to enjoy (teaching, preaching, small group lessons, etc.). Of course, many at this level begin to learn the original languages of the Bible (Hebrew, Aramaic, and Greek) so they can better access the nuances of the inspired text in terms of verb tense, word order, and other literary devices (think poetry and prophecy) that are not so obvious in English Bible translations.

1. Look up John 13:16, 20, and 21 in a Study Bible and summarize below one study note that you found especially interesting or insightful.

_____

_____

_____

2. Look up John 13:34-35 in a Bible Commentary. What do you notice is the primary concern of your chosen commentary?

_____

_____

_____

THE TRUTH

Wherever you are in your spiritual journey, we want to encourage you to progress in your "ingestion" of the Word of God. Once you habitually read through sections of Scripture, your personal goal shifts to Bible study. You need to take the time to understand and evaluate the Historical-cultural context behind a Bible book. The tools above are designed to help you do this (Study Bibles, Study Guides, Bible Apps, Commentaries, etc.) This includes the social, geographical, topographical, and political factors that are relevant to the authors and audience's setting. To grasp the larger picture the student of the Bible needs to understand the Bible background of a text. It is very important to remember that Scripture was God's Word to other people before it became His Word to you. The exact moment recorded in a certain text of Scripture occurred thousands of years ago. Peter, for instance, preached his sermon in Acts 2:36-39 in an ancient language to a culture that is even foreign to modern Israelis. Peter's words rang in the ears of men who were first-hand witnesses to the crucifixion of Christ (Acts 2:36). They had seen His tattered flesh and His broken body as it struggled for breath upon the cross. Inspired by the Holy Spirit, Peter's message of repentance, salvation, and baptism was first for those in this ancient Jewish crowd. And by the amazing grace of God, this message continued to resonate through time until it rang within the ears of countless others.

> Therefore let all the house of Israel know for certain that God has made Him both Lord and Christ—this Jesus whom you crucified."

Acts 2:36

THE TRUTH

MEDITATE Fill in the blanks as you continue committing this week's verse to memory.

> "For the _____ of God is alive and active. _____ than any double-edged sword, it _____ even to dividing _____ and spirit, joints and marrow; it _____ the thoughts and attitudes of the heart."
>
> *Hebrews 4:12*

ENGAGE

Praise God for being Truth (John 14:6). Confess how you sometimes look to your own experience and understanding to form your opinions of what is true, right, and good. Thank God for providing insight into who He is, all He has done, and what He has called you to. Ask Him to help you faithfully interpret His Word so that you may understand and obey.

Week 10 • Day 04
BIBLE STUDY AND MEDITATION

EXAMINATION

READ
Psalm 19:7-11   ☐ Want More? Read John 14

WATCH
Week 10 - Bible Study and Meditation

To watch the video, scan the QR code below by opening your phone's camera and holding your device so that the QR code appears on the screen. Click the link associated with the QR code, and choose this week's video. https://qrco.de/be3SWs

1. What are the dangerous approaches to Bible study that Dr. Moody laid out in this week's video?

2. How has the **HEAR** method helped you dig deeper into God's Word this week? What struggles are you having with the method? Address those within your d-group.

_____
_____
_____

3. How will you continue to focus on Bible study within your personal time in the Word? How might you encourage those in your group to continue growing in their Bible study discipline?

_____
_____
_____

EXERCISE

READ   Psalm 19:7-11

Psalm 19 encourages believers to commit themselves to the spiritual disciplines of Bible study and meditation. When people understand the value of their goal, they are far more likely to commit to the work it takes to reach the goal.

Psalm 19 reveals the value of God's Word in the believer's life. It is perfect – flawless and undefiled–and capable of restoring and rescuing. Scripture can build up the believer who studies to receive the truth humbly. It's capable of enabling the believer's eyes to see and understand. It is pure, reliable, and enduring. As you spend time studying and meditating, you will experience the value that will keep you consistently returning for more. As you meet God within the words of Scripture and faithfully interpret its contents, the Holy Spirit enables you to understand and be transformed by its truth.

> The precepts of the Lord are right, rejoicing the heart; The commandment of the Lord is pure, enlightening the eyes."
>
> Psalm 19:8

MEDITATE — Below, attempt to write out this week's verse from memory.

ENGAGE

Praise God for being perfect. Confess the ways you don't trust the authority of His Word in your life. Thank God for making a way to communicate everything you need for life through His living Word. Ask God to help you see the value of His Word so that you commit yourself to study and meditation and that He would allow you to delight in your time in the Word.

Week 10 • Day 05

BIBLE STUDY AND MEDITATION

EXERCISE

READ *John 15:1-11*
☐ Want More? Read John 15

EXEGESIS

Practice the Bible study method we learned this week (**H.E.A.R.** method) on John 15:1-11. Write at least one sentence for each word below. Consult the notes from a study Bible if you need help.

HIGHLIGHT   What I see:

(Need more help? Read through John 15:1-11 with a highlighter marking every occurrence of the word "you." Make a list below of the verse number, putting into your own words what Jesus is saying to His twelve followers.)

_____
_____
_____

EXPLAIN   What it means:

(Need more help? In one to two sentences see if you can express what Jesus is trying to communicate to the twelve. Use a study Bible for help if you have one.)

_____
_____
_____

ACKNOWLEDGE   The timeless truths:

(Need more help? What timeless truth(s) do we learn from this text about the kind of service Jesus wants from His disciples? What do you learn about God?)

_____
_____
_____

RESPOND   With specific action:

(Need more help? What is one action that you think God wants you to take after studying this text? Say when and where you will take the action.)

_____
_____
_____

While the **H.E.A.R** method is the one that we will use to help ensure that a proper interpretation method is followed, there are other helpful plans to follow. As you become more comfortable we suggest trying other good Bible study methods.

EXAMPLE

Mark Twain, the renowned lecturer, writer, and humorist had a complex relationship with the Bible. He was often skeptical, comical, and even hostile towards scripture. However, Twain could not ignore the Bible. No matter how far Twain circled away from Christian faith, he continually circled back to scripture. At times denying its validity and upon other occasions quoting it as *law*. To that latter point he once wrote, "Most people are bothered by those passages of Scripture they do not understand, but the passages that bother me most are those I do understand." If more skeptics were to be honest, they would have to admit that they are less skeptical of God and more skeptical of their ability to exist apart from their sin. Looking at the highlighted aspects of a passage, a proper Bible method seeks to explain its meaning and acknowledge its truths. This leaves the reader with only one alternative. How will they respond?

MEDITATE Practice reciting this week's verse from memory and be prepared to say them aloud to your d-group.

ENGAGE

Praise God for being the Way (John 14:6). Confess that there is no other way to salvation apart from Jesus Christ. Thank God for making you "wise for salvation through faith in Christ Jesus" (2 Timothy 3:15). Ask God to use Scripture in your life to teach, convict, correct, and train you. Pray that He will make you complete and equipped for every good work (2 Timothy 3:16-17).

ENCOURAGE

Use this checklist as a guide for your weekly d-group time. Refer to the discipler's guide at the front of the book for more encouragement and practical advice.

- Work through questions from the accountability page.
- Spend time praying specifics for one another.
- Take turns reciting the memory verses.
- Discuss answers to the questions throughout the week that are marked with this symbol. ⊙

PRAYER REQUESTS

ACCOUNTABILITY QUESTIONS

These questions are to be asked of one another in a spirit of accountability (Proverbs 27:17). They are intended to stimulate conversations of character and confession of sin in a safe environment that values honesty, vulnerability, confidentiality, and grace.

1. Have you spent quality time in your spiritual disciplines this week?

2. Have you taken advantage of opportunities to share your faith this week? Explain.

3. Have your words and actions been a good testimony this week to the gospel of Jesus?

4. Have your thoughts and speech been pure (cussing, criticism, negativity, etc.)?

5. Have you been sexually pure this week? Have you been exposed to sexually alluring material? (For those who are married: Have you prioritized quality romantic time with your spouse?)

6. Have you been a good steward of your finances? Have you lacked integrity in the handling of your finances?

7. Have you been honoring and generous in your meaningful relationships this week (Family, friends, etc.)?

8. Have you given in to any addictive behavior this past week? Explain.

9. Have you been completely honest with me?

I'm praying for the salvation of the following two people and prayerfully considering how to share Christ with them myself: _____

> "Therefore, confess your sins to one another, and
> pray for one another, so that you may be healed."
>
> *James 5:16a*

Week 11 • Day 01
PRAYER

ESSENTIAL TRUTH

The critical task of personal prayer is being disciplined to maintain a continual God-consciousness—"a connectedness"—where all our acts in life become a kind of prayer. Toward this end, the Lord Jesus gave us a model prayer (The Lord's Prayer) whose various elements can be summarized with the acrostic **A.C.T.S.**

- **A**doration initiates prayer with the right attitude and praises God for who He is.
- **C**onfession is agreeing with God about our sin struggles and their remedies.
- **T**hanksgiving expresses gratitude for our blessings of life, both spiritual and physical.
- **S**upplication focuses on the personal requests made in prayer for ourselves and others.

1. Read the Essential Truth, identify two phrases that stand out, and write them below. Why do you believe these phrases are significant?

_____
_____
_____

2. Considering the elements of this model prayer (**A.C.T.S.**), which do you engage in most frequently, and which do you neglect?

_____
_____

3. Do you feel connected to God throughout your days? If not, what hinders you from maintaining a continual God-conscious prayer life?

___

___

___

EXERCISE — memory verses

> "Pray, then, in this way: 'Our Father who is in heaven, Hallowed be your name. Your Kingdom come. Your will be done, on earth as it is in heaven. Give us this day our daily bread. And forgive us our debts, as we also have forgiven our debtors. And do not lead us into temptation, but deliver us from evil. [For yours is the Kingdom and the power and the glory forever. Amen.]'"
>
> *Matthew 6:9-13*

Communication is an essential aspect of any relationship. God speaks to believers through His Word and Spirit, and they communicate with Him through prayer. Like other relationships, communicating with God requires an intentional investment. As we grow up in life and faith, we learn to communicate more concisely and develop the ability to express ourselves through different situations and in various ways. From early childhood, we realize that each relationship requires differing forms and levels of communication.

How we speak to our parents differs from how we talk to our spouses or children. Jesus taught His disciples about prayer so they could approach their Heavenly Father appropriately and effectively. While the revelation of God as a "Father" was present in the Old Testament (Exodus 4:22-23, Deuteronomy 1:31; Isaiah 43:6; Jeremiah 3:4), it is primarily a New Testament concept that requires more clarification. In this memory verse, Jesus gives a model prayer for believers to follow as they approach God in the intimacy that Jesus and the Spirit secures for them (Romans 8:15-16). Disciples of Jesus do not pray to draw attention to themselves, nor do they want their prayers to be flashy or extravagant. This model prayer comes from a place and leads to a place of intimacy and authenticity. Disciples of Jesus are afforded an intimate level of communication with God as "Father" that was hardly imaginable to even the high priests and prophets of the Old Testament.

EXAMPLE

Throughout literature, the bulk of love stories tend to build toward the passionate intimacy of a relationship that crescendos and then abruptly ends at the wedding. The marriage ceremony is often the climax, and the relationship goes downhill. Production companies like Disney and Hallmark frequently neglect to produce any love story demonstrating the healthy reality of long-term marital life—a growing enjoyment of deeper intimacy, commitment, and understanding. Like other relationships, good marriages require intentional investment and maintenance. One would rightfully question the intentions of a couple who celebrated their wedding only to live separate lives and never speak. A healthy personal relationship requires two-way communication. If Bible study opens the lines of communication from God to us, prayer forms the avenue of communication the other way, from us to God. Both Bible study and prayer are required to enjoy what Christ has secured. We spend personal time with God through prayer and Bible study. They actually should color each other. We should read the Bible prayerfully and pray biblically. As such, one would rightfully question the intentions of someone who proclaims to love God but has no prayer life.

MEDITATE Write out this week's verses below as you spend time committing them to memory.

MORE If you'd like to increase your time in Scripture, commit to this optional weekly Bible reading plan.
Read (or listen via an audio Bible)

- ☐ (Day 1) John 16
- ☐ (Day 2) John 17
- ☐ (Day 3) John 18
- ☐ (Day 4) John 19
- ☐ (Day 5) John 20

ENGAGE

Thank God for the freedom to communicate with Him. Confess where you lack authenticity or intimacy in your relationship with Him. Thank Him for wanting to hear from you. God is willing and able to help. Thank Him for listening when you speak to Him. Ask Him to help you pray more consistently, authentically, and effectively.

Week 11 • Day 02
PRAYER

EXERCISE

READ *1 Thessalonians 5:12-22*

☐ Want More? Read John 17

1. Highlight the elements of appropriate conduct for the disciple found in 1 Thessalonians 5:12-22. List them below.

___
___
___

2. Read Colossians 4:2, and **Explain** the type of attitude that a believer should keep in his or her prayer life.

___
___
___

Paul was writing to the church in Thessalonica to prepare them for Jesus' return and God's righteous judgment. Jesus' first coming was in mercy and grace, but He will come again in justice and glory. In this letter, Paul commands disciples of Jesus to live in a specific way so that they might be sanctified and ready for His return (1 Thessalonians 5:23). He gives a long list of behaviors that the belief in the return of Christ in judgment should create: appreciating leaders (5:12), living in peace with one another (5:13), encouraging those struggling (5:14), helping the weak (5:14), being patient with everyone (5:14), doing good for one another (5:15), rejoicing always (5:16), giving thanks (5:18), not quenching the Spirit (5:19), not despising prophetic utterances (5:20), examining everything and holding fast to what is good (5:21), and abstaining from every kind of evil (5:22). In the glaring middle of this list of appropriate behaviors is the command to pray without ceasing (1 Thessalonians 5:17). Jesus's first coming secured our consistent and courageous access to God in prayer. We can pray because Jesus came the first time. We should pray without ceasing because Jesus is coming again in justice, and we have work to do through Him until He does.

People often correlate the idea of continual prayer with a recited series of mumbled words, chants, or mantras when nothing could be farther from the truth. Praying without ceasing implies that the default mental state of a believer should be "O God...." Continual prayer looks to God for help, celebration, approval, strength, perspective, encouragement, and affirmation throughout the day. A default, Christ-focused mental state finds peace and purpose in His truths. Continual prayer is not mindless repetition; it intentionally monopolizes every opportunity to pray.

The Bible consistently presents three elements required for a disciple of Jesus to engage in continual prayer. These elements are confessing sin, focusing the mind, and abiding in love. As sinful people with an innate attraction to sin (James 1:14-15), confession of sin is an essential acknowledgment of both personal fault (Ecclesiastes 5:20) and God's perfection (James 1:17). A mind molded within the environment of sinful cultures and constantly influenced by the temptations of the flesh does not stand a chance without the grace of Christ and a consistent focus on God's character. Finally, to build the proper impulse required to "pray without ceasing," a disciple of Jesus must abide in love (1 John 4:16). Love often motivates us to pray, and prayer causes us to be more aware of God's love. Sadly, believers are often seen as passionate about God on Sundays while passionate about the world the rest of the week. The discontinuity of our prayer lives adds to this dispassionate display of our love for God. Do not easily give your energy and attention to the idolatry of this age.

Continual prayer implies living in continual awareness of God's character and presence. This lifestyle of persistent prayer creates a consistency in our own character that a watching world notices. A growing awareness of God's investment and involvement in our daily life shifts our perspective and influences behavior. Continual prayer holds our temptations before God and asks for His deliverance from the tempter. Continual prayer allows a disciple of Jesus to acknowledge God's good work and immediately thank Him for the goodness and beauty around them. Continual prayer is a pursuit to be continually in the presence of God.

1. Acknowledge the timeless truth of why a disciple of Jesus can come boldly and continually to God in prayer (See Hebrews 4:14-16; 6:19).

_____
_____
_____

2. Which element do you struggle with the most in your prayer life: confession, focus, or abiding in love? Why do you think that is the case?

_____
_____
_____

3. Respond to challenge to "pray without ceasing" (1 Thessalonians 5:17). What practical steps can you take today to live in a continual God-consciousness?

_____
_____
_____

MEDITATE Fill in the blanks as you continue committing this week's verses to memory.

> "Pray, then, in this way: 'Our _____ who is in heaven, Hallowed be your name. Your Kingdom come. Your will be done, on earth as it is in _____. Give us this day our daily bread. And _____ us our debts, as we also have forgiven our debtors. And do not lead us into temptation, but _____ us from evil. [For yours is the Kingdom and the power and the glory forever. Amen.]'"
>
> *Matthew 6:9-13*

ENGAGE

Praise God for His love. Confess how you look to things of the world to satisfy yourself in the way that only God can. Thank Him for His continual presence in your life—He always hears and is always with you. He is willing and able to help. Ask God to help you consistently be aware of and confess your sin, focus your mind on Him in the busyness of life, and abide in His love regardless of your circumstances.

Week 11 • Day 03
PRAYER

EXERCISE

READ *Ephesians 6:18-21*

☐ Want More? Read John 18

1. Ephesians 6:18 uses the word "all" multiple times. **Highlight** the instance and what they emphasize in the believer's prayer life.

_____
_____
_____

2. Use Ephesians 6:20-21 to **Explain** the benefit of prayer in the life of the Christian soldier who is equipped in the armor of God.

_____
_____
_____

Throughout Paul's letter to the Ephesians, he demonstrates that the free gift of salvation in Jesus Christ (the gospel) is the starting point for continued and compounding change. Like a rock thrown into a still body of water, the ripple effect of the gospel progressively affects every aspect of the Christ-centered life. Today's reading in Ephesians demonstrates the "big splash" that our security in Christ (Ephesians 2:6) creates in our service of Christ (Ephesians 4:1). Paul connects the word "stand" in Ephesians 6:13 to the "prayers" of Ephesians 6:18. This reminds us that our victory on the battlefield of life—a victory over sin and its consequences—begins with prayer. The strength to stand firm (2:14), wear the armor of God (2:13), and wield the sword of the Spirit (2:17) directly correlates to continual prayer (2:18).

When the fires of adversity and affliction overtake, the facades of Christian cultural life quickly burn up, but the faithful prayers of Christ's followers remain. In this sense, prayers are more than mere "flare prayers" shot up into the air in a moment of distress. They are the "life support" system provided by Christ for us as we walk with Him "through" the challenging valleys of life (Psalm 23:4). If followers of Christ better understood the power of victory in prayer, they would not remain silent. The letter to the Ephesians celebrates a powerful truth. We do not fight for victory. We fight from victory. We pray from victory. This is the ripple effect of the gospel. If we desire to enjoy the victory over sin that Jesus has already secured, Paul says we must "pray" a certain way to tap into that victory. Praying "without ceasing" (Ephesians 6:18) comes as a result of the permanent presence of God in our lives secured by Christ's complete victory over sin and death. Praying "in the Spirit" means praying in the power and sphere of the Spirit, which is another way to describe the new covenant reality of a believer's connectedness to God. The new dynamic of "the Spirit of life in Christ Jesus" has set us free from the old dynamic of "sin and of death" (Romans 8:2).

The phrase "watch and pray" occurs often in the Bible. When Nehemiah was repairing the walls of Jerusalem and the enemy opposed the work, Nehemiah defeated the enemy by watching and praying (Nehemiah 4:9). Obedience to the command to "watch and pray" is part of the secret of victory over all three enemies of the Christian—the world (Mark 13:33), the flesh (Mark 14:38) and the devil (Ephesians 6:18). Incidentally, Peter went to sleep when he should have been praying, and the result was victory for Satan (Mark 14:29-31, 67-72).

Think of prayer as a "war-time walkie-talkie" always set to "On." Jesus has secured a trustworthy and timely connection to the headquarters of God's Kingdom, and we are called and equipped to battle for the things of God and the people we love. God's Word commands us to pray on behalf of all the believers ("the saint" in Ephesians 6:18-19). The Lord's prayer begins with "Our Father"—not "My Father." In a culture that overvalues individuality and autonomy, Jesus designed His Church to be interdependent upon one another. The prayer life of a disciple of Jesus affects and impacts the lives of their brothers and sisters in Christ. Intercessory prayer (praying for others) is one of the most selfless acts of love.

Besides praying for ourselves and others, where else should we direct our prayer lives? Jesus' model prayer calls on His followers to pray, "Your kingdom come" (Matthew 6:10). This prayer is used to advance missions and evangelism. Paul adds that the disciple of Jesus should specifically pray for the boldness to live out and speak out the good news of Jesus themselves (Eph. 6:19-20). Note that Paul did not ask them to pray for his comfort or safety but for the effectiveness of his witness. Paul's request was for boldness and clarity to declare the mystery of the gospel during his trial before Caesar.

1. If you struggle to pray, how might your understanding of the power of prayer be skewed? **Acknowledge** what you learned today that challenged your understanding of prayer?

_____

_____

_____

2. Respond with specific action to the challenge above. How might you pray for insight ("watch and pray") to know what God is doing around you? How can you more consistently pray for your brothers and sisters in the faith and their ministry?

_____

_____

_____

MEDITATE   Fill in the blanks as you continue committing this week's verses to memory.

> Pray, then, in this way: 'Our _____ who is in heaven, _____ be your name. Your _____ come. Your will be done, on earth as it is in _____. Give us this day our daily bread. And _____ us our debts, as we also have forgiven our _____. And do not lead us into temptation, but _____ us from evil. [For yours is the Kingdom and the _____ and the glory forever. Amen.]'"
>
> Matthew 6:9-13

ENGAGE

Praise God for victory over Sin, Death, and Satan. Confess the ways you look to overcome the world by your abilities instead of resting in the victory of Christ. Thank God for giving you the ability to "watch and pray" and the opportunity to intercede for your brothers and sisters. Ask Him to help you understand the power of prayer so that you will not neglect it. Pray that He will make you aware of the needs around you so that you may effectively pray to benefit His Kingdom.

Week 11 • Day 04
PRAYER

EXAMINATION

READ
Matthew 6: 5-8

☐ Want More? Read John 19

WATCH
Week 11 - Prayer

To watch the video, scan the QR code below by opening your phone's camera and holding your device so that the QR code appears on the screen. Click the link associated with the QR code, and choose this week's video. https://qrco.de/be3SWs

1. Reference Matthew 6:5-7. Prayer is the most intimate of disciplines—It should be done privately and publically, but you are not to put on a show. Do you struggle more with private or public prayer? How can you grow in each of these areas?

_____
_____
_____

2. As a child of God, speaking to your Father, you should pray with the authority given to you. Does this characterize your prayer life currently? If so, how? If not, what changes do you need to make to how you approach prayer?

_____
_____
_____

3. Like many other disciplines, prayer is fueled by your time in the Word. How can the disciplines you've learned through Bible reading and Bible study enhance your prayer life?

_____
_____
_____

EXERCISE

READ   Matthew 6: 5-8

"Lord, You are my God." What an excellent way to begin prayer. When we start with adoration, we immediately put everything in perspective. As a disciple of Jesus, you have access to your God. Your Father in Heaven loves you enough to make Himself available to hear you through prayer. You can talk to Him—God, the Lord, your Father, the Creator of all things, our Protector, Provider. When studying the Word of God, we learn more about who He is. When we approach Him in prayer, we should recall these truths. Our words should be centered on who He is. So, we begin our prayer with adoration—praising God for who He is. In praise, we admire His character and marvel over the God who hears us. It reminds us of who we are and all He's done for us. Prayer centered on adoration of God becomes worship. We commit to acknowledging who He is and elevate His name. We thank Him for His work throughout history, specifically in our lives. We remember His faithfulness. Then, we make our requests known to Him.

MEDITATE Below, attempt to write out this week's verses from memory.

ENGAGE

Praise God for being exactly who He is. Confess the ways your prayer life is self-centered instead of God-centered. Thank Him for hearing you when you pray. Ask Him to grow your adoration of Him so you can focus your heart and mind on the truth of His character.

Week 11 • Day 05
PRAYER

EXERCISE

READ *Philippians 4:6-9*
☐ Want More? Read John 20

EXEGESIS

Study Philippians 4:6-9 (from yesterday's Bible reading) using the **H.E.A.R.** method of inductive Bible study. Write at least one sentence for each letter below. Consult the notes from a study Bible if you need help.

HIGHLIGHT What I see:

Practice the Bible study method we learned this week (**H.E.A.R.** method) on Philippians 4:6-9. Write at least one sentence for each word below. Consult the notes from a study Bible if you need more help.

___
___
___

EXPLAIN What it means:

(Need more help? In one to two sentences see if you can express what Jesus is trying to communicate to the twelve. Use a study Bible for help if you have one.)

_____
_____
_____

ACKNOWLEDGE The timeless truths:

(Need more help? What timeless truth(s) do we learn from this text?)

_____
_____
_____

RESPOND With specific action:

(Need more help? What is one action that you think God wants you to take after studying this text?)

_____
_____
_____

While the **H.E.A.R** method is the one that we will use to help ensure that a proper interpretation method is followed, there are other helpful plans to follow. As you become more comfortable, we suggest trying other good Bible study methods.

WEEK 11

EXAMPLE

On January 29, 1986, a severe cold front swept through Cape Canaveral, Florida, blanketing the surrounding region in ice. Above this frozen and flat terrain, a marvel of modern invention and the crowning jewel of the American Aeronautics and Space Administration was quickly gaining altitude. Propelled by over seven million pounds of thrust, the space shuttle Challenger rocketed to 46,000 feet in under seventy-two seconds. What appeared to be a successful launch was tragically engulfed in flames seconds later. Investigators subsequently discovered what they deemed to be a significant communication gap between the engineers who warned against the cold weather launch and the flight managers.

On that tragic day in 1986, a series of miscommunications claimed seven lives and cost more than 3.2 billion dollars. For many believers, their spiritual journey falters greatly because of a significant communication gap in their prayer life. Whether out of ignorance ("I do not know how to pray") or discipline ("it is too tough/boring to pray"), they chalk this lack of communication up to a common limitation that simply cannot be overcome. Without any accusation of over statement, the greatest indication of a believer's faith is their time communicating with God in a personal relationship with Him. This is a core result of what Jesus Christ accomplished through His life, death, resurrection, and ascension. The English Poet Alexander Pope notably said, "to err is human." In contrast, the Bible reminds us of God's absolute power and knowledge. It proclaims the mission of God as more crucial and the mission's headquarters as more capable than any human endeavor. How much difficulty and suffering would be avoided if Jesus' disciples chose prayer (communication with God) over their limited and rushed calculations?

MEDITATE   Practice reciting this week's verses from memory and be prepared to say them aloud to your d-group.

ENGAGE

Praise God for being all-knowing, all-powerful, ever-present, and all loving. Confess how you withhold your needs from God because you think they are insignificant or you do not believe He will hear you. Thank Him for rescuing, restoring, and relating to His people. Ask Him to give you confidence in your communication with Him. Pray that you will become a person who prays consistently, confidently, and candidly throughout your entire life and that He will be magnified because of it. Pray about the kingdom work that God has laid on your heart as you worked through today's material.

ENCOURAGE

Use this checklist as a guide for your weekly d-group time. Refer to the discipler's guide at the front of the book for more encouragement and practical advice.

- Work through questions from the accountability page.

- Spend time praying specifics for one another.

- Take turns reciting the memory verses.

- Discuss answers to the questions throughout the week that are marked with this symbol.

PRAYER REQUESTS

_____
_____
_____
_____
_____
_____

EXTRA

PRACTICE If you struggle to stay focused or to know where to start in your prayer life you are not alone. The best way to get started is to get started.

LEVELS OF PRAYER

Level One: If you are new to your Christian walk, then we highly suggest you start by setting aside a specific amount of time each day to practice the **method of prayer** taught here. Schedule it and time it. Pray before all meals, thanking Him for providing for you so faithfully. Pray as you go to bed at night and get up in the morning. Pray through your day's events and expectations. Pray when you face fears and anxieties (Philippians 4:6-7). At first, it might seem strange to pray, but as you do, acknowledge that you DO see Him working in numerous places in your life (through Scripture, providence, preaching, certain people, internal tugs on your heart, etc.). Point out those places where you witness His work in your life and brag on what He is doing. Use the A.C.T.S. acrostic to pray through various aspects of your life.

Level Two: If you have some experience and success with a responsive prayer life that enjoys the fruitfulness of confident and continual prayers, then seek to take your prayer life up a notch by adding a prayer journal to **make note of your prayers.** Purchase a blank journal and use the first few pages to set some prayer goals and schedule out a prayer calendar for the week. In the following journal pages, list or even script your prayer requests (write a letter to God). Many prayer warriors have found it quite beneficial and worshipful to use one color pen for the request and another color to come back later and write out God's answer to their prayer.

Level Three: The next level of involvement for a mature prayer life would be to target your prayer life as a part of **missions involvement.** This could be in the form of hosting prayer meetings for missionaries or mission efforts at specific times of the year or as they come along. One of the most fruitful expressions of this level of a mature prayer life is prayer walking through a targeted mission field like a new town, neighborhood, school, or public area where the gospel will be strategically shared or a new church will be purposefully planted. Praying on site with insight seeks to soften up an area for evangelistic missionary efforts. Whether in a special called prayer meeting for a specific movement of missions or a prayer walk through that particular mission field. If this level of prayer already interests you as a group, we suggest you **take an extra week and have a dedicated prayer meeting as a Disciple Group.** Pause the study for next week, choose a quiet location, and spend an entire hour (time it) praying through a list (family, leaders, missions, etc.) as a group out loud. You will be amazed at how fast the hour goes by and how powerful the experience is.

ACCOUNTABILITY QUESTIONS

These questions are to be asked of one another in a spirit of accountability (Proverbs 27:17). They are intended to stimulate conversations of character and confession of sin in a safe environment that values honesty, vulnerability, confidentiality, and grace.

1. Have you spent quality time in your spiritual disciplines this week?

2. Have you taken advantage of opportunities to share your faith this week? Explain.

3. Have your words and actions been a good testimony this week to the gospel of Jesus?

4. Have your thoughts and speech been pure (cussing, criticism, negativity, etc.)?

5. Have you been sexually pure this week? Have you been exposed to sexually alluring material? (For those who are married: Have you prioritized quality romantic time with your spouse?)

6. Have you been a good steward of your finances? Have you lacked integrity in the handling of your finances?

7. Have you been honoring and generous in your meaningful relationships this week (Family, friends, etc.)?

8. Have you given in to any addictive behavior this past week? Explain.

9. Have you been completely honest with me?

I'm praying for the salvation of the following two people and prayerfully considering how to share Christ with them myself: _____

> "Therefore, confess your sins to one another, and
> pray for one another, so that you may be healed."
>
> *James 5:16a*

Week 12 • Day 01
WORSHIP

ESSENTIAL TRUTH

Worship is our response to what matters most to us. God created us in love to be worshippers and everyone worships something. Worship, simply stated, is knowing and loving God back. A disciple of Jesus loves God above all else and gives back to Him thoughtful, passionate, and practical worship. The depth of our worship is directly related to our view of God and His glory.

1. Read the Essential Truth, identify two phrases that stand out to you, and write them below. Why do you believe these phrases are significant?

_____
_____
_____

2. How would you define worship?

_____
_____
_____

3. Does your personal worship of God reflect this essential truth? Why or why not?

_____
_____
_____

EXERCISE memory verse

> "Therefore I urge you, brethren, by the mercies of God, to present your bodies a living and holy sacrifice, acceptable to God, which is your spiritual service of worship."
>
> *Romans 12:1*

Each day, countless interactions through relationships, experiences, and circumstances cause reactions that either diminish or inspire us. Within this context, disciples of Christ have experienced and interacted with Jesus in a way that has forever changed who they are. Once an enemy of God (Romans 5:10), separated from goodness (Colossians 1:21-23), they become increasingly aware of how they are saved by grace (Ephesians 2:8-9) and made children of God and coheirs with Christ (Romans 8:17). They experience the transformative power of being made a new creation (2 Corinthians 5:17) and being invited into a deeper understanding of God. The harmony and love found in God's triune nature—Father, Son, and Spirit—inspire believers on a level that surpasses explanation. A disciple of Jesus exists in fellowship with Him and longs to see Him face-to-face. The inward and outward response to these incredible truths is called worship. Worship is how we respond to who God is and what He has done and continues to do in and through our lives. Authentic worship encompasses thoughts, feelings, behaviors, and actions in response to the love of God.

EXAMPLE

The theater and cinema overflow with narratives of love and devotion, but none has become more iconic and perhaps ironic than that of William Shakespeare's *Romeo and Juliet*. At first glance, the tragic story of Romeo and Juliet's love and commitment is inspirational. However, deeper examination stumbles over great irony. These star-crossed lovers, willing to risk it all, had only been in a relationship for under twenty-four hours. With limited shared experience or weathered circumstances, Romeo and Juliet committed to a secret marriage and a poisonous ploy to fool their families. It could be argued that Romeo and Juliet is less of a love story and more of a warning against emotional infatuation and sensational behaviors. Such antics and contradictions should not be present in a believer's worship. Worship can be emotional, but authentic worship is not the fleeting fancy or immaturity of a short-term relationship. Authentic worship springs from the realization that God knew and loved you before you were created, even though you would rebel against Him and even as you learn to love Him back.

WEEK 12

MEDITATE — Write out this week's verse below as you spend time committing them to memory.

MORE — If you'd like to increase your time in Scripture, commit to this optional weekly Bible reading plan.
Read (or listen via an audio Bible)

- ☐ (Day 1) John 21
- ☐ (Day 2) 1 John 1
- ☐ (Day 3) 1 John 2
- ☐ (Day 4) 1 John 3
- ☐ (Day 5) 1 John 4

ENGAGE

Praise God for being your Creator, Redeemer, and Savior. Confess how your heart and mind focus on life circumstances and other relationships and miss opportunities to focus on and respond to who God is and what He has done. Thank Him for His goodness towards you in life. Ask Him to help you understand more of who He is and His specific work in your life so that you may appropriately respond with a worshipful life.

Week 12 • Day 02
WORSHIP

EXERCISE

READ *Mark 12:28-34*

☐ Want More? Read 1 John 1

1. The Great Commandment to "Love God" and "Love Others" is found in three of the four Gospels. Compare Mark 12:28-34 to Deuteronomy 6:4-9 in order to clarify the Scripture that Jesus is quoting. **Highlight** two observations from the Deuteronomy passage and note them below.

___

2. Reference Mark 12:30 and then **Explain** what Jesus commands us to do. What does it mean to love God with our hearts? With our souls? With our minds? With our strength?

___

When asked which command was the most important (Mark 12:28), Jesus summarized the entirety of the Law of Moses and the prophets into a single statement. For perspective, Jesus was present at the creation of the universe, the formation of Adam from dust, and the establishment of all souls from a singular exhale. Jesus—who witnessed the fall of man, spoke with Abraham, wrestled with Jacob, and led His chosen people from Egypt, encouraged Joshua before the battle of Jericho—reduced the vast cumulative of God's Law to a singular imperative "to love." God designed you to love Him passionately from the "heart and soul," thoughtfully from "the mind," and practically from your "strength" (Mark 12:30a). God created us to worship like this. We love Him because He first loved us (1 John 4:19). Worship is loving God back. It is an appropriate response to His gracious love given to us in the person and work of Jesus.

Knowing God leads to loving God. By studying who God is and what He has done (Theology), one gains personal knowledge of God's character and thus comes to know Him more intimately (2 Peter 1:2-9). As the Holy Spirit equips disciples of Christ to understand deeper truths of God (1 Corinthians 2:13), their hearts and minds become even more attuned to His love. The volume and depth of response to God through worship directly relate to our knowledge and understanding of who He is. Within this context, how does a disciple of Jesus justify a lack of worship in their lives? The inability to praise God is a potential sign of a lack of spiritual maturity, poor spiritual health, or a season of spiritual distress. Our relationship with God should move us to worship Him passionately. If we feel nothing, we will do nothing. Passionate worship involves feelings of intimate affection with Jesus that can be seen through our expressions, emotions, and excitement.

Worship of God, however, is not solely an emotional or sensational experience. God wants you to "love Him back" with your attention—with "all of your mind"—not just with your affection—with "all your heart and soul." Loving with all your mind requires focusing your senses on God. It requires some measure of study and meditation. Psalm 139 displays how God loves us with His attention. "O Lord, You have searched me and known me. You know when I sit down and when I rise up; You understand my thought from afar. You scrutinize my path and my lying down, and are intimately acquainted with all my ways" (Psalm 139:1-3). Love pays attention. The list does not stop there. Worship requires affection, attention, and ability—loving God "with all your strength." Loving God back in worship includes loving Him in practical ways. Wherever you find strength in your life (skills, actions, talents, etc.), use those things to love God back. Your affection, attention, and abilities are precious commodities that you can give to God as a "reasonable" offering of worship (Romans 12:1-2).

Do you see how broad the Bible defines worship? Worshiping God might include reading, studying, memorizing Scripture, praying, singing, dancing, or any other outpourings of a worshipful heart and mind. But it also includes loving God by serving God. This is what it means to love God "with all your strength." God is the source of strength (Isaiah 40:29), and these strengths and abilities should be utilized to display your love for Him. I can love God back by serving His people and His kingdom. The contemporary church expects musicians to share their gifts in worship. The local church should similarly expect the artist to paint, the writer to compose, the caregiver to support, and so on. All these are forms of biblical worship. It could be argued that the worshipful service of nursery workers and children's department volunteers has been directly involved with the salvation of more souls than professional evangelists. Jesus did not come to be served but to serve others (Matthew 20:28). As His disciples, we also accept the call to serve others with the strength and gifts God has invested into our lives (1 Peter 4:10).

1. Singing is about expressing your affection for God to God. Do you worship God passionately through song and prayer? Name a current worship song that moves your heart? **Acknowledge** the timeless truth about God found in that song that stirs your passion for God.

_____

_____

_____

2. Focusing on one thing at a time is difficult in our busy and distracted world. Evaluate your time with God through reading and studying His Word and in prayer. How do you struggle to give your attention to God in thoughtful worship?▼

_____

_____

_____

3. Respond to the call to love God practically—with your "abilities." Are there any skills or talents that you are not using—but could be using—to show God your love and demonstrate His love to the people around you?

_____
_____
_____

MEDITATE Fill in the blanks as you continue committing this week's verse to memory.

> "Therefore I urge you, brethren, by the _____ of God, to present your bodies a living and holy _____, acceptable to God, which is your spiritual _____ of worship."
>
> Romans 12:1

ENGAGE

Praise God for demonstrating love. Confess how you struggle to love Him passionately, thoughtfully, and practically. Thank Him for loving you first and enabling you to feel, think, and act in ways that show Him love back. Ask Him to help you grow in worship by revealing areas of your life that you live for yourself instead of Him.

Week 12 • Day 03
WORSHIP

EXERCISE

READ *Matthew 5: 13-16*

☐ Want More? Read 1 John 2

1. Reference Matthew 5:13-16. Jesus calls His disciples the "salt of the earth" and challenges them to retain the attributes of salt. **Highlight** ways that the image of "salt" relates to the Christian life? Worship?

_____
_____
_____

2. Matthew 5 also gives the image of "light" as an appropriate analogy for the authentic Christian life. **Explain** ways that the image of "light" relates to the Christian life? Worship?

_____
_____
_____

When we sing God's praises among fellow believers, we call it "worship." When we sing God's praises among unbelievers, we call it "witness." One is preparatory for the other. Both attempt to give Him His rightful glory and honor. William Temple said, "To worship is to quicken the conscience by the holiness of God, to feed the mind with the truth of God, to purge the imagination by the beauty of God, to open the heart to the love of God, to devote the will to the purpose of God." The depth of a believer's worship directly relates to their understanding of God. The one who wrongly perceives God as small will convey their poor theology through diminished worshipfulness. Likewise, the one who knows God as the infinite, immutable creator and sustainer celebrates God's great glory.

By definition, a Doxology is an expression of praise to God. The word doxology originates from the Greek words *doxa* (glory, splendor) and logos (work, speak). Worship conveys God's glory by expressing His goodness (Matthew 5:16) and glorifies God by demonstrating His beauty and believability. Everyone worships someone or something through ritual, song, adoration, and offering. Likewise, everyone has a theology, but this does not imply that their theology is accurate or biblical. Examining the correlation between worship and theology reveals that the study of God is worship and produces worship.

All people are created for God's glory (Isaiah 43:6-7). God made us for this purpose alone—to glorify Himself. As such, it is every person's duty to live for God's glory (1 Corinthians 10:31). To glorify God is to live and speak in such a way as to raise other peoples' opinion of Him—to display His beauty and believability. Likewise, Jesus instructed His first disciples to be the salt of the earth and a light on a hill (Matthew 5:13-15). Of course, this is colossal struggle in life. From the first sin in the garden, humanity has put itself before God. By nature, we want to glorify ourselves, not God. Because of this selfish nature, Jesus clarified that His disciples could only live lives defined by proper worship through the salvation and sanctification that He provides.

1. In what ways have you lost your saltiness or hidden your light from the world?
   _____
   _____
   _____

2. **Acknowledge** specific ways you see God's beauty and believability in your life right now. Where do you see His goodness and greatness displayed these days?
   _____
   _____
   _____

3. **Respond** to the call to go further in your worship and witness. How is God specifically prompting you to put His glory on display in your life?
   _____
   _____
   _____

MEDITATE Fill in the blanks as you continue committing this week's verse to memory.

> "Therefore I urge you, brethren, by the _____ of God, to _____ your _____ a living and holy _____, acceptable to God, which is your spiritual _____ of _____."
>
> Romans 12:1

ENGAGE

Praise God for His beauty and believability. Confess how you do not display God's glory in your life because of your own self-centeredness. Thank God for using you and all of creation to reveal His glory to others. Ask Him to give you a proper view of Himself (theology) so that He may be magnified in all you think, say, and do (doxology).

Week 12 • Day 04
WORSHIP

EXAMINATION

READ
Mark 12: 28-31

☐ Want More? Read 1 John 3

WATCH
Week 12 - Worship

To watch the video, scan the QR code below by opening your phone's camera and holding your device so that the QR code appears on the screen. Click the link associated with the QR code, and choose this week's video. https://qrco.de/be3SWs

1. Mark 12:30 says, "You shall love the Lord your God with all your heart, and with all your soul, and with all your mind, and with all your strength." Consider how you currently use your affection, attention, and abilities to worship God. What are some ways that you can love God passionately (with your heart), thoughtfully (with your mind), and practically (with your strength)?

_____
_____
_____

2. We were created for God's glory and to enjoy His glory. We glorify God by displaying his beauty and believability. How have you seen God glorified through other believers in your life?

_____
_____
_____

3. Worship and Word are connected. How are your current spiritual disciplines regarding time in the Word fueling your worship? What changes do you need to make?

_____
_____
_____

EXERCISE

READ   *John 4:24; Psalm 105:4*

We were made for God's enjoyment. In God's perfect design, he could enjoy a loving relationship with His people. Sin distorted that relationship, but we know the story didn't end there. God made a way to rescue His people so their relationship with Him could be restored. When we worship, we respond to who He is and what He's done and give back to Him. What is a gift worthy of who God is and what He's done? Worship. Believers are to glorify God through continual worship that connects Spirit and truth. As you've invested in and grown in spiritual disciplines, these things should result in a life of rich worship. Through the truth studied in His Word and the Holy Spirit inside of you enabling and empowering you, you can worship God and reflect His goodness to Him. You enjoy His presence, provision, and protection in life, and He enjoys your worship. Not just when things are going well or on Sunday mornings, but continually. Let your life be one of worship by continually glorifying God in Spirit and truth.

MEDITATE Below, attempt to write out this week's verse from memory.

ENGAGE

Praise God for being praiseworthy. Confess the ways you miss opportunities to worship Him continually. Thank God for providing all you need to worship Him: Spirit and Truth. Ask God to transform your life into one full of worship so you can give everything back to God in continual worship.

Week 12 • Day 05

WORSHIP

EXERCISE

READ *Revelation 4:5-11*
☐ Want More? Read 1 John 4

EXEGESIS

Study Revelation 4:5-11 using the H.E.A.R. method of inductive Bible study. Write at least one sentence for each letter below. Consult the notes from a study Bible if you need help.

HIGHLIGHT What I see:

_____
_____
_____

EXPLAIN What it means:

_____
_____
_____

ACKNOWLEDGE The timeless truths:

_____
_____
_____

RESPOND With specific action:

_____
_____
_____

While the **H.E.A.R** method is the one that we will use to help ensure that a proper interpretation method is followed, there are other helpful plans to follow. As you become more comfortable we suggest trying other good Bible study methods.

Revelation 4:11 says, "Worthy are You, our Lord and our God, to receive glory and honor and power; for You created all things, and because of Your will they existed and were created." In this sense, worship means to ascribe "worth." Jesus Christ alone is worthy of praise. His enemies said He was worthy of death (John 19:7), but the angels say He is worthy of praise. Men accused Him of working by the power of Satan (Matthew 12:24), but the angels say He is worthy of power. He became poor for our sakes (2 Corinthians 8:9), but He deserves all riches. "The preaching of the cross is foolishness" to sinful man (1 Corinthians 1:18), but it is wisdom to the angels and to us who have been saved by it. On earth, Jesus was "crucified in weakness" (2 Corinthians 13:4), but in heaven He is lauded for His power. Dishonored on earth, He is honored in glory. He was made a curse on the cross, but He is today both the recipient and bestower of blessing. So, they sang this new song, this second coming Christmas carol. It is a praise song of His worth, a missionary song sent forth, an angelic song of rebirth, and a coronation song of the earth. It is a marvelous, balanced hymn. Instead of songs that are "me-centered" and emphasize the believer's experience, we can sing praise to God in this way—Christ-focused and emphasizing God's glory.

EXAMPLE

An atheist who is opposed both to the notion of God and to human spirituality will deny that their life expresses any form of worship. In actuality, everyone worships someone or something. We surround ourselves with what we are most passionate about. You need only look and listen to identify someone's object of worship. The self-proclaimed "Christian" who habitually chooses fishing over corporate worship and takes every opportunity in conversation to discuss their boat passionately, by definition, worships recreational angling. Of course, they would never say this, but the passionate expression of their speech and the investment of their time and money demonstrate their heart of worship. It is not hard to tell what people worship. They brag about it, spend money on, and give their time to it. It could be a favorite sports team, vacation spot, health fad, movie, or book series. With such an evident rubric in mind, what would those who know you say you worship? Within the context of examining actions and speech, Jesus would say in Matthew 6 that "for where your treasure is, there your heart will also be."

MEDITATE   Practice reciting this week's verse from memory and be prepared to say them aloud to your d-group.

WEEK 12

ENGAGE

Praise God for His worth (Revelation 5:9, 12). Confess how you are focused on receiving praise instead of giving it to God alone. Thank Jesus for enduring what He DID NOT deserve on our behalf—the cross. Offer Him what He DOES deserve now—our thoughtful, passionate, and practical worship. Ask Him to use your life to glorify Himself in every way.

ENCOURAGE

Use this checklist as a guide for your weekly d-group time. Refer to the discipler's guide at the front of the book for more encouragement and practical advice.

- Work through questions from the accountability page.
- Spend time praying specifics for one another.
- Take turns reciting the memory verses.
- Discuss answers to the questions throughout the week that are marked with this symbol. ▼

PRAYER REQUESTS

_____
_____
_____
_____
_____
_____
_____

ACCOUNTABILITY QUESTIONS

These questions are to be asked of one another in a spirit of accountability (Proverbs 27:17). They are intended to stimulate conversations of character and confession of sin in a safe environment that values honesty, vulnerability, confidentiality, and grace.

1. Have you spent quality time in your spiritual disciplines this week?
2. Have you taken advantage of opportunities to share your faith this week? Explain.
3. Have your words and actions been a good testimony this week to the gospel of Jesus?
4. Have your thoughts and speech been pure (cussing, criticism, negativity, etc.)?
5. Have you been sexually pure this week? Have you been exposed to sexually alluring material? (For those who are married: Have you prioritized quality romantic time with your spouse?)
6. Have you been a good steward of your finances? Have you lacked integrity in the handling of your finances?
7. Have you been honoring and generous in your meaningful relationships this week (Family, friends, etc.)?
8. Have you given in to any addictive behavior this past week? Explain.
9. Have you been completely honest with me?

I'm praying for the salvation of the following two people and prayerfully considering how to share Christ with them myself: _____

> "Therefore, confess your sins to one another, and pray for one another, so that you may be healed."
>
> *James 5:16a*

Week 13 • Day 01
WITNESS

ESSENTIAL TRUTH

If glorifying God among believers is called worshipping, then glorifying God among unbelievers is called witnessing. A witness merely expresses what they have seen and know to be true. Successful witnessing is simply sharing Jesus in the power of the Holy Spirit and leaving the results to God. Walking with God in evangelism is less about confrontation and more about relationships, love, and lifestyle.

1. Read the Essential Truth, identify two phrases that stand out to you, and write them below. Why do you believe these phrases are significant?

_____
_____
_____

2. Restate in your own words the definition of "successful witnessing" above. Do any of the three elements surprise you?

_____
_____
_____

3. In your experience, is evangelism often associated with confrontation or relationships? Explain your evaluation.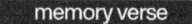

_____
_____
_____

EXERCISE memory verse

> You will receive power when the Holy Spirit has come upon you; and you shall be My witnesses both in Jerusalem, and in all Judea and Samaria, and even to the remotest part of the earth."
>
> *Acts 1:8*

As we stated previously, we "glorify" someone or something when we "raise another's opinion" of them. As we worship God among fellow believers, we collectively "lift up" our opinions about His beauty and believability. Worship and witness perform similar actions among different types of audiences. Witness is glorifying God among unbelievers. A disciple of Jesus who demonstrates worship without witness is not fulfilling the commission Jesus gave His disciples (Matthew 28:16-20). Attending corporate worship on Sunday but not bearing witness to the good news of salvation on Tuesday is equivalent to sitting at a feast but not inviting the starving. When we share our faith with the lost world around us we are "beggars sharing with other beggars where the food is." We would not dare keep that to ourselves. The souls of the lost matter to God, and they should matter to us. Authentic witnessing flows from authentic worship. It, by definition, defies a compartmentalized life and involves glorifying God by being His worshippers in our homes, neighborhoods, and workplaces. He has strategically placed you in these places to "raise people's opinions" of Himself. In the first chapter of the Gospel of John, we are told that John the Baptist was not the light, but he came to bear witness to the light (John 1:8). In John 8:12, Jesus says He is "the light of the world." Later in Matthew 5:14, Jesus tells His first disciples that they are "the light of the world. Both are true. Jesus is the light, but like John the Baptist, a disciple of Jesus reflects that light (Matthew 5:16).

EXAMPLE

The effects of seasonal depression are recorded in the writings of Hippocrates as early as 377 BC. In his work, Hippocrates explained a connection between the changes of the seasons and mood swing issues such as mania and melancholy. In more modern times, countless medical studies associated seasonal depression with regions that experience extended periods of darkness (i.e. less sunlight exposure). It was not until the 1980s that Dr. Norman Rosenthal, a South African-born psychologist, began experimenting with light therapy. Dr. Rosenthal found that scheduled exposure to specific light waves drastically reduced the effects of seasonal depression.

In a world characterized by spiritual darkness and depression, God reflects His light through His children's lived-out testimonies (behaviors and speech). As His light "shines" through us in word and deed, we provide those living in darkness around us with spiritual "light therapy."

THE TRUTH

MEDITATE — Write out this week's verse below as you spend time committing them to memory.

MORE — If you'd like to increase your time in Scripture, commit to this optional weekly Bible reading plan.
Read (or listen via an audio Bible)

- ☐ (Day 1) 1 John 5
- ☐ (Day 2) 2 John
- ☐ (Day 3) 3 John
- ☐ (Day 4) Ephesians 1
- ☐ (Day 5) Ephesians 2

ENGAGE

Praise God for being Light amid a dark and broken world. Confess how you do not reflect God's light through witnessing to the unbelievers around you, whether in word or deed. Thank God for His call on your life to be light in the world and the power to accomplish it through the Holy Spirit. Ask God to give you a desire to glorify Him through witnessing.

Week 13 • Day 02
WITNESS

EXERCISE

READ *1 Corinthians 2: 1-9*

☐ Want More? Read 2 John

1. Reference 1 Corinthians 2:1-5: **Highlight** the qualities that characterize Paul's witness and record them below. ▼

_____
_____
_____

2. According to 1 Corinthians 2:5, Paul's goal in witnessing was to have their faith rest on God's power and not on men's wisdom. **Explain** how Paul relied on the Spirit for power and not on his knowledge or skillsets.

_____
_____
_____

Paul's resume demonstrates an extreme level of education and a mastery of philosophy, religious history, and theology. His genealogy, achievements, and accolades are beyond impressive (Philippians 3:4-6). Paul could have easily presented the good news of Jesus to the people of Corinth with showmanship, swagger, and a strategically refined presentation. Instead, Paul tells the Corinthians that he spoke simply about Jesus Christ. The Greek culture was obsessed with philosophy, intellectual prowess, and pursuing so-called "human wisdom." Paul chose to keep his witness simple and relevant. This does not imply that Paul never used the intellect God provided him from birth or the education God granted him through study. Evidence of this is found in Acts 17, as Paul addresses those present at Mars Hill with cultural relevance and scholastic expertise. Neither Jesus nor Paul were hesitant to reach people through intellectual appeal (e.g. John 3, Acts 16).

Paul had real emotions, struggles, weaknesses, and shortcomings. Paul is one of the greatest evangelists and church planters in Christian history, but his witness was not dependent on his abilities or feelings. Paul's witness depended on the death and resurrection of Jesus Christ and the unfailing Spirit of God. In his frail humanity, Paul trusted the Holy Spirit to work in the heads and hearts of those who heard the good news of Jesus through his witness. This leads us to a straightforward and concise definition of witnessing. Success in witnessing is simply taking the initiative to share Jesus in the power of the Holy Spirit and leaving the results to God.

All disciples of Jesus can share the gospel. The first and most challenging step is acknowledging that you do not do the "saving." Employing the illustration of light again, it is sunlight that grows the plant. We merely reflect that light into dark places around us. Disciple-making starts with the intentionally going to people in dark places and pointing them to the love of Christ that brings salvation. The Holy Spirit does the incredible work of convicting sin, revealing truth, and offering comfort (John 16: 5-15). This is why leaving the results to God is so important. We do not want to be prideful if someone receives Christ as Savior, nor be discouraged or guilty if they do not.

> " But when He, the Spirit of truth, comes, He will guide you into all the truth; for He will not speak on His own initiative, but whatever He hears, He will speak; and He will disclose to you what is to come."
>
> *John 16:13*

1. How have your emotions (weakness, fear, inadequacy, etc.) hindered you from being a witness to the people around you?

_____
_____
_____

2. Say Acts 1:8 out loud. **Acknowledge** the huge difference having God's "power" makes in being a witness for Jesus Christ. Share a story of the difference it has made in your evangelistic efforts if you have one to tell.

_____
_____
_____

3. Respond specifically to how this definition has changed the way you should approach witnessing (sharing Jesus in the power of the Holy Spirit and leaving the results to God)?

_____
_____
_____

MEDITATE   Fill in the blanks as you continue committing this week's verse to memory.

> You will receive _____ when the Holy Spirit has come upon you; and you shall be My _____ both in Jerusalem, and in all Judea and Samaria, and even to the remotest part of the _____."
>
> Acts 1:8

ENGAGE

Praise God for His power. Confess the ways that you are weak, fearful, and in need of His power. Thank God for the Holy Spirit in your life. Ask God to give you the boldness to witness to those around you and that He would display His power through your obedience.

Week 13 • Day 03
WITNESS

EXERCISE

READ *John 3: 1-21*

☐ Want More? Read 3 John

1. Jesus modeled a method of evangelism as He spoke to Nicodemus in John. **Highlight** some of the things Jesus said that would challenge Nicodemus' thinking.

_____
_____
_____

2. In John 3:14-15, Jesus connects the truth that Nicodemus knows and understands (Moses lifted up the serpent in the wilderness) with the gospel's truth (so the Son of Man be lifted up so that everyone who believes will have eternal life in Him). Perhaps you know the following verse by memory, John 3:16. **Explain** this verse in your own words to speak this truth to a friend.

_____
_____
_____

In today's reading, Jesus was approached at night by a moral, religious, lost man named Nicodemus (John 3:1-21). In the next chapter of John, Jesus approaches an immoral, heretical woman from Samaria (John 4:1-26). In each case, Jesus had a specific strategy and used precise tools to witness. Nicodemus was an intelligent Jewish leader who came to Jesus in the night trying to understand the works He was doing. He believed that Jesus was from God but was perplexed by Jesus' identity.

Nicodemus felt secure in his religiosity, but his arrogance hindered his understanding of Jesus as the Messiah. As Jesus logically presented a series of truths to Nicodemus, he was placing metaphorical pebbles in Nicodemus' shoes. Each following step caused Nicodemus to slow down and reconsider his assumptions. After a few pebbles, Jesus told Nicodemus the truth necessary for salvation—"The Son of Man must be lifted up, so that everyone who believes will have eternal life in Him" (John 3:14b-15). In John 3:16, Jesus gave Nicodemus the central truth that should be shared in any evangelistic conversation. Out of God's great love, He sent forth His Son, Jesus Christ, to rescue people from sin and death. They need to have faith in Him to receive this salvation. Disciple-making, by definition, includes the act of evangelism, as we see in the Great Commission (Matthew 28:18-20), whereby we lead a non-disciple of Jesus to receive the free gift of salvation in Jesus.

The two most important tools used to "share Jesus" with those around us are **His Story and Your Story.**

WEEK 13

1. Acknowledge that there are people near you who need to hear the truth of John 3:16 and Romans 6:23. Write out 2-3 of their names below. How could you "place pebbles in their shoes" to help them reconsider what they know to be true about God and who they are?

_____

_____

_____

2. Respond to the blessing of such a tool by practicing it. Draw out the 3 Circles illustration. Reference page 270. When your Disciple group meets practice talking through the circles as you would with a friend.

_____

_____

_____

MEDITATE — Fill in the blanks as you continue committing this week's verse to memory.

> You will receive _____ when the _____ has come upon you; and you shall be My _____ both in Jerusalem, and in all _____ and Samaria, and even to the _____ part of the _____."
>
> Acts 1:8

ENGAGE

Praise God for His power made present in your life through the Holy Spirit. Confess how you struggle to speak up for God and feel inadequate to share "His Story" at times. Thank God for blessing you and using you as a blessing to others. Ask Him to help you actively participate in the rescue of the people around you.

EXTRA

PRACTICE Sharing the gospel can be frightening. A simple and visual method like the Three Circles is both helpful and concise.

"**The 3 Circles**." This quick and easy illustration can be done in just a few minutes, or you can dig in and elaborate on the truths found within each circle depending on where the conversation goes and how much time you have. You can quickly adapt it to accommodate any conversation or situation.

Drawing the **First Circle**, write "**God's Design**" and draw a heart. God has a wonderful plan for our lives and wants to see people live in that plan. God originally planned a perfect world free from pain and sadness. In this world, people would live in perfect harmony with God and one another (Genesis 1:31, Psalm 19:1). The gospel conversation begins with God's perfect design (First Circle), but sin causes brokenness to enter our world.

Drawing a **Second Circle,** write "**Brokenness**" and draw three squiggly lines. Sin distorts God's perfect design because people choose to trust in themselves. Because of sin, we are no longer in perfect harmony with God but eternally separated from Him (Romans 3:23, 6:23). Explain to the other person in the conversation that the three lines represent such places of brokenness as our purpose, peace, and relationships. Connect the two circles with and arrow from the first to the second and add the word "Sin" above the line. Jesus came, lived a perfect life, and suffered the death that sin deserves. Brokenness allows us to see our need for rescue (Romans 1:25, Proverbs 14:12), and this is where the good news comes into the conversation.

Drawing a **Third Circle** below and in between the first two circles, write the word "**Gospel**." Share from a Bible or memory John 3:16 and Romans 6:23. As you share these two Bible verses and talk about the Gospel (Good News) of Jesus Christ, draw

THE TRUTH

three arrows that represent the work of Christ on our behalf. The arrow goes down showing the life of Christ when He was born of a virgin that first Christmas. The second arrow goes to the right depicting Jesus's death on the cross to take away our sin as our sacrificial substitute (draw another line down to make the symbol of the cross complete). The third arrow goes up to demonstrate the resurrection of Jesus Christ into glory, securing our salvation. God loved His people too much to leave them separated from Him forever. He came to them. Jesus Christ—fully God, fully man—lived a perfect life and died the death that we deserve for our sin. By paying the penalty for our sin, Jesus is the only way to restore us to God (John 3:16, Colossians 2:14, 1 Corinthians 15:3-4).

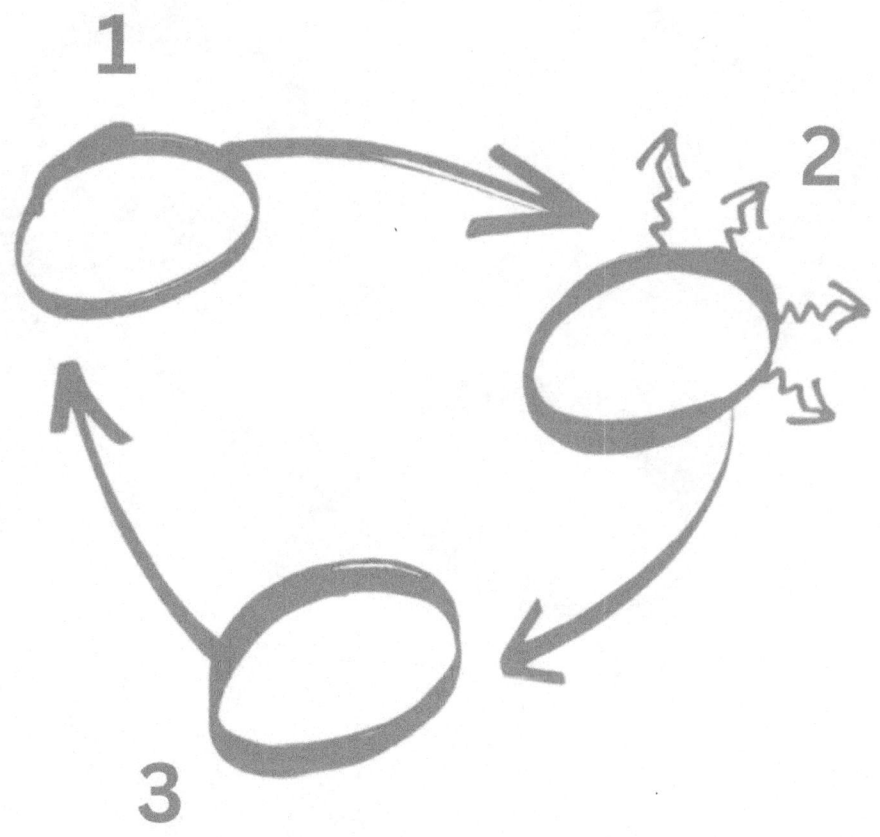

WEEK 13

EXTRA

PRACTICE Familiarize yourself with the gospel truths expressed through the Three Circles. by filling in the blank diagram below.

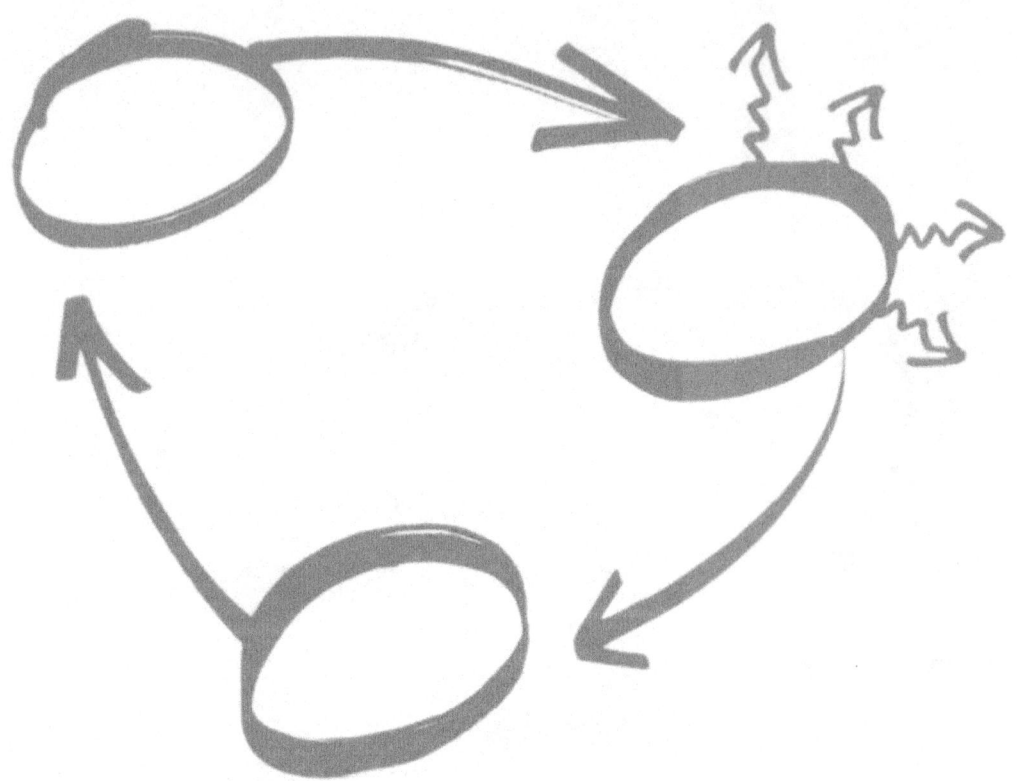

Week 13 • Day 04
WITNESS

EXAMINATION

READ
John 4:7-26

☐ Want More? Read Ephesians 1

WATCH
Week 13 - Witness

To watch the video, scan the QR code below by opening your phone's camera and holding your device so that the QR code appears on the screen. Click the link associated with the QR code, and choose this week's video. https://qrco.de/be3SWs

1. Highlight throughout the story of the Samaritan woman in John 4 how her titles for Jesus change? What does this demonstrate about her growing perception of Jesus?

_____
_____
_____

2. Explain what the woman at the well did after speaking with Jesus (John 4:28-29)? Why is this important to understand?

_____
_____
_____

EXERCISE

READ   John 4:7-26

John 4 gives us another example of Jesus modeling effective evangelism. While Nicodemus came to Jesus in John 3, Jesus went out of his way to have this encounter with the Samaritan woman at the well. Jesus challenged Nicodemus theologically in order to share the truth of the gospel with him, but with this woman, Jesus redirected her thinking. Jesus used what could be called "water-to-water evangelism" with her. He introduced a spiritual topic (living water) through an earthly topic (water). In our lives, we will encounter many hurting people feeling lonely or ostracized. Sharing our story with them is an excellent way to bridge the gap between our lives. When God rescued us from our sin and struggles, he gave us each a unique and powerful testimony of His faithfulness. We can share the parts of our story that will relate to others and open doors for us to share the gospel . "Your Story" is the second tool we can use in our gospel conversations to make disciples for Jesus.

THE TRUTH

MEDITATE Below, attempt to write out this week's verse from memory.

ENGAGE

Praise God for His presence and guidance in your life. Confess how you forget how God has been faithful to you. Thank Him for pursuing you in your relationship and making His story personal to you by transforming your story. Ask Him to help you reflect on the realities of His work in your life and faithfully present that story in a way that allows others to see the goodness of God.

WEEK 13

EXTRA

PRACTICE By organizing your testimony (the story of how Jesus rescued you) you will be better equipped to share it with others.

When prepared and familar, you can share your story in two minutes or thirty minutes. It helps to understand how our story should flow to be efficient and effective. When working through your story, you'll want to focus on three main questions. **BC, Christ,** and **AD**.

"**BC**" stands for what life was like **"Before Christ."** First, what was your life like before Jesus rescued you? Before Jesus, what did you believe about God? What dictated your decisions and how you lived your life? What held you captive in thinking or action? What fears ruled your life? What did you live for? The point is, what did God rescue you from? The answer is sin and brokenness, but you know exactly what that looked like in your life, and this is a way to relate to people who may be struggling with the same things.

BC (What was my life like before Jesus rescued me?)

_____

_____

_____

"Christ" stands for the part of your story where you share how you came to know and trust Jesus Christ as your personal Savior? At this point in the conversation, talk about the significant circumstances, experiences, and people surrounding your "coming to faith" story. How were you made aware of your need for a Savior? What truth did a friend share to help you understand who Jesus is? Which Scripture convicted your heart or revealed something about God to you? This question is about God's work in your life. What did He do to make Himself known to you? While this is a personal story, God is the hero of your story. You want to make that known.

Christ (How was I introduced to Jesus Christ?)

_____
_____
_____

"AD" stands for the Latin phrase *Anno Domini* which means "the year of our Lord" and reminds you to conclude your conversation with a description of what has God done in and through your life as a disciple of Jesus? After submitting to Jesus in faith, your life changed. You were once… (your answer to question one), but now you are (answer this question). What has He restored? What has He redeemed? What has He transformed? Tell the person you are witnessing to about your new identity in Him. Tell them about how Jesus has given you purpose in life. Tell them how He's using the difficult parts of your life for your good and His glory. Create a segue to share "His Story" at this point. While "Your Story" is authentically about you, it is also your personal experience of the faithfulness of God. So, do not miss out on an opportunity to share "His Story." Help them see themselves in "Your Story," and then help them see the salvation available to them in Jesus Christ and "His Story."

AD (What has life been like since I began my relationship with Jesus?)

_____
_____
_____

Week 13 • Day 05

WITNESS

EXERCISE

READ *John 4:1-15*
☐ Want More? Read Ephesians 2

EXEGESIS

Study John 4:1-15 using the **H.E.A.R.** method of inductive Bible study. Write at least one sentence for each letter below. Consult the notes from a study Bible if you need help.

HIGHLIGHT   What I see:
_____
_____
_____

EXPLAIN   What it means:
_____
_____
_____

ACKNOWLEDGE The timeless truths:

_____
_____
_____

RESPOND With specific action:

_____
_____
_____

While the **H.E.A.R.** method is the one we use to help ensure that a proper interpretation method is followed, there are other helpful plans to follow. As you become more comfortable, we suggest trying other good Bible study methods.

First John 2:6 teaches us that "the one who says he abides in Him ought himself to walk in the same manner as He walked." Followers of Christ study Jesus' teachings and actions "to walk as He walked." Jesus modeled how to live, love, and witness throughout His ministry and daily life. The third and fourth chapters of the Gospel of John show how Jesus shared the gospel with two different people—Nicodemus and the woman at the well. Nicodemus was a morally intelligent Jewish man seeking truth but struggling to see past culture, religion, and tradition. In contrast, the Samaritan woman was an individual defined by immorality who lacked education or social acceptance.

By contrasting these meetings between Jesus and these two lost persons, we realize that although Jesus utilized different approaches, His core method and message were the same. With both Nicodemus and the Samaritan women, Jesus allowed the righteousness of His behaviors and reputation to interlace with His gospel presentation. Jesus' personal story matched God's big story. Meeting both people within the constructs of their understanding, Jesus invested compassion and truth into every aspect of His interaction with them. First Timothy 2:4 tells us that God "desires all men to be saved and to come to the knowledge of the truth." Equip yourself with the ability to share His story (the gospel) and your story (personal testimony).

EXAMPLE

During a time when Native American people groups were often looked down upon in movies and popular culture, Alice Cunningham Fletcher's faith in Christ inspired her to action. Guided by her faith in Christ, she dedicated her life to improving the education and welfare of Indigenous peoples. Fletcher often lived among the tribes she served, including the Omaha, whose customs and traditions were deeply foreign to her. During a famine, Fletcher used her funds and influence to secure supplies and advocate for assistance. Despite the criticism, Fletcher's lived among those she felt called to share the good news of Jesus with.

MEDITATE   Practice reciting this week's verse from memory and be prepared to say them aloud to your d-group.

THE TRUTH

ENGAGE

Praise God for His heart for humanity. Confess the ways that you neglect sharing the story of your salvation. Thank God for the unique story that He has given you—what He has rescued you from and what He's rescued you for. Ask Him to give you the willingness and boldness to share His story and your story with everyone around you.

ENCOURAGE

Use this checklist as a guide for your weekly d-group time. Refer to the discipler's guide at the front of the book for more encouragement and practical advice.

- Work through questions from the accountability page.

- Spend time praying specifics for one another.

- Take turns reciting the memory verses.

- Discuss answers to the questions throughout the week that are marked with this symbol. ⊙

PRAYER
REQUESTS
_____
_____
_____
_____
_____
_____

ACCOUNTABILITY QUESTIONS

These questions are to be asked of one another in a spirit of accountability (Proverbs 27:17). They are intended to stimulate conversations of character and confession of sin in a safe environment that values honesty, vulnerability, confidentiality, and grace.

1. Have you spent quality time in your spiritual disciplines this week?
2. Have you taken advantage of opportunities to share your faith this week? Explain.
3. Have your words and actions been a good testimony this week to the gospel of Jesus?
4. Have your thoughts and speech been pure (cussing, criticism, negativity, etc.)?
5. Have you been sexually pure this week? Have you been exposed to sexually alluring material? (For those who are married: Have you prioritized quality romantic time with your spouse?)
6. Have you been a good steward of your finances? Have you lacked integrity in the handling of your finances?
7. Have you been honoring and generous in your meaningful relationships this week (Family, friends, etc.)?
8. Have you given in to any addictive behavior this past week? Explain.
9. Have you been completely honest with me?

I'm praying for the salvation of the following two people and prayerfully considering how to share Christ with them myself: _____

> "Therefore, confess your sins to one another, and pray for one another, so that you may be healed."
>
> *James 5:16a*

Week 14 • Day 01

TRUST AND OBEDIENCE

ESSENTIAL TRUTH

The Christian life can be summarized with two simple, yet connected, behaviors: trust and obey. As a believer learns to trust God entirely, exclusively, and extensively, they will also grow in obedience to Him—heart, mind, soul, and strength. In other words, one's trust in the trustworthiness of God fundamentally leads to obedience. Life, then, is full of faith tests that display the motivation behind our obedience, whether faith or fear.

1. Read the Essential Truth, identify two phrases that stand out to you, and write them below. Why do you believe these phrases are significant?

_____
_____
_____

2. How would you describe your trust in God and obedience to His Word? Has it changed over time?

_____
_____
_____

3. Have you experienced faith tests? How have they impacted your faith?

_____
_____
_____

EXERCISE memory verses

" Trust in the Lord with all your heart, and do not lean on your own understanding. In all your ways acknowledge Him, and He will make your paths straight."

Proverbs 3:5-6

When a lawyer (an expert in the Mosaic Law) asked Jesus about the greatest command, Jesus' two-part answer was, "You shall love the Lord your God with all your heart, and with all your soul, and with all your mind" (Matthew 22:37). In this, Jesus was making it clear that love and law work together. This answer directs His audience to the foundational truth, which comprises the first four of the Ten Commandments (tablet 1). How do you love God with all your heart, soul, mind, and strength? Answer? Have no other gods, do not make idols, do not take His name in vain, etc. Love is more than obedience to the law, but it is not less than that. In the Gospel of Matthew, the rich young ruler stated that he had kept these and other commands since his youth (Matthew 19:20). But what does loving God on this level imply? For this young man of wealth and power, loving God did not include loving God more than the lifestyle his possessions and position afforded him. This young man approached Jesus with authenticity, only to depart sadly. Throughout the Gospels, only the rich young ruler approached Jesus optimistically and departed sorrowfully. When facing the cost of loving God with the entirety of one's heart, soul, and mind, some will have to admit that they are merely followers of religion and ritual. Many would be better described by the fickle term "fan" than the more faithful term "follower." A true follower of God trusts in the Lord with their attention (mind), affection (heart and soul), and abilities (strength). They obey God because they trust Him.

EXAMPLE

Faith is fascinating because so many examples exist of how we live by faith. We trust our vehicles to get us safely to work and back home again, even if we do not know how the engines work. We trust our doctors' medicines, even though we cannot pronounce their chemical formula names. Skydiving provides an excellent analogy for faith. Upon take off, skydivers inspect their equipment for the third or fourth time as they think through the jump flow. Leaning forward to open the door, they are instantly overtaken by the cool air of increasing altitude. The unobstructed view from 13,000 feet offers an arched horizon spanning hundreds of miles. Below them, the terrain is a collage of different colors and textures reminiscent of a patchwork quilt. They will complete several maneuvers over 60 seconds of free fall, demonstrating accuracy and control while reaching a terminal velocity exceeding 120 mph. When asked why they would take such a high risk, many respond, "I have confidence in my parachute." A skilled skydiver's parachute is well-designed and professionally maintained; they inspect every inch of it. By comparison, a gasoline or electric vehicle contains the materials and systems required to produce a tremendous explosion. Still, we rarely consider this risk when turning the key or pressing the start button. This is because you trust your car. More seriously, Jesus' disciple should trust in the Lord.

MEDITATE   Write out this week's verses below as you spend time committing them to memory.

MORE   If you'd like to increase your time in Scripture, commit to this optional weekly Bible reading plan.
Read (or listen via an audio Bible)

☐ (Day 1) Ephesians 3
☐ (Day 2) Ephesians 4
☐ (Day 3) Ephesians 5
☐ (Day 4) Ephesians 6
☐ (Day 5) Philemon

ENGAGE

Praise God for being trustworthy. Confess how you lean on your understanding in life. Thank Him for loving you, even when you struggle to give Him your love, trust, and obedience. Ask Him to reveal more of Himself and incline your heart, soul, and mind to trust Him completely.

Week 14 • Day 02
TRUST AND OBEDIENCE

EXERCISE

READ *Proverbs 3:1-10*

☐ Want More? Read Ehesians 4

1. Read Romans 1:5-7 and 16:26. **Highlight** what these "bookends" of the book of Romans reveal about obedience. ▼

_____
_____
_____

2. Reference the larger context of the week's memory verse (Proverbs 3:1-10). List below the "calls to action" in one column and the fruit that the action will produces in another. (Example: calls to action: v.1 – do not forget my teaching, keep my commandments; fruit: v. 2 – will add days and peace to your life.)

_____
_____
_____

"What is God's will for my life?" This is a question that every Christ follower struggles with occasionally. Trust is God's divine purpose for the lives of His children (Psalm 37:5). The divine order of this text demonstrates how believers first trust God personally and then trust Him to guide and direct them. Following God is not an assembly of rules or religious policies and procedures. Walking with God is a relationship developed through trust and obedience. In today's reading, God doesn't simply command kindness and truth as mechanical behaviors. The primary teaching point of verses 1 through 4 demonstrates how a righteous heart catalyzes godly action (Proverbs 4:23; 1 Timothy 1:5).

In verse 5, you are given a positive admonishment–to trust the Lord with all your heart. This is a call to trust God entirely. Before getting into bed tonight, you won't run a stress test on the bedframe or calculate the cycle rate of the mattress springs. You trust your bed to support your weight and fall into bed. Similarly, God encourages you to trust Him and fall into His love. He can bear the weight of your heart just as Jesus has already taken the weight of your sin.

The second section of verse 5 warns not to trust your understanding. While human reasoning relies on limited knowledge and experience, trusting God involves relying on His infinite wisdom and understanding. Our understanding can often lead us astray, as emotions, biases, and incomplete information influence it. In contrast, God's perspective is all-encompassing, and placing our trust in Him ensures that we are guided by a source far more significant than our capabilities. Your "understanding" is the "logical" mental process through which you analyze circumstances. Trusting Jesus, Peter stepped out of the boat and walked a few steps upon a turbulent sea. It wasn't until Peter analyzed the data from his experiences as a professional fisherman that he doubted Jesus and began to sink (Matthew 14:22-36). If Jesus says, "Come to Me," trust Him, He will defy physics. He is the creator and sustainer of all things (Hebrews 1:3).

Trusting God means acknowledging Him in all your ways (Proverbs 3:6a), which refers to everything you do. In the present context, it is not simply an intellectual awareness of God's existence but acceptance of God's presence to guide and direct your life. "And He will make your paths straight" (Proverbs 3:6b). Notice the plural, "paths." This is general, not specific. Whatever path you choose, you must trust God entirely, exclusively, and extensively, and He will guide and be with you.

> "But the goal of our instruction is love from a pure heart and a good conscience and a sincere faith."
>
> *1 Timothy 1:5*

1. Explain what it means to put all your weight on God "with all your heart?"

_____
_____
_____

2. Acknowledge the specific ways people tend to put too much trust in their "own understanding?"

_____
_____
_____

3. Do you trust God entirely, exclusively, and extensively? **Respond** to this question by listing evidence from your life below that supports your answer. How is God specifically challenging you right now?

_____
_____
_____

THE TRUTH

MEDITATE Fill in the blanks as you continue committing this week's verses to memory.

> Trust in the Lord with all your _____, and do not lean on your own _____. In all your ways acknowledge Him, and he will make your paths _____."
>
> *Proverbs 3:5-6*

ENGAGE

Praise God for bearing the full weight of our hearts, minds, souls, and strengths. Confess how you tend to be cautious about your trust in God. Thank Him for caring for you intimately and offering leadership. Ask God to reveal areas where your trust is not entirely, exhaustively, and extensively fixed on Him. Pray that He will convict and transform your heart and mind as you learn to obey His Word.

Week 14 • Day 03
TRUST AND OBEDIENCE

EXERCISE

READ *Romans 3:21-31*

☐ Want More? Read Ephesians 5

1. **Highlight** the verses from Romans 3:21-31 that include the word "faith" below and what they add to our understanding of faith.

___

2. **Explain** what "faith in Jesus Christ" means in the context of Romans 3.
___

Faith is a common denominator between people of all cultures and belief systems. Everyone holds to some form of faith. The question is, "Where is your faith placed?" You exercise faith daily when flipping a light switch, starting a vehicle, or mailing a letter. We trust that the light will come on, the car will start, and the letter will arrive at its destination. Apart from the small daily tasks and choices that require faith, everyone puts their faith in someone or something larger than themselves. Buddhists believe in self-enlightenment. Muslims believe in Allah, the Koran, and Mohammed. Those who worship religion place their faith in rules and their own "good works" (Titus 3:5; Matthew 23:15-33). Because the object of faith is wrong in these cases, this faith cannot lead to salvation (Acts 4:12). The Bible insists that we should place all of our faith and trust in Jesus (John 14:6).

Hebrews 11:1 says, "Now faith is the assurance of things hoped for, the conviction of things not seen." To better understand this verse, we need to look back six verses to Hebrews 10:34. When Hebrews was penned, the local Church endured persecution for their faith in Christ. Some within the Church were imprisoned, leaving other believers with the difficult decision of whether to help them or risk losing their property and maybe even their lives. Verse 34 demonstrates how the early Church responded to this adversity. "For you showed sympathy to the prisoners and accepted joyfully the seizure of your property, knowing that you have for yourselves a better possession and a lasting one." Following God obediently can be costly, but in this way, obedience is an investment in trust and faith. The book of Hebrews is about living a faith-filled life that looks at the high price of love and then accepts the potentially high cost with joy, knowing the nature of a believer's inheritance in Christ.

Such unshakable trust and obedience to God extends beyond this life. This life is a brief preparation for eternal joy—a "better possession and a lasting one"(Hebrews 10:34). You can risk your life and property in this world. This is for "the sufferings of this present time are not worth comparing with the glory to be revealed to us" (Romans 8:18). Hebrews 11:1 reminds followers of Jesus that faith is a deep confidence founded on the knowledge that God's promises are true (2 Peter 3:9; 2 Corinthians 1:20). With each significant decision evaluated through the optics of faithfulness to God, the disciple of Jesus gains insight into the importance of trust and obedience.

> "For you showed sympathy to the prisoners and accepted joyfully the seizure of your property, knowing that you have for yourselves a better possession and a lasting one."
>
> *1 Timothy 1:5*

1. Acknowledge the truth that God grants us tests of faith to help us embrace His kingdom agenda. A faith that cannot be tested cannot be trusted. When have you experienced this, and how have you grown in your trust and obedience to the Lord?

_____
_____
_____

2. Respond to the call to live a "faith-filled" life. Is your life characterized by faith, as Scripture defines it? How is God challenging your heart to trust and obey right now?

_____
_____
_____

MEDITATE Fill in the blanks as you continue committing this week's verses to memory.

> "_____ in the Lord with all your _____, and do not lean on your own _____. In all your ways _____ Him, and he will make your paths _____."
>
> *Proverbs 3:5-6*

ENGAGE

Praise God for being such a "trustworthy" object for our faith. Confess your tendency to put your faith only in what you see and understand. Thank God for your promised inheritance—to be with Him forever. Ask Him to give you more faith. Ask Him to provide you with a faith that allows you to surrender your past and future, choose the imperishable, see the invisible, and do the impossible.

Week 14 • Day 04
TRUST AND OBEDIENCE

EXAMINATION

READ
Proverbs 3:5-6

☐ Want More? Read Ephesians 6

WATCH
Week 14 - Trust And Obedience

To watch the video, scan the QR code below by opening your phone's camera and holding your device so that the QR code appears on the screen. Click the link associated with the QR code, and choose this week's video. https://qrco.de/be3SWs

1. Proverbs 3:5- 6 is not about rules and maps but relationships and trust. Do you tend to approach God and His Word looking for rules to follow or for your Father whom you want to hear from? Describe the implications of how you approach God's Word. ▼

_____
_____
_____

2. Evaluate yourself honestly. Do you trust God? Where do you place your faith?

_____
_____
_____

3. Can God trust you? Have you proven you are trustworthy and competent in dealing with what He has given you?

_____
_____
_____

EXERCISE

READ *Jeremiah 17:7-8*

You must decide who or what to rely on in every circumstance that life brings. You may not slow down enough to consider whether you will trust in God or yourself, but you still make a choice. In everything we do, we trust. But there is no one as trustworthy as God. You probably know this well from your experiences of being let down by friends, family, or coworkers. However, we still want to trust ourselves and others over God. Over the past several weeks, you have developed and grown in spiritual disciplines. Your time in His Word, prayer, worship, and witness all work together to form this relationship between you and God. This relationship is based on trust and obedience. You grow in trust and obedience as you grow in His Word. Knowledge and experience transform your heart, thoughts, and decisions. Trusting God in difficult times and obeying His Word in the face of adversity is evidence of the Holy Spirit's power in your life. This is not something you can generate. In every moment, you must make a choice, but God has given you everything you need to know and believe that He is trustworthy, so you can trust Him.

MEDITATE Below, attempt to write out this week's verses from memory.

ENGAGE

Praise God for His goodness. Confess how you seek other avenues to put your trust in difficult situations. Thank God for proving His character through a personal relationship with you. Ask Him to help you trust and obey Him in every moment. Pray that He will allow you to see when you are making a decision and that you will always choose to trust Him.

Week 14 • Day 05
TRUST AND OBEDIENCE

EXERCISE

READ   *Romans 4:16-25*
☐ Want More? Read Philemon

EXEGESIS

Study Romans 4:16-25 using the **H.E.A.R.** method of inductive Bible study. Write at least one sentence for each letter below. Consult the notes from a study Bible if you need help.

HIGHLIGHT   What I see:
_____
_____
_____

EXPLAIN   What it means:
_____
_____
_____

ACKNOWLEDGE   The timeless truths:
_____
_____
_____

RESPOND   With specific action:
_____
_____
_____

While the **H.E.A.R.** method is the one that we will use to help ensure that a proper interpretation method is followed, there are other helpful plans to follow. As you become more comfortable we suggest trying other good Bible study methods.

God's covenant with Abraham (Genesis 12:1-3) was a one way covenant and did not require him to carry out a series of "good deeds" for it to be fulfilled. God's request of Abraham was to have faith. Even when Abraham's faith waned, God remained true. Long after Abraham's death, God continues to honor His promises. The English word promise is based on the Latin *promittere*, a word weighted in the context of the absolute. In the original Greek of the New Testament, the word for promise is *epaggelia*, which means "to announce." This word usage illustrates the power and reliability of God's promises. The emphasis in the Bible is not on humans keeping promises but rather on God's ability to give His promises. Faith occurs when you stop trying to do something through your own efforts and instead trust God and obey Him. In this way, faith is the practical acknowledgment that God's ways are greater than yours (Isaiah 55:8-9).

Faith is the singular attitude that stands in direct opposition to trusting yourself. Through 10 years of waiting for the fulfillment of a seemingly impossible promise, Abraham's faith grew stronger as he continued to glorify God. Martin Luther testified, "I have held many things in my hands, and I have lost them all; but whatever I have placed in God's hands, that I still possess." Both salvation and sanctification require authentic trust in the promises of God. Saving faith is what you do when there is nothing left to do, when there is nothing you can do. Sanctifying faith is trusting God no matter what. Promises fuel the life of faith, not explanations. Within His perfect nature, God is not capable of breaking His promises. Although this creates what appears to be a paradox in the lives of many proclaimed Christians, the fault is not with God or His Word. The error is found in the poor theology of those who attempt to cast God more as a genie or a vending machine than the Singular God of Creation.

EXAMPLE

In 1944, during World War 2, a small battalion of Japanese soldiers was deployed to islands in the Philippines. Within these ranks was a soldier named Hiroo Onoda. Commissioned by Major Yoshimi Taniguchi, Hiroo was commanded "never" to surrender. In August 1945, Japan formally surrendered, and it was authenticated aboard the USS Missouri on 2 September 1945. However, news of this surrender never reached Hiroo and his fellow soldiers. As such, without resupply, continued orders, or formal leadership, Hiroo and his men continued to fight. Over the years, Hiroo's peers surrendered or were captured until Hiroo was all that remained. From 1944 to 1974, Hiroo survived from what he could find in the jungles of Lubang island. Hiroo only laid down his rusted rifle when a student convinced the Japanese government to send Major Yoshimi Taniguchi. Taniguchi had long since retired and become a book salesman. With the tragedy of a wasted life aside, how could Hiroo have obeyed so faithfully for so many years? For centuries, Japanese dynasties were viewed as divine beings. This false teaching was used to radicalize soldiers such as Hiroo and Kamikaze pilots who flew suicidal missions. Japanese soldiers faced a faith conflict. If they physically lay down their arms, they thought they were spiritually laying down their gods. Of course, when we choose to follow Jesus, we face a conflict of faith, but the false gods of our lives tend to be gods of politics, nationality, celebrity, religion, or self-sufficiency. Is God the fulfillment of your faith? Do you need to lay down your arms? Here is a great acrostic: F.A.I.T.H... Forsaking All I Trust Him!

> The Lord is good,
> A stronghold in the day of trouble,
> And He knows those who take refuge in Him."
>
> *Nahum 1:7*

MEDITATE — Practice reciting this week's verses from memory and be prepared to say them aloud to your d-group.

ENGAGE

Praise God for being a promise keeper. Confess the ways that you might struggle to trust God based on your experience with people breaking promises. Thank Him for the promises of forgiveness of sin, eternal life with Him in heaven, and the permanence of presence in your life. Ask God to strengthen you into a person who trusts His promises and obeys His Word no matter what.

ENCOURAGE

Use this checklist as a guide for your weekly d-group time. Refer to the discipler's guide at the of the book for more encouragement and practical advice.

- Work through questions from the accountability page.

- Spend time praying specifics for one another.

- Take turns reciting the memory verses.

- Discuss answers to the questions throughout the week that are marked with this symbol.

PRAYER REQUESTS

_____
_____
_____
_____
_____
_____
_____

ACCOUNTABILITY QUESTIONS

These questions are to be asked of one another in a spirit of accountability (Proverbs 27:17). They are intended to stimulate conversations of character and confession of sin in a safe environment that values honesty, vulnerability, confidentiality, and grace.

1. Have you spent quality time in your spiritual disciplines this week?

2. Have you taken advantage of opportunities to share your faith this week? Explain.

3. Have your words and actions been a good testimony this week to the gospel of Jesus?

4. Have your thoughts and speech been pure (cussing, criticism, negativity, etc.)?

5. Have you been sexually pure this week? Have you been exposed to sexually alluring material? (For those who are married: Have you prioritized quality romantic time with your spouse?)

6. Have you been a good steward of your finances? Have you lacked integrity in the handling of your finances?

7. Have you been honoring and generous in your meaningful relationships this week (Family, friends, etc.)?

8. Have you given in to any addictive behavior this past week? Explain.

9. Have you been completely honest with me?

I'm praying for the salvation of the following two people and prayerfully considering how to share Christ with them myself: _____

> "Therefore, confess your sins to one another, and pray for one another, so that you may be healed."
>
> *James 5:16a*

THE TRUTH

BODY OF CHRIST

305
WEEK 15
The Church

1 Peter 2:9

327
WEEK 16
Spiritual Gifts

1 Corinthians 12:7

347
WEEK 17
Filled with the Spirit

Ephesians 5:18-20

367
WEEK 18
Spiritual Warfare

Matthew 6:9-13

389
WEEK 19
Spiritual Fruit

Galatians 5:22-23

409
WEEK 20
Biblical Justice & Giving

2 Corinthians 9:7

429
WEEK 21
Disciple Making

1 Thessalonians 2:8

THE TRUTH

Week 15 • Day 01
THE CHURCH

ESSENTIAL TRUTH

The Church is the body of Christ and consists of everyone, everywhere, who has a personal relationship with Jesus Christ. The Church functions as the people of God on the mission of God and is, therefore, both invisible and visible, local and universal. The Church accomplishes its work through the message of Jesus (the gospel) and the method of Jesus (personal disciple-making).

1. Read the Essential Truth, identify two phrases that stand out to you, and write them below. Why do you believe these phrases are significant?

_____
_____
_____

2. Based on this definition, use your own words to define the word Church.

_____
_____
_____

3. How does this explanation of the Church differ from your current understanding and usage of the word?

_____
_____
_____

EXERCISE `memory verse`

> "But you are A CHOSEN RACE, A royal PRIESTHOOD, A HOLY NATION, A PEOPLE FOR God's OWN POSSESSION, so that you may proclaim the excellencies of Him who has called you out of darkness into His marvelous light."
>
> *1 Peter 2:9*

What do you think of when you hear the word "Church?" Some may imagine rules, programs, bylaws, buildings, and worship services. When defining the word "Church," others might describe it as a place or structure. Biblically, the Church is not an "it" or a "what," but a "who." As Jesus designed it, the Church is a people on mission for Him. The Church is a family (1 Timothy 3:15) comprised of the chosen people of God (John 15:16), who have been set apart for His purpose (Colossians 3:12-17). God called the Church out of darkness and into His marvelous light to proclaim His excellencies (1 Peter 2:9). Because speech is indicative of belief, followers of Jesus should be careful not to refer to the Church as anything other than the people of God on the mission of God. It is poor theology to say that you are "getting ready for Church," or that you are "attending Church." The Church is WHO we are in Christ. We ARE the Church, a royal priesthood, a holy nation, a people for God's possession (1 Peter 2:9).

EXAMPLE

In 1492, Christopher Columbus wrongly assumed that he and his crew had successfully circumnavigated the globe. However, the landmass he saw on the distant horizon was not the East Indies, but the sizable, unmapped continents of North and South America. Operating under the false assumption that he had landed in India, Columbus referred to the indigenous people he encountered as "Indios," meaning "Indians" in Spanish. This misunderstanding shaped centuries of identity, policy, and cultural interactions with indigenous peoples. What appears to be a minor language error can escalate into a significant shift in cultural understanding. Similarly, we take a considerable risk when we wrongly assume that the Church is only a building or organization. What may seem like an innocent misstatement has evolved into a significant shift in how the world around us, and even believers, perceive the personage and mission of the Church. Jesus did not come and die for a building or an organized event. Jesus came to seek and save the lost. The Church is not a place or a thing; the Church is a people.

THE TRUTH

MEDITATE — Write out this week's verse below as you spend time committing them to memory.

MORE — If you'd like to increase your time in Scripture, commit to this optional weekly Bible reading plan.
Read (or listen via an audio Bible)

- ☐ (Day 1) 1 Timothy 1
- ☐ (Day 2) 1 Timothy 2
- ☐ (Day 3) 1 Timothy 3-4
- ☐ (Day 4) 1 Timothy 5
- ☐ (Day 5) 1 Timothy 6

ENGAGE

Praise God for being relational with His people. Confess the ways you struggle to commit to your brothers and sisters in Christ. Praise God for His grace in welcoming you into His family and for providing a community of faith where you can worship, learn, serve, and live. Pray for His guidance in understanding "the Church" as the community of believers to whom you are dedicated, rather than merely a building you visit for Sunday services.

Week 15 • Day 02
THE CHURCH

EXERCISE

READ *Matthew 16:18; Matthew 18:15-17*

☐ Want More? Read 1 Timothy 2

1. Read Matthew 16:13-17 and highlight the context that led Jesus to declare the establishment of His Church in 16:18.

_____
_____

2. Explain how the word "Church" is used in Matthew 18:15-17. Do these two early references to Jesus' Church (16:18 and 18:17) indicate a place where God's people go or a group of God's people? How does this passage shed light on how you should use the term "Church?"

_____
_____

Matthew 13-16 provides detailed insights into the religious leaders' rejection of Jesus as the Messiah and King. Numerous prophecies throughout the Old Testament point to Jesus as the Son of God, Messiah, and King of the Jews (Isaiah 7:14, Zechariah 9, and Micah 5:2). In the New Testament, the Gospel of Matthew begins with genealogy, which proves that Jesus was the promised Son who would reign on the throne of David (Matthew 1). Jesus' messianic claim is further supported by the account of the Magi (also known as the Wise Men) and the early ministry of John the Baptist (Matthew 2-3). After He was tempted in the wilderness, Jesus presented the tenets of His coming Kingdom in the Sermon on the Mount (Matthew 5-7). In the face of Jewish leaders dismissing Jesus as the Messiah and prophesied King, Jesus began to teach about a Kingdom beyond politics and pride. He spoke of a Kingdom comprised of the overlooked, the downcast, and the weary (Matthew 11).

From that point forward, Jesus revealed the "mysteries" of His Kingdom to those He would affectionately call His Church. Jesus proclaimed, "To you it has been granted to know the mysteries of the Kingdom of Heaven, but to them it has not been granted" (Matthew 13:11). Jesus first uses the term "Church" in Matthew 16:18. The word Church is translated from the Greek word *ekklesia*, meaning "assembly." *Ekklesia* refers to the citizens of a city, or soldiers, assembling for a specific purpose (such as work or war). This theme is also found in the Old Testament, typically referenced by the Hebrew word *qahal*, which is derived from the word for "voice" (i.e., "to a call to assemble"). *Ekklesia* and *qahal* provide an essential link between the Church of the New Testament and the nation of Israel of the Old Testament: the people of God called to assemble for the work of the Kingdom.

Several church metaphors connect the Old and New Testament concepts of *ekklesia* and *qahal*. 1Peter 2:9 describes Jesus' Church as the nation of God—the people of God, organized to proclaim the Father's excellencies. Ephesians 1:22-23 and 1 Corinthians 12:27 refer to the Church as the body of Christ—a unified whole living out the life of Christ in their diverse functions with the Son as the head of the Church. Ephesians 2:19-22 and 1 Peter 2:5 portray Jesus' Church as the temple of the Spirit—a group of people who have the Holy Spirit within them and whose purpose is to represent Him to a watching world. It is crucial to recognize that the disciple of Jesus plays a role in each of these metaphors. Jesus' choice to use the word *ekklesia* and His continued explanation demonstrate that being part of Jesus' Church is more than a membership; it is a partnership.

THE TRUTH

In the modern mind, membership implies expectations of services, perks, and advantages. A gold or platinum membership to a cruise line grants special treatment and privileges, such as access to the captain's table. In many ways, the sense of entitlement and privilege associated with "membership" was at the core of the Jewish religious leaders rejection of Jesus. Most of these men were so focused on their family heritage, education, and social status that they could not imagine a captain's table or "wedding feast" open to everyone. Unable to overcome their perceived privileges, they could not comprehend Jesus' offer to partner with Him to complete the Kingdom work of the Church. The Church, as Jesus designed it, is not a cruise ship separated by levels of access and privilege. As Jesus designed it, the Church is a battleship where everyone serves a critical role.

1. Based on today's study, **Acknowledge** the timeless truth found in Jesus' choice of the word "Church" in your own words.

_____
_____
_____

2. Jesus planned His Church the way He wants it and He wants His Church the way He planned it. **Respond** to this expanded understanding of the concept of the Church. What do you think is your specific part in Jesus' Church?

_____
_____
_____

3. Do you trust God entirely, exclusively, and extensively? **Respond** to this question by listing evidence from your life below that supports your answer. How is God specifically challenging you right now?

_____
_____
_____

MEDITATE   Fill in the blanks as you continue committing this week's verse to memory.

> "But you are a chosen race, a royal priesthood, a holy nation, a people for God's own _____, so that you may proclaim the _____ of Him who has called you out of darkness into His marvelous _____.'"

1 Peter 2:9

ENGAGE

Praise Jesus for building His Church. Confess the ways that you have undervalued the body of Christ. Thank Jesus for loving the Church and giving Himself up for her. Ask God to use you to build up His Church and to be an active and productive part of a local body of believers. If you do not know your S.P.O.T. (special place on the team) within your local church, ask God to reveal it to you now.

THE TRUTH

Week 15 • Day 03
THE CHURCH

EXERCISE

READ *Acts 2:1-13, 41-47*

☐ Want More? Read 1 Timothy 3-4

1. As you read Acts 2:42-47, **Highlight** the characteristics of the early Church. Write a list below.

_____
_____
_____

2. **Explain** the role of the Holy Spirit found within the Acts 2 Church. ▼

_____
_____
_____

The accounts following Jesus' ascension into heaven demonstrate a period of continued spiritual growth and unity in the early Church. Jesus did not leave His Church alone when He ascended. His disciples followed His commands to gather in prayer and await the *parakletos* (Helper) that He promised to send them. Aware of the need to replace Judas, the apostles demonstrated their continued trust in God's sovereignty by selecting Matthias as the twelfth apostle through a drawing of lots (Acts 1:23-26). Such actions indicate that Jesus' first disciples understood His teaching about His Church and the need to assemble in unity for the purposeful work of God's Kingdom.

In Acts 2:3, God's Spirit descended as tongues of fire, indwelling and empowering His people. In some Christian circles, the coming of the Holy Spirit is over-emphasized, and in others it is entirely overlooked. If the work of the Holy Spirit is overly sensationalized, one risks missing the purpose of the Holy Spirit's work and intention for spiritual gifts. On the other hand, those who choose to underemphasize or even ignore the presence and work of God's Spirit risk attributing the work of God to themselves. A more balanced teaching of the Holy Spirit emphasizes the incredible help and comfort the Holy Spirit provides while acknowledging His work and God's greater glory. In Old Testament times, people were instructed "to go" to God's Temple to be near God's presence. A significant shift occurred in the New Testament era—disciples of Jesus became temples of the Holy Spirit upon conversion and were called "to go to the people" on mission.

What Paul would later describe as spiritual gifts set the stage for Peter's great sermon in Acts 2. This text demonstrates how the Holy Spirit (the Helper) empowered an ordinary fisherman with a moderate education to preach the gospel with a power far exceeding his natural talents. To further glorify God and validate Peter's gospel presentation, the Holy Spirit gifted many with the ability to teach and preach in the native dialects of those in attendance. Scripture tells us that thousands in attendance repented and acknowledged Jesus as their Lord.

Acts provides us with four key "birthmarks" that define what it means to be part of a Christ-centered community (Church). First, the early Church was totally **DEVOTED** to Jesus and the teachings of the Apostles (Acts 2:42). They were continually committed to learning and obeying Jesus' commands and to serving within His Church. Their devotion was not occasional or superficial. Those in the early Church persistently studied God's Word in order to obey Gods passionately.

Secondly, this text demonstrates how the Holy Spirit supernaturally **EMPOWERED** the Church. Acts 2:43 teaches that awe came upon everyone as the Spirit empowered the apostles to perform many wonders and signs. The presence of the Holy Spirit also brought depth and unity to their gatherings, thereby further revealing God's presence among His people for His work. The early Church did not merely attend a Sunday morning event as a compartmentalized version of a spiritual activity; they lived empowered lives.

Third, the actions of the early Church displayed an irrational **COMMITMENT** to one another. Acts 2 describes how the early Church shared with each other in the blessings and burdens of daily life (Acts 2:44-47). The wealthy sold their properties to meet the needs of their fellow Christians. Such acts erased barriers of gender, race, and social class while creating a community defined by love, unity, and equality. Because these expressions of selflessness and compassion were irrational by social and secular standards, these acts of love and unity became a powerful testimony demonstrating the Church's commitment to Christ and His callings.

Lastly, the early Church was outrageously **FOCUSED** on the propagation of the gospel. They were so motivated to share the Good News of Jesus that it continued the Church's primary mission despite facing extreme persecution. When faced with imprisonment, martyrdom, and incredible hardship, the early Church continued, all-the-more, to boast of Jesus and His great work of salvation.

> And there appeared to them tongues as of fire distributing themselves, and they rested on each one of them."
>
> *Acts 2:3*

THE TRUTH

1. Acknowledge the timeless truth about why God invites new people into the family of God. Why does He give His Church His Spirit?

_____
_____
_____

2. Respond to the four characteristics discussed. Which of the four marks of an Acts 2 Church is the most convicting to you?

_____
_____
_____

3. Are there any other believers who know you are devoted to them? Are there any lost people who know you are devoted to them? Name them below and take some time to pray for them.

_____
_____
_____

THE TRUTH

MEDITATE Fill in the blanks as you continue committing this week's verses to memory.

> "But you are a _____ race, a royal priesthood, a holy nation, a _____ for God's own _____, so that you may proclaim the _____ of Him who has called you out of _____ into His marvelous _____."
>
> *Proverbs 3:5-6*

ENGAGE

Praise God for the power of His Spirit within you. Confess a few of the places in your life where you do not take advantage of His Spirit's power, but instead trust in your own abilities. Thank Him for His presence in your life and for enabling you to obey God and be an active and vital part of His Church. Ask Him to help you be devoted to Him, empowered by the Holy Spirit, committed to your community of believers, and focused on the propagation of the Gospel.

Week 15 • Day 04
THE CHURCH

EXAMINATION

READ
Acts 2:37-47

☐ Want More? Read 1 Timothy 5

WATCH
Week 15 - The Church

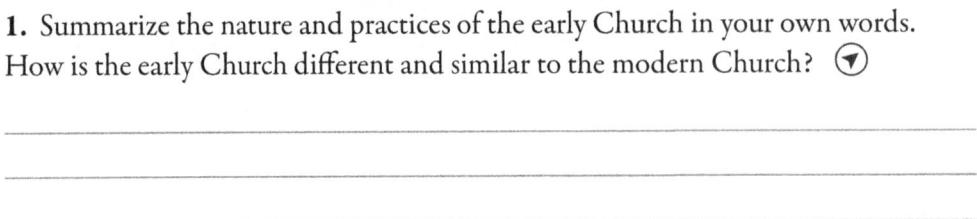

To watch the video, scan the QR code below by opening your phone's camera and holding your device so that the QR code appears on the screen. Click the link associated with the QR code, and choose this week's video. https://qrco.de/be3SWs

1. Summarize the nature and practices of the early Church in your own words. How is the early Church different and similar to the modern Church? ▼

_____
_____
_____

2. How did Dr. Christopher Moody's teaching on the word "Church," as used in the Bible enrich or refine your understanding of the word?

_____

_____

_____

EXERCISE

READ   Acts 2:37-47

In Acts 2, we see the "family of God" for the first time. Family is a term we use to describe those to whom we are closest, for whom we care the most, especially our spouse and children. We cannot control the people our children will become, but we can influence the aspects of life to which they are exposed, both good and bad. The "family of God" activities described in Acts 2 are those to which we want our immediate family, especially our biological and spiritual children, exposed. Exposure to these activities reinforces the godly habits and Christ-centered examples they are learning through their disciple-making process. Again, Acts 2:37-47 mentions various religious activities that the early church family participated in as a group.

1. Baptism

2. Biblical Teaching

3. Fellowship (more than just being together; it means having in common, probably referring to the sharing of material goods)

4. Lord's Supper (breaking bread together)

5. Prayer

6. Sharing Resources and Serving

7. Eating Together (that is the second breaking of bread)

8. Generous Giving

9. Worship

10. Making More Disciples

Although this list is not exhaustive, it represents a series of worshipful actions and behaviors that Jesus commonly modeled for his disciples. While all of these activities are important, Jesus paid special attention to two, which we now identify as ordinances of the Church. By Jesus' design, Christ-centered disciple-making places the practice of Baptism and the Lord's Supper on public display. These ordinances are not merely empty religious rituals but holy behaviors that help connect us in relationships while teaching about biblical faith. A commonly expressed sentiment says, "Tell me, and I forget; teach me, and I may remember; involve me, and I learn." One's learning cannot be passive, and these various activities listed in Acts 2:37-47 are the holy habits that characterized the early church. Regarding Baptism and the Lord's Supper, all the Gospels and many of the epistles pointed to these two things as commanded by Jesus.

In this spiritual context, rituals such as Baptism and the Lord's Supper are forms of worship. They are physical representations (water in Baptism, bread and juice in the Lord's Supper) of spiritual events we participate in. Celebrating someone's Baptism, for instance, allows the church to join in the drama of a new believer's spiritual regeneration (a death-to-life story, Colossians 2:12). The Lord's Supper symbolizes our daily intimacy with the living Christ. Celebrating the "Table" as we do reminds us that He lived, was crucified, resurrected, and ascended, while also foreshadowing the coming future when He will once again break bread with us, His followers, in His Kingdom (Revelation 19).

THE TRUTH

MEDITATE Below, attempt to write out this week's verses from memory.

ENGAGE

Praise God for giving you a family of believers to do life with. Confess the ways you struggle to live on mission in partnership with the Church or in unity with other believers. Thank God for loving, equipping, and using us right where we are. Ask Him to deepen your love for Him and the people around you.

Week 15 • Day 05
THE CHURCH

EXERCISE

READ *Galatians 3:23-29*
☐ Want More? Read 1 Timothy 6

EXEGESIS

Study Galatians 3:23-29 using the H.E.A.R. method of inductive Bible study. Write at least one sentence for each letter below. Consult the notes from a study Bible if you need help.

HIGHLIGHT   What I see:
___
___
___

EXPLAIN   What it means:
___
___
___

THE TRUTH

ACKNOWLEDGE The timeless truths:

_____
_____
_____

RESPOND With specific action:

_____
_____
_____

While the **H.E.A.R.** method is the one that we will use to help ensure that a proper interpretation method is followed, there are other helpful plans to follow. As you become more comfortable we suggest trying other good Bible study methods.

Are you a part of the family of God? One cannot risk assuming the answer to this crucial question. It is inaccurate to think that everyone attending a worship service or listed on a church roll is part of God's family. God gives one condition, as seen in Galatians 3:26, "For you are all sons of God through faith in Christ Jesus." Faith is required for adoption as God's son. If you have not confessed with your mouth and believed in your heart that Jesus Christ is your Savior and Lord, you can make that decision today (Romans 10:9-10). Upon faith in Jesus, all are welcomed into the family of God. Not only do you become a child of God, but you are also given a family of believers to support you. The local Church is your family. As a believer, you are a part of that family, whether you are active and present or not. Do not neglect your family and miss out on the ability to be the Church. A follower of Jesus without a Church family is a contradiction in terms—like a football player without a team, a soldier without an army, a bee without a hive, or a tuba player without an orchestra.

EXAMPLE

The infamous story of the Titanic stands as a testament to misunderstanding. Despite being hailed as "unsinkable," the crew continually dismissed crucial warnings about icebergs, leading to catastrophic consequences and tragic deaths. This tragedy serves as a stark reminder of the consequences of failing to comprehend and process factual information effectively. Similarly, misunderstandings about the identity and purpose of Jesus' Church carry significant risks. Who is the Church? The Bible describes the Church as the body of Christ, living out the life of Christ—the people of God on a mission from God. It is a community of believers called to embody His love, share the gospel, and serve others. Misrepresenting or misunderstanding this truth can hinder its mission and distort its purpose.

MEDITATE Practice reciting this week's verses from memory and be prepared to say them aloud to your d-group.

ENGAGE

Praise God for being your Father. Confess how you have forgotten your identity in the family of God. Confess the ways in which you fail to partner with the family of God. Thank Him for bringing you into relationship with Himself and giving you a family of brothers and sisters in the faith. Ask Him to enable you to be an active part of the Church each day of your life..

ENCOURAGE

Use this checklist as a guide for your weekly d-group time. Refer to the discipler's guide at the front of the book for more encouragement and practical advice.

- Work through questions from the accountability page.
- Spend time praying specifics for one another.
- Take turns reciting the memory verses.
- Discuss answers to the questions throughout the week that are marked with this symbol. ▼

PRAYER REQUESTS

_____
_____
_____
_____
_____
_____

ACCOUNTABILITY QUESTIONS

These questions are to be asked of one another in a spirit of accountability (Proverbs 27:17). They are intended to stimulate conversations of character and confession of sin in a safe environment that values honesty, vulnerability, confidentiality, and grace.

1. Have you spent quality time in your spiritual disciplines this week?

2. Have you taken advantage of opportunities to share your faith this week? Explain.

3. Have your words and actions been a good testimony this week to the gospel of Jesus?

4. Have your thoughts and speech been pure (cussing, criticism, negativity, etc.)?

5. Have you been sexually pure this week? Have you been exposed to sexually alluring material? (For those who are married: Have you prioritized quality romantic time with your spouse?)

6. Have you been a good steward of your finances? Have you lacked integrity in the handling of your finances?

7. Have you been honoring and generous in your meaningful relationships this week (Family, friends, etc.)?

8. Have you given in to any addictive behavior this past week? Explain.

9. Have you been completely honest with me?

I'm praying for the salvation of the following two people and prayerfully considering how to share Christ with them myself: _____

> "Therefore, confess your sins to one another, and pray for one another, so that you may be healed."
>
> *James 5:16a*

Week 16 • Day 01
SPIRITUAL GIFTS

ESSENTIAL TRUTH

To maximize His glory, God supernaturally enables each believer with at least one spiritual gift in order to serve the local Church and make a valuable contribution. Spiritual gifts are not to be confused with natural talents, but both talents and gifts should be used to serve the Kingdom of God. Every ability has a kingdom application. Scripture encourages us to discover and develop our spiritual gifts. The lists of gifts are found in four places: 1 Corinthians 12:1-11, Romans 12:3-8, Ephesians 4:11-12, and 1 Peter 4:10-11.

1. Read the Essential Truth, identify two phrases that stand out, and write them below. Why do you believe these phrases are significant?

___

___

___

2. List a few of your natural talents that could be used to serve God's Kingdom.

___

___

___

3. Do you have a place of personal ministry, service, or leadership within the Church that you can evaluate to help understand your spiritual gifts? List them below.

_____

_____

_____

EXERCISE `memory verse`

> "But to each one is given the manifestation of the Spirit for the common good."
>
> *1 Corinthians 12:7*

God has united His people under Jesus' authority and given them the commission to make disciples of all nations. The ministry philosophy of every local church should be the same: "the equipping of the saints" for the work of this ministry (Ephesians 4:12). Jesus designed His Church as an "equipping" church, and He gathers into one body a community of diverse individuals with unique natural talents and supernatural spiritual gifts. It is mission-critical to distinguish between spiritual gifts and natural talents. While natural talents can benefit the local church, spiritual gifts are given by the Holy Spirit for the sole purpose of strengthening and serving the body of Christ. Empowered by the Holy Spirit, spiritual gifts are essential to the Church's mission to make disciples. If spiritual gifts remain unused, the local church remains incomplete and often inept. God has provided everything the local church needs to make disciples locally and abroad (Acts 1:8). If a local church body is lacking, it is likely due to underutilized spiritual gifts. As you reflect and study spiritual gifts this week, approach the process prayerfully. Reflect on your service, leadership, or ministry roles within your local church. Where has your contribution to the work of the local church benefited others? Strive to discover and develop your unique spiritual gift(s) while aligning your service of Christ with God's divine design of your life, both naturally and supernaturally.

> But you will receive power when the Holy Spirit has come upon you; and you shall be My witnesses both in Jerusalem, and in all Judea and Samaria, and even to the remotest part of the earth."
> *Acts 1:8*

EXAMPLE

The baseball legend Mark McGwire once said, "When I feel the ball hit right on the sweet spot, a home run is just around the corner." When we lean into our spiritual gifts and the unique abilities God has given us, we find our sweet spot in serving Him. Using spiritual gifts allows us to step into a purposeful life as disciple-makers. In the same way, McGwire's sweet spot propelled the ball to incredibly long distances. We find ourselves being used in incredible ways when we utilize our spiritual gifts. These gifts enable us to connect with others more profoundly, fostering community and enriching the Church. Moreover, they empower us to make a meaningful impact on the world, reflecting God's love and purpose. Every gift has the potential to impact the world around us as well as eternity itself, whether it is teaching, encouraging, giving, exhorting, serving, comforting, or leading.

WEEK 16

MEDITATE Write out this week's verse below as you spend time committing it to memory.

MORE If you'd like to increase your time in Scripture, commit to this optional weekly Bible reading plan.
Read (or listen via an audio Bible)

- ☐ (Day 1) 1 Peter 1
- ☐ (Day 2) 1 Peter 2
- ☐ (Day 3) 1 Peter 3
- ☐ (Day 4) 1 Peter 4
- ☐ (Day 5) 1 Peter 5

ENGAGE

Praise God for creating a family of believers to which you could belong and for which you could serve. Confess any struggle you have in contributing to or serving your local church. Thank Him for uniquely equipping each believer in a way that will benefit the entire family of God. Ask God to help reveal your spiritual gift to you and to clarify how you can use it for His glory.

THE TRUTH

Week 16 • Day 02
SPIRITUAL GIFTS

EXERCISE

READ *1 Corinthians 12:1-11*

☐ Want More? Read ¨1 Peter 2

1. As you read through 1 Corinthians. 12:4-7, **Highlight** the four terms used to denote different aspects of spiritual gifting. Give a few synonyms for each word. If you have access to a Bible dictionary or concordance, look these words up and record some observations below. ⊙

_____
_____
_____

2. **Explain** Paul's logic in this passage. What does this diversity serve to promote in Jesus' Church? Why is this important?

_____
_____
_____

God provides spiritual men and women with spiritual gifts. These spiritual gifts are a vital resource for His Church—for the expansion of His Kingdom. Numerous biblical passages demonstrate how spiritual gifts contribute to the benefit of the local and global Church (1 Corinthians 12:1-11, Romans 12:3-8, Ephesians 4:11-12, and 1 Peter 4:10-11). 1 Corinthians 12:7 teaches us that every disciple of Jesus receives the Holy Spirit and is endowed with at least one spiritual gift. These gifts are not for personal gain, but for the Church's "common good" to maximize the glory of God. Jesus' Great Commission was not intended to be accomplished apart from His Spirit. Disciples of Christ are not capable of carrying out the incredible work of making disciples of all nations without the empowerment of Christ's Spirit (Cf. Acts 1:8; John 15:5). Therefore, He instructs them to remain in Jerusalem and await the "gift my Father promised" (Acts 1:4).

For perspective, Jesus' first disciples had spent nearly three years with Him. While following Jesus as their Rabbi, they hung on His every Word, witnessed Him teach with power, and experienced firsthand as He performed many different miracles. These men had sat under the instruction of the most incredible teacher, preacher, and communicator who ever existed. The Apostles had learned from the Rabbi of Rabbis, but were still lacking. Apart from the supernatural gifting of the Holy Spirit, no amount of education or natural talent alone was sufficient to complete the work of the Church of Jesus Christ.

Understanding the distinctions between learned skills, natural talents, and spiritual gifts remains critical for a fruitful Christian life. A learned skill is acquired and refined over time through education and application. In comparison, a natural talent is primarily influenced by genetics and inclination. One can undoubtedly contribute to a local church by employing natural talents and learned skills. However, those who rely only on natural talents and abilities in their service of Christ are often tempted to take credit for the work of the Kingdom. A spiritual gift is bestowed by God independent of genetics at the point of every believer's conversion to benefit the Church. Less temptation exists to take credit for such supernatural empowerment. A gifted vocalist or talented musician could compose and execute an incredible performance. Still, apart from spiritual giftings, they are likely to focus on themselves instead of the God their music is designed to worship. For this reason, humility proves crucial for maximizing God's glory in this sinful world.

1 Corinthians 12 reminds us that spiritual gifts leverage the diversity of the Church while concentrating on the unity of its work to make disciples. In today's

reading, Paul underscores the unity of spiritual gifts by pointing to the "same Spirit," same Lord," and "same God" as their source. While each disciple of Jesus possesses different "gifts," "ministries," "effects," and "manifestations" of the Spirit (1 Cor. 12:4-7), all of these gifts originate from God. This arrangement most effectively encourages both diversity and unity within the Church. Spiritual gifts equip and unify the Body of Christ, promoting interdependence and harmony. One exercises the gift of hospitality, another of teaching, and yet another demonstrates the gift of mercy. Individually, each of these gifts benefits the Church's work. United, these various gifts form the foundation of every healthy Bible Study, Sunday School, Community Group, or local church.

Since there was division in the Corinthian church, Paul began 1 Corinthians 12 by emphasizing the oneness of the Church. The larger context of the chapter is unity, and the ministry gifts of the Spirit encourage unity through diversity and interdependence. The Holy Spirit gives spiritual gifts for the good work and harmony of the Church. Paul did not intend for 1 Corinthians 12 to be an exhaustive list of all spiritual gifts. He lists a great variety of gifts, such as knowledge, faith, miracles, discernment, and various languages. Paul concludes by comparing the Church to a body composed of many parts. In this analogy, each body member plays a unique role.

1. What does Scripture teach us about the purpose and use of spiritual gifts for the work of the Church?

2. What are the key differences between learned skills, natural talents, and spiritual gifts, and how does humility play a role in ensuring that these gifts are used to glorify God rather than oneself?

___

MEDITATE Fill in the blanks as you continue committing this week's verse to memory.

> But to _____ one is given the manifestation of the _____ for the common good."
>
> *1 Corinthians 12:7*

ENGAGE

Praise God for equipping the saints for the work of ministry. Confess the ways you struggle to serve the Church with the spiritual gifts God has given you. Thank Him for providing various giftings to meet the needs of His people. Ask Him to help you understand how He's gifted you and how He intends to use you.

Week 16 • Day 03
SPIRITUAL GIFTS

EXERCISE

READ *Romans 12:4-8*

☐ Want More? Read 1 Peter 3

1. Consider the Church as described in Romans 12:1-3, and **Acknowledge** at least two theological truths that provide the basis for a believer exercising their spiritual gifts in the body of Christ (Romans 12:4-8).

_____
_____
_____

2. **Respond** to the list of seven spiritual gifts in Romans 12:6-8. These different "passions" motivate the various members of Christ's "one" body to serve in different ways (12:5). Is there one of the seven that drives your service of Christ and His body (passion to tell, help, clarify, motivate, supply, guide, comfort)?

_____
_____
_____

Romans 12:4-8 is one of several biblical texts that demonstrate how God uniquely gifts every believer to fulfill a specific role in the body of Christ. Like 1 Corinthians 12, Romans 12 is not intended to be viewed as an exhaustive list of spiritual gifts. Over the last few days, you have studied the purpose and practical application of spiritual gifts. A deeper understanding of spiritual gifting can often ignite a believer's enthusiasm for disciple-making and personal ministry. But how does a disciple of Jesus discover and use the spiritual gifts the Holy Spirit has given them?

For some, discovering their spiritual gifts will be a straightforward process. In contrast, most individuals will require some experimentation to find their giftings. As you seek to define your spiritual gifts, remember that each individual is gifted differently. Jesus designed His Church to comprise people who act and serve in different ways. Identify a need in your local church that aligns with your skills, passion, and calling, and then prayerfully consider addressing it. Create an environment that gives you the freedom to grow and serve the needs of others. Many new believers are surprised that their spiritual gifts do not always align directly with the skills they have learned or the natural talents they possess. Spiritual surveys and other tools can be helpful, but experience is the best teacher. Through trial and error, alongside the evaluation of a trusted discipler, one often discovers one's spiritual gifts.

In today's reading, Paul emphasizes the unique role each gift plays in the Church and the various passions that drive us to serve in these specific ways:

1. **Prophecy (Passion to Proclaim)** –Those gifted with prophecy can speak truth in timely, convicting ways, guiding others toward God's Word.

2. **Serving (Passion to Help)** –These individuals readily discern the unfulfilled needs of others and cheerfully intervene to help without seeking recognition.

3. **Teaching (Passion to Clarify)** –Teachers bring understanding to the Word, making Scripture tangible and applicable for others.

4. **Exhortation (Passion to Motivate)** –Exhorters encourage and challenge others, often bringing correction coupled with kindness.

5. **Giving (Passion to Supply)** –Those with this gift often seek opportunities to give generously, going above and beyond to meet needs quietly and without fanfare.

6. **Leading (Passion to Guide)** –Leaders can organize and mobilize others,

guiding teams toward a shared purpose.

7. **Mercy (Passion to Comfort)** – Those gifted in mercy are inherently aware of the pain of others and respond with compassion and care.

The purpose of every spiritual gift is to enrich the work of the Church. Identifying the gifts God has given you is of little value if you do not use them. The parable of the talents in Matthew 25:14-30 exhibits how God intends for His children to multiply what He has entrusted them. Whether your gift is prophecy or mercy, find ways to act on your gifting intentionally to serve those in your local church. Prophets might inspire others through writing or public speaking, while those with the gift of mercy may find fulfillment in counseling or supporting those in need. God created you with a purpose and with specific passions. Embracing your spiritual gifts is one of the keys to both longevity and unity. People rarely keep doing things for which they are not passionate. Step into your role, serve with enthusiasm, and use your spiritual gifts to glorify Him. Together, these contributions build His Kingdom.

1. How do disciples of Jesus begin exploring their spiritual gifts if they are unsure where to start?

_____
_____
_____

2. Which of the seven spiritual gifts mentioned—prophecy, serving, teaching, exhortation, giving, leading, or mercy—resonates most strongly with your heart's passion to serve others?

_____
_____
_____

WEEK 16

MEDITATE   Fill in the blanks as you continue committing this week's verse to memory.

" But to _____ one is given the _____ of the _____ for the _____ good."

1 Corinthians 12:7

ENGAGE

Praise God for being the head of the Church. Confess the ways you try to serve from your own power and abilities rather than trusting God and walking in obedience. Thank Him for His provision for the Church. Ask God to help you see Him at work in and through His people and deepen your faith in and dependence on Him.

Week 16 • Day 04
SPIRITUAL GIFTS

EXAMINATION

READ
Romans 12:1-8

☐ Want More? Read 1 Peter 4

WATCH
Week 16 - Spiritual Gifts

To watch the video, scan the QR code below by opening your phone's camera and holding your device so that the QR code appears on the screen. Click the link associated with the QR code, and choose this week's video. https://qrco.de/be3SWs

1. Explain how spiritual gifts are different from natural talents.
___
___
___

2. How does the variety of spiritual gifts create an interdependence within the local church? Explain.

_____

_____

_____

EXERCISE

READ Romans 12:1-8

In Romans 12, Paul emphasizes the importance of humility, unity, and the stewardship of spiritual gifts within the body of Christ. Painfully aware that these selfless attributes are contrary to the sinful nature, followers of Christ must acknowledge that their lives are not their own (Galatians 2:20). To this point, Paul begins by urging believers to present their bodies as a living sacrifice (Romans 12:1). He then explains that doing so is both pleasing to God and an act of spiritual worship. These verses demonstrate that a worshipful life springs from a close relationship with Jesus and a love for what Jesus loves. Some may be tempted to view this passage as a list of emotional or moral goals achieved only through self-discipline. However, Paul reminds the Church that although the believer submits to the transformation, Jesus is the one who renews the minds of His disciples.

The analogy of a physical body compared to the local church reveals the interconnected and interdependent nature of the Church Jesus designed. Within this body of believers, each believer is commissioned to serve the Lord with their natural and spiritual gifts, attentive to the greater mission of the local church and the service of one another. In this way, the local church becomes the combined hands and feet of Jesus within their community (1 Corinthians 12:27). Each member of the body is encouraged to use their unique spiritual gifts with dedication and sincerity, whether prophesying, serving, teaching, encouraging, giving, leading, or showing mercy. When one selfishly sees oneself above others or selfishly refuses to serve with their gifts, the local church body suffers.

THE TRUTH

MEDITATE Below, attempt to write out this week's verse from memory.

ENGAGE

Praise God for giving you the ability to partner with Him in Kingdom work. Confess the ways you doubt the gifts He's given you or your ability to do the work He's called you to. Thank Him for knowing you fully, providing for your needs, equipping you supernaturally, and using you right where you are. Ask God to deepen your trust in Him and maximize your obedience to His Word.

Week 16 • Day 05
SPIRITUAL GIFTS

EXERCISE

READ *Matthew 25:14-30*
☐ Want More? Read 1 Peter 5

EXEGESIS

Study Matthew 25:14-30 using the H.E.A.R. method of inductive Bible study. Write at least one sentence for each letter below. Refer to the notes from a study Bible if you need assistance.

HIGHLIGHT   What I see:
_____
_____
_____

EXPLAIN   What it means:
_____
_____
_____

ACKNOWLEDGE   The timeless truths:

_____
_____
_____

RESPOND   With specific action:

_____
_____
_____

While the **H.E.A.R.** method is the one that we will use to help ensure that a proper interpretation method is followed, there are other helpful plans to follow. As you become more comfortable we suggest trying other good Bible study methods.

God has given His children incredible gifts intended to enrich His family and bring Him glory. In Matthew 9:37, Jesus reminds His followers that "the harvest is plentiful, but the workers are few." As children of God (John 1:12) and coheirs with Christ (Romans 8:17), believers are adopted into the heritage of Jesus' great work of reconciliation (Ephesians 2:10). When criticized by the religious leaders of His day for investing in Zacchaeus, Jesus responds by saying, "For the Son of Man has come to seek and to save that which was lost." The purposeful work of the Church is to grow in relationship with Jesus while doing the work of His Kingdom. Where many seek to grow spiritually through self-investment, there is a measure of spiritual maturity that can only be achieved by investing what God has given you into the lives of others.

Such an investment requires work and involves risk. However, one is not expected to do more than they are enabled to do through the power of the Holy Spirit. The work of making disciples is not a solo mission. God has given His children His Spirit, His Word, and His Church. Like the parable of the talents, God has given each of His children the opportunity to use their gifts for the benefit of others or to hide them selfishly. One is obedience to your Father and faith in His power; the other is disobedience and a lack of trust. Choose wisely.

EXAMPLE

In the late 1880s, a small boy in Munich struggled to keep up with his class. Young Albert experienced developmental difficulties to the point that he could not construct a complete sentence until he was four years old. Albert's parents worried that learning difficulties would define his life. Today, we know this young man as Albert Einstein, the renowned physicist, mathematician, and Nobel Prize winner. Despite his towering intellect and resourcefulness, Einstein struggled to learn effectively in a formal educational environment. Einstein's story is an excellent example of a round peg trying to fit into a square hole. God created you in His image for His glory. In His infinite wisdom, He gave you a distinct personality and specific spiritual gifts. Discovering your spiritual gifts and God's calling for your life is often like finding the right block that fits in the right space. Once you discover your space, you will find your calling. God has an incredible plan for all His children; you are no exception.

MEDITATE   Practice reciting this week's verse from memory and be prepared to say it aloud to your d-group.

ENGAGE

Praise God for His providence. Confess the ways you struggle to trust Him and live by faith. Thank Him for gifting you and your family of faith in ways that will build one another up and continue the ministry of Jesus. Ask Him to show you the specific action steps to take to obey Him and invest what He has given you.

ENCOURAGE

Use this checklist as a guide for your weekly d-group time. Refer to the discipler's guide at the of the book for more encouragement and practical advice.

- Work through questions from the accountability page.
- Spend time praying specifics for one another.
- Take turns reciting the memory verses.
- Discuss answers to the questions throughout the week that are marked with this symbol. ▼

PRAYER REQUESTS

_____
_____
_____
_____
_____
_____
_____

WEEK 16

ACCOUNTABILITY QUESTIONS

These questions are to be asked of one another in a spirit of accountability (Proverbs 27:17). They are intended to stimulate conversations of character and confession of sin in a safe environment that values honesty, vulnerability, confidentiality, and grace.

1. Have you spent quality time in your spiritual disciplines this week?

2. Have you taken advantage of opportunities to share your faith this week? Explain.

3. Have your words and actions been a good testimony this week to the gospel of Jesus?

4. Have your thoughts and speech been pure (cussing, criticism, negativity, etc.)?

5. Have you been sexually pure this week? Have you been exposed to sexually alluring material? (For those who are married: Have you prioritized quality romantic time with your spouse?)

6. Have you been a good steward of your finances? Have you lacked integrity in the handling of your finances?

7. Have you been honoring and generous in your meaningful relationships this week (Family, friends, etc.)?

8. Have you given in to any addictive behavior this past week? Explain.

9. Have you been completely honest with me?

I'm praying for the salvation of the following two people and prayerfully considering how to share Christ with them myself: _____

> "Therefore, confess your sins to one another, and pray for one another, so that you may be healed."
>
> *James 5:16a*

Week 17 • Day 01

FILLED WITH THE SPIRIT

ESSENTIAL TRUTH

Walking in obedience to God in life and ministry comes mainly from the help of the Person of the Holy Spirit. The Holy Spirit indwells, infills, insures, and enables a believers through their spiritual journey. A "spiritual" person seeks to be led by the Spirit moment by moment, finding joy in the spiritual intimacy and influence that God provides.

1. Read the Essential Truth, identify two phrases that stand out to you, and write them below. Why do you believe these phrases are significant? ⌖

_____
_____
_____

2. Using your own words, what does it mean to be filled with the Holy Spirit?

_____
_____
_____

3. How have you experienced being led by the Holy Spirit? Have you struggled to experience the presence and help the Holy Spirit promises?

_____
_____
_____

EXERCISE — memory verses

> "And do not get drunk with wine, for that is dissipation, but be filled with the Spirit, speaking to one another in psalms and hymns and spiritual songs, singing and making melody with your heart to the Lord; always giving thanks for all things in the name of our Lord Jesus Christ to God, even the Father."
>
> *Ephesians 5:18-20*

Although some consider the Holy Spirit a purely New Testament concept, the Holy Spirit's ministry is evident throughout the entire Bible, not just the New Testament. Jeremiah prophesied of the New Covenant, in which God's Law will be written on the hearts of His people (Jeremiah 31). Ezekiel also spoke about the future indwelling of God's Spirit, which will sanctify His people, giving them new, softer hearts instead of those made of stone (Ezekiel 36). God fulfilled this level of intimacy between Himself and His children through the regeneration of the Spirit and His permanent presence with those who accepted the saving grace of Jesus Christ. Under the Old Covenant, the Spirit of God withdrew from the presence of disobedience and sinfulness (Ezekiel 10:18-22; Psalm 51:11). However, because of Jesus' atoning work, the New Covenant guarantees the Spirit's permanent presence with believers. The Holy Spirit teaches disciples of Jesus about the nature of God through "inward guidance," while drawing believers closer to God. Through the indwelling work of the Spirit of God, disciples of Jesus live out God's purpose for their lives.

> Do not cast me away from Your presence
> And do not take Your Holy Spirit from me."
>
> *Psalm 51:11*

EXAMPLE

For decades, an elderly Romanian woman unknowingly used a seven-pound nugget of amber as a doorstop. In its unrefined state, she had assumed this nugget of amber was little more than a rock. It was only after her passing that her family discovered that what she thought was a worthless rock was worth an astonishing one million dollars. This story sadly demonstrates how many in the Church approach their understanding and engagement with the Holy Spirit. God has given us an immeasurable depth of power, wisdom, and comfort in the Holy Spirit. However, we are often so focused on our daily lives and short-term plans that we fail to realize the great value of God's continual presence and power in us. Before ascending to Heaven, Jesus told His first disciples that He was sending them a Helper. Jesus fulfilled His promise on the day of Pentecost, and today, this promise is applied to all those who follow Him.

WEEK 17

MEDITATE Write out this week's verses below as you spend time committing them to memory.

MORE If you'd like to increase your time in Scripture, commit to this optional weekly Bible reading plan.
Read (or listen via an audio Bible)

☐ (Day 1) Ephesians 1-2
☐ (Day 2) Ephesians 3
☐ (Day 3) Ephesians 4
☐ (Day 4) Ephesians 5
☐ (Day 5) Ephesians 6

ENGAGE

Praise God the Holy Spirit. Confess the ways you struggle with isolation and loneliness, forgetting the presence and power of the Spirit within you. Thank God for His nearness and comfort. Ask Him to deepen your intimacy with Him through His Word and His Spirit.

Week 17 • Day 02
FILLED WITH THE SPIRIT

EXERCISE

READ *Jeremiah 31:31-34, Ezekiel 36:25-27*

☐ Want More? Read Ephesians 3

1. As you read through Jeremiah 31:31-34 and Ezekiel 36:25-27, **Highlight** the various promises of the New Covenant in a list below.

_____
_____
_____

2. Explain how the New Covenant might be considered "new." In what ways did the Old Covenant (Mosaic Covenant) not provide these blessings?"

_____
_____
_____

As those new to faith begin to understand and experience the Holy Spirit, they often perceive the Spirit as a New Testament event or as a new source of power unavailable to those of the Old Testament. This diminished view of God's Spirit overlooks numerous Old Testament references. Both the person and purpose of the Holy Spirit are present throughout the Bible. The first mention of God's Spirit occurs as early as Genesis 1. In this reference, God's Spirit is said to hover over the waters at the dawn of creation. With some variance in translations, God's Spirit is mentioned as many as 136 times in the Old Testament. The two prophets from today's reading—Jeremiah and Ezekiel—lived hundreds of years before the coming of the Holy Spirit at Pentecost in Acts 2, and yet they were enlightened and comforted by the Holy Spirit as they carried out God's will and penned divinely inspired Scripture. Even while living under the Old Covenant, the Holy Spirit gave these men a glimpse into the future and the incredible promises of the New Covenant of Christ.

The primary difference between the Holy Spirit's relationship with God's people living under the Old Covenant versus that of the New Covenant is that the Spirit of God came and went under the Old Covenant (Ezekiel 10:18-22; Psalm 51:11). Consequently, they did not enjoy the permanence of the Holy Spirit's presence. One might wrongfully assume that the Holy Spirit somehow changed. To this point, it is essential to understand that the Holy Spirit is the third Person of the Trinity, co-equal, co-eternal with the Father and Son. As God is perfect and unchanging (immutable), so is the Holy Spirit (Numbers 23:19). The difference is not the Holy Spirit. Due to the saving grace of Jesus Christ and the resulting final, full, and forever forgiveness of believers, the Holy Spirit can now permanently indwell those under the New Covenant (1 Corinthians 3:16). The difference is the saving grace and covering atonement of Jesus Christ. Sin has been permanently forgiven, so God's Spirit can now permanently remain "with" and "in" a New Covenant believer (John 14:16-17).

The work and character of the Holy Spirit remain consistent throughout Scripture. The Holy Spirit facilitates a connection between God and His people, enabling spiritual growth, empowering personal ministry, and sanctifying relationships with Him. The Holy Spirit does this by revealing divine truth in God's Word (1 Corinthians 2:10-11), thus making God's Word living and active (Hebrews 4:12). He leads people to repentance by convicting the world of sin and judgment (John 16:8-11). God's Spirit also guides, comforts, and encourages followers of Christ through the joys of ministry and seasons of persecution and rejection (John 14:16-21, Acts 20:22-23).

Furthermore, the Holy Spirit actively equips believers with spiritual gifts according to His will (1 Corinthians 12:11). As discussed last week, these supernatural gifts strengthen the Church and glorify God in their usage. Paul reminds us that even the greatest spiritual knowledge or abilities amount to little apart from the Holy Spirit (1 Corinthians 13:2). The primary intention of the Holy Spirit is not empowerment for its own sake, but to serve others through the love of Christ.

> "If I have the gift of prophecy, and know all mysteries and all knowledge; and if I have all faith, so as to remove mountains, but do not have love, I am nothing."
> *1 Corinthians 13:2*

1. Acknowledge the timeless truth that connects the perfection of your salvation to the permanence of the Holy Spirit's presence inside of you. Put this connection into your own words below?

_____
_____
_____

2. Respond to the list of actions of the Holy Spirit in the section above and note two aspects of the Spirit's work that you could use more of in your life.

_____
_____
_____

WEEK 17

MEDITATE Fill in the blanks as you continue committing this week's verses to memory.

> " And do not get _____ with wine, for that is dissipation, but be _____ with the Spirit, speaking to one another in psalms and _____ and spiritual songs, singing and making melody with your heart to the Lord; always _____ thanks for all things in the name of our Lord Jesus Christ to God, even the Father."
>
> *Ephesians 5:18-20*

ENGAGE

Praise God for the permanence of His Spirit within you. Confess the ways you quiet the Holy Spirit by neglecting the Word of God or walking in sin. Thank Him for His teaching, convicting, guidance, comfort, and encouragement through the Holy Spirit. Ask Him to empower you to the work of ministry through His Spirit so you can walk in obedience and live a life of faithfulness.

Week 17 • Day 03

FILLED WITH THE SPIRIT

EXERCISE

> **READ** *Ephesians 5:15-21*

☐ Want More? Read Ephesians 4

1. Ephesians 5:15-21 gives several implications about what it looks like to "walk" carefully (5:15) since the day are "evil" (5:16). **Highlight** at least three of these implications below.

___
___
___

2. **Explain** what it means to be "filled" with the Spirit (5:18a). Why does Paul contrast it to drunkenness (5:18a) and compare it to singing (5:19). ⊙

___
___
___

The person and work of the Holy Spirit are essential in the life of every follower of Christ. The Hebrew word *ruach* and the Greek word *pneuma* are both translated as "Spirit," and both carry imagery of "breath" or "wind." This rich imagery of vitality and empowerment reminds the disciples of Jesus of the importance of the Holy Spirit. Similarly, the Greek word *parakletos*, translated as "Comforter" (John 14:16), literally means the "called alongside" one. This word depicts the Spirit as someone sent to "come alongside" a Christ follower to assist, support, guide, and encourage. The Spirit of God "helps" disciples of Jesus through their pursuit of fruitfulness (John 16:7-11). He also provides comfort and encouragement during times of adversity that inevitably come as we serve Jesus' kingdom interests in this fallen world (Romans 8:26). During seasons of difficulty, one becomes acutely aware of the personal and divine presence of the Holy Spirit. If you have ever experienced a sweeping sense of peace, the sensation that God has drawn you near, or that the Holy Spirit is interceding for you when you do not know what to pray, you have likely experienced the comforting work of the Holy Spirit.

Ephesians 5:18 paints a profound contrast between the emptiness of self and the overflowing fulfillment of the Spirit. Note the explicit command found in the verse: "And do not get drunk with wine, for this is dissipation, but be filled with the Spirit." By contrasting the inward and outward effects of inebriation (drunkenness) with those of being filled with the Spirit, Paul demonstrates the incredible difference between a carnal man and a sanctified follower of Christ. Being under the influence of alcohol temporarily augments one's inhibitions, often resulting in inappropriate behaviors, thoughts, and actions (ie. "dissipation" or "debauchery"). In contrast, being under the influence of the Spirit means surrendering to His divine control, resulting in both spiritual growth and the overflowing joy of the Lord (Romans 14:17-18). Incidentally, the Greek verb for "be filled" in Ephesians. 5:18 is both passive and in the present tense. This word usage indicates that a disciple of Jesus must "keep on" being filled with the Spirit as they submit to the Spirit's "control" in their lives.

Paul's contrast between drunkenness and being filled with the Spirit juxtaposes humanity's futile search for fleeting happiness against that of God's lasting joy. During the recovery process, addicts and alcoholics often acknowledge that their emotional and psychological dependency on addictive substances stems from self-disdain, doubt, regret, or grief. As people self-medicate with these substances, they diminish self-awareness and offer fleeting moments of escape. The Holy Spirit, however, provides lasting joy, peace, comfort, and a sense of purpose. The Greek word *asótia* translated as "dissipation" or "debauchery" can also be associated with wastefulness.

Paul's admonition in Ephesians 5 is about walking in wisdom and redeeming the time "because the days are evil." In this way, Ephesians 5:18 demonstrates the wasted time, energy, and resources of a self-filled life. Far too many younger believers spend years attempting to mix who they were before Jesus with who God has made them as "a new creation" in Christ (2 Cor. 5:17). Like oil and water, the two will not mix. The Spirit of God will not embrace evil, but He will "transform" you into a new creation (2 Corinthians 3:18).

Ephesians. 5:19-21 adds that a believer "filled with the Spirit" is empowered to worship, serve, and give thanks even in the face of challenging circumstances. Paul encourages followers of Jesus to speak to one another in psalms and hymns, singing joy to the Lord. The Spirit of God offers a deep and genuine contentment that overflows into outward expressions of encouragement. These concepts are not just theological notions but a lived-out reality as the Spirit of God works in the heart of a believer. Ultimately, the Holy Spirit is the believer's sufficiency in all things. Paul demonstrates the foolishness of seeking fulfillment in fleeting substitutes while encouraging followers of Christ to submit to the Spirit of God as He transforms them to live worthy of their calling (Ephesians 4:1).

1. Acknowledge a main theological truth about the "filling" of the Spirit that has proved the most insightful to you as you seek to obey the command of Ephesians. 5:18 this week. Summarize it below.

_____

_____

_____

2. Respond to the notion of fleeting "substitutes" to the Spirit-filled life. Where do you tend to go when you experience "evil days?" Make a list below of areas of self-medication and self-fulfillment in which you need repentance.

_____

_____

_____

MEDITATE

Fill in the blanks as you continue committing this week's verses to memory.

> " And do not get _____ with wine, for that is dissipation, but be _____ with the Spirit, speaking to one another in psalms and _____ and spiritual songs, _____ and making melody with your heart to the Lord; always _____ thanks for all things in the name of our _____ Jesus Christ to God, even the Father"

Ephesians 5:18-20

ENGAGE

Praise God for being our Comforter. Confess the ways you look to yourself or the world for assistance, support, guidance, and encouragement. Thank Him for providing all you need and for never leaving you without help. Ask Him to increase your awareness and intimacy with Him so you will become sensitive to the Holy Spirit at work within you.

THE TRUTH

Week 17 • Day 04
FILLED WITH THE SPIRIT

EXAMINATION

READ
Romans 8:26-28 ☐ Want More? Read Ephesians 5

WATCH
Week 17 - Filled With The Spirit

To watch the video, scan the QR code below by opening your phone's camera and holding your device so that the QR code appears on the screen. Click the link associated with the QR code, and choose this week's video. https://qrco.de/be3SWs

1. According to Romans 8:26-28, what do believers need, and how does the Spirit provide?

2. List some ways that you are encouraged by the truth that the Spirit searches your heart, knows your mind, and prays for your needs? How are you prompted to trust and obey God more deeply because of this truth?

_____

_____

_____

EXERCISE

READ   Romans 8:26-28

When discussing the work of the Holy Spirit, one often primarily focuses on spiritual gifts, conviction of sin, or enlightenment through God's Word. Yet, Romans 8:26-28 highlights the profound role of the Holy Spirit as counselor and advocate. God is not distant from the sufferings of His children, nor is His Spirit. The children of God are reminded that Jesus lived among them and has experiential knowledge of the adversities of this world. Jesus' understanding of grief and pain is evident throughout the Gospel books, affirmed in the fact that "Jesus wept" (John 11:35). Within the depths of despair, loss, mourning, confusion, or dejection, God's Spirit groans with His children. In what appears to be a dark image, God's Spirit paints an uplifting portrait of divine advocacy through His unwavering presence and ministry of spiritual and emotional comfort. Verse 26 explicitly reassures a disciple of Jesus that He has not abandoned them, as His Spirit intercedes on their behalf in times of weakness (John 14:18).

Today's reading reminds disciples of Jesus that God is aware of the inmost aspects of their minds and hearts. Psalm 34:18 assures God's children that the Lord is near to those who are brokenhearted. It is through the work of the Holy Spirit that believers experience this nearness. As a Counselor, the Spirit provides clarity and direction during times of confusion (John 16:13). The Holy Spirit offers clarity and enlightenment as one studies the Word of God. He brings peace and unity to the local church body as it assembles to fellowship, celebrate, and worship. God's Spirit also provides discernment, wisdom, and spiritual gifts as the Church continues its commissioned work of making disciples. Romans 8:26 ensures that even when words fail, God knows the hearts of His children. It is through the ministry of the Holy Spirit that God grants His Church the profound peace that sustains it through life's significant challenges (Philippians 4:7).

MEDITATE Below, attempt to write out this week's verses from memory.

ENGAGE

Praise God for His nearness. Confess how you don't always acknowledge His awareness of and advocacy for you. Thank Him for knowing you perfectly and for giving you peace in His presence. Ask Him to help you see how He's working all things for good—that is making you look more like Him.

Week 17 • Day 05

FILLED WITH THE SPIRIT

EXERCISE

READ *John 14:15-19*
☐ Want More? Read Ephesians 3

EXEGESIS

Study John 14:15-19 using the **H.E.A.R.** method of inductive Bible study. Write at least one sentence for each letter below. Consult the notes from a study Bible if you need help.

HIGHLIGHT   What I see:
_____
_____
_____

EXPLAIN   What it means:
_____
_____
_____

ACKNOWLEDGE   The timeless truths:

_____
_____
_____

RESPOND   With specific action:

_____
_____
_____

While the **H.E.A.R.** method is the one that we will use to help ensure that a proper interpretation method is followed, there are other helpful plans to follow. As you become more comfortable we suggest trying other good Bible study methods.

Jesus guaranteed His first disciples that the Father would send them "another Helper" of the same kind as Him (John 14:16). This "Spirit of truth" would stay "with" them forever and be "in" them (John 14:16-17). Thus, He assures His followers that although He will soon be unseen, they will not be left as orphans. In Acts 2, Jesus fulfills this promise as the Spirit comes and begins to indwell the children of God permanently. Having lived in close community with Jesus, it was difficult for His first disciples to understand how Jesus' departure could be to their "advantage" (John 16:7). Jesus had intentionally invested the mass of His ministry efforts into a small group of men. Yet as the early Church quickly grew beyond the boundaries of Israel, the Holy Spirit was capable of continually working in and through the lives of all believers in all regions of the world. On the day of Pentecost in Acts 2, for the first time, the Spirit of God permanently indwelt the children of God. Under the Old Covenant of the Law, one man would prepare himself to enter the presence of God once a year. The notion that God's Spirit would remain among His people, or present Himself to more than a select few, amazed prophets such as Jeremiah and Ezekiel. Now, Jesus allows believers to become living, breathing temples of the Spirit (1 Corinthians 6:19; 2 Corinthians 6:16; Ephesians 2:21-22; 1 Peter 2:5).

EXAMPLE

In 1992, the devastating forces of Hurricane Andrew made landfall in Southern Florida and Central Louisiana. Conservative estimates place the combined property and infrastructure damages in the United States at over $26 billion. These damages included widespread power outages, impacting approximately 1.4 million people. Some residences remained without power for over a month as repairs were underway. However, an elderly resident named Norena did not have her power restored for 15 years! Due to unfinished repairs and a lack of personal resources, Norena remained in the dark. For 15 years, she endured the winter cold and summer heat until a news outlet ran her story. After a local mayor of the nearby Florida city discovered her situation, an electrical contractor restored her power within hours. In later interviews, Norena shared her excitement about flipping light switches and taking a warm bubble bath for the first time in over a decade.

Norena's account reminds us of the incredible hope of restoration. Just as her quality of life and home functionality were transformed by having her power restored, the spiritual life of the disciple of Christ can be transformed or renewed by the presence and power of the Holy Spirit. God's power is readily available to His children, and He is very aware of your needs.

MEDITATE Practice reciting this week's verses from memory and be prepared to say them aloud to your d-group.

ENGAGE

Praise God for being our Helper. Confess the ways you deny your weaknesses and look to your own strength in difficult seasons. Thank God for His strength and care for His people at all times and in all seasons. Ask Him to give you security in His strength, love, care, and provision in your life.

ENCOURAGE

Use this checklist as a guide for your weekly d-group time. Refer to the discipler's guide at the front of the book for more encouragement and practical advice.

- Work through questions from the accountability page.
- Spend time praying specifics for one another.
- Take turns reciting the memory verses.
- Discuss answers to the questions throughout the week that are marked with this symbol. ▼

PRAYER REQUESTS

_____
_____
_____
_____
_____
_____

ACCOUNTABILITY QUESTIONS

These questions are to be asked of one another in a spirit of accountability (Proverbs 27:17). They are intended to stimulate conversations of character and confession of sin in a safe environment that values honesty, vulnerability, confidentiality, and grace.

1. Have you spent quality time in your spiritual disciplines this week?

2. Have you taken advantage of opportunities to share your faith this week? Explain.

3. Have your words and actions been a good testimony this week to the gospel of Jesus?

4. Have your thoughts and speech been pure (cussing, criticism, negativity, etc.)?

5. Have you been sexually pure this week? Have you been exposed to sexually alluring material? (For those who are married: Have you prioritized quality romantic time with your spouse?)

6. Have you been a good steward of your finances? Have you lacked integrity in the handling of your finances?

7. Have you been honoring and generous in your meaningful relationships this week (Family, friends, etc.)?

8. Have you given in to any addictive behavior this past week? Explain.

9. Have you been completely honest with me?

I'm praying for the salvation of the following two people and prayerfully considering how to share Christ with them myself: _____

> "Therefore, confess your sins to one another, and pray for one another, so that you may be healed."
> *James 5:16a*

Week 18 • Day 01
SPIRITUAL WARFARE

ESSENTIAL TRUTH

There are spiritual realities at the root of every physical reality. Sooner or later every believer discovers that the Christian life is a battleground, not a playground, and that a believer faces an enemy who is much stronger than they are, apart from the Lord. We need SPIRITUAL STRENGTH and that requires spiritual weaponry like wielding the sword of God's Word (Eph. 6:14-18). We do not fight, however, "for" victory—we fight "from" victory. Battles in the Spiritual realm are largely fought in the prayer realm.

1. Read the Essential Truth, identify two phrases that stand out to you, and write them below. Why do you believe these phrases are significant?

_____
_____
_____

2. Using your own words, what does it look like to fight "from" victory as opposed to "for" victory?

_____
_____
_____

3. Does your life feel like a battleground? Do you tend to look to spiritual strength or human strength in the midst of battle?

EXERCISE — memory verses

> "Stand firm therefore, having girded your loins with truth, and having put on the breastplate of righteousness, and having shod your feet with the preparation of the gospel of peace; in addition to all, taking up the shield of faith with which you will be able to extinguish all the flaming arrows of the evil one. And take the helmet of salvation, and the sword of the Spirit, which is the Word of God."
>
> *Ephesians 6:14-19*

The Word of God clearly acknowledges the validity of spiritual warfare (Daniel 10:12-14, Ephesians 6, James 4:7). To its detriment, the modern Church often overvalues or undervalues the authenticity of spiritual warfare. Where one group attributes every hardship to the work of an unseen spiritual enemy, another group completely dismisses the notion of spiritual attacks entirely. Some people find themselves seemingly obsessed with studying angelic beings to the detriment of overlooking the gospel. At the same time, others choose to ignore biblical teachings of spiritual warfare to the point of diminishing the validity of Scripture itself. The Word of God underscores the reality of forces of spiritual darkness: (1) Satan tempted Jesus (Matthew 4:1-11), (2) Jesus cast out demons (Matthew 12: 22 32;

Mark 5: 1-20; Luke 11:14-20), and Jesus' disciples cast out demons (Matthew 10:1; Luke 9:1). Outlined in Ephesians 6, the armor of God provides excellent insight into the nature of the spiritual battle, the nature of the enemy, and the resources available to the followers of Jesus. Of course, these instructions and provisions make it clear that victory is not rooted in a believer's abilities or power. Jesus has already won the war against the forces of darkness and their demonic leadership (Colossians 2:15). Disciples of Jesus fight "from" this victory, not "for" it. Jesus has already won the war.

EXAMPLE

Designed in the late 1940s as the world's fastest and most equipped troop carrier, the S.S. United States stands as a profound example of wasted potential. With an estimated construction cost of over $78 million (approximately $928 million today), the S.S. United States could carry 15,000 troops and their required equipment over 10,000 miles without refueling. On her maiden voyage in 1952, she earned the still uncontested Blue Riband for the highest average speed crossing the Atlantic Ocean. Yet, despite such incredible potential and innovative design, she never fulfilled its intended purpose. Although designed for war, a shift in political policy and popular opinion led to its repurposing as a luxury liner for presidents and dignitaries. With the armaments removed and the systems adapted, the greatest warship of time became little more than a cruise ship. Operating as a luxury liner, the ship was equipped to carry just under 2,000 passengers, a stark contrast to her capacity of 15,000 troops. Passengers could enjoy extensive amenities, including 695 staterooms, four dining salons, three bars, two theaters, and five acres of open deck space with a heated pool. It also featured 19 elevators and the pioneering comfort of complete air conditioning. Ultimately, the S.S. United States served as a luxurious escape for wealthy travelers on peaceful Atlantic journeys, rather than a military transport.

Much like the S.S. United States, many followers of Christ live solely for personal comfort while squandering the resources and calling entrusted to them by God. The purposeful life of a disciple of Jesus is not self-indulgence, but faithful engagement in the spiritual battle that rages unseen and often ignored. God's Word reminds His children that an invisible, yet very real, war is raging on countless fronts (Ephesians 6:12). The Church, as Jesus designed it, is not a cruise ship but a battleship.

WEEK 18

MEDITATE

Write out this week's verses below as you spend time committing them to memory.

MORE

If you'd like to increase your time in Scripture, commit to this optional weekly Bible reading plan.
Read (or listen via an audio Bible)

- ☐ (Day 1) 2 Corinthians 1
- ☐ (Day 2) 2 Corinthians 2
- ☐ (Day 3) 2 Corinthians 3
- ☐ (Day 4) 2 Corinthians 4
- ☐ (Day 5) 2 Corinthians 10

ENGAGE

Praise God for securing the victory for us. Confess the ways you look to your own strength to overcome adversity, rather than trusting the spiritual strength provided through God and His Word. Thank Him for giving you everything you need to battle in the broken world. Ask Him to deepen your dependence on Him and encourage your heart with His victory.

THE TRUTH

Week 18 • Day 02
SPIRITUAL WARFARE

EXERCISE

READ *2 Corinthians 10:3-5, Ephesians 6:10-12*

☐ Want More? Read 2 Corinthians 2

1. Highlight what these two passages say about the "flesh." Reword and list them below. ▼

_____
_____
_____

2. Paul states, "For though we walk in the flesh, we do not war according to the flesh" (2 Cor. 10:3). **Explain** what it means to "walk in the flesh" and yet not "wage war according to the flesh"?

_____
_____
_____

3. Both passages emphasize that our battle is not against "flesh and blood." Explain the implications of this for how we view conflicts and disagreements, both within the church and in the world. ▼

_____

_____

_____

Spiritual warfare is a consistent theme throughout the New Testament, with examples in the Spirit-inspired writings of James, Luke, John, Peter, and Paul. These biblical texts encourage disciples of Christ to acknowledge that their spiritual struggles are rooted in an unseen supernatural conflict. It is unlikely that you daily ponder the magnitude of being a singular person among billions of people on a small planet set adrift in an ever-expanding universe. Similarly, most people do not take the time to consider that an invisible spiritual battle is happening all around them, just beneath the surface of everyday life. In Ephesians 6:10-13 and 2 Corinthians 10:3-5, Paul teaches that although we live in a physical world, these unseen spiritual battles are not fought with earthly weapons.

The most significant conflicts of life occur on the battlefield of the mind and the heart. The Greek word *logismos*, translated into English as "arguments" or "speculations" in 2 Corinthians 10:5, demonstrates the internal dispute of thoughts and assumptions. This theater of war is most evident in the lives of the depressed, anxious, downtrodden, and addicted. Yet self-examination reveals the presence of spiritual conflict in all thoughts and consequent behaviors. Although many followers of Christ turn to self-help processes, God does not expect His children to muster the innate power to overcome what is beyond their ability. Therefore, God has granted His people the support of His Son, Spirit, Word, and Church. Ephesians 6:10-13 reminds the follower of Christ that the strength to face spiritual warfare comes from Christ alone.

2 Corinthians 10:5 encourages the follower of Christ to "take every thought captive to make it obedient to Christ," further establishing that the conflict resides between one's knowledge of God (their theology) and every other human thought or ideology (egoism). In Genesis 3, Eve is the first human casualty on this spiritual battlefield. Understanding the fall of humanity requires us to acknowledge that

Satan did not strike a physical blow in the battle for Adam and Eve's souls. Instead, the Serpent of old launched a poisonous ideology into the theater of their hearts and minds: "and you will be like God" (Genesis 3:5). Her desire to be her own god was her downfall. And it is this pollution of thought and desire that has infected the whole human race ever since.

How are we to fight such an invisible spiritual battle? What are our weapons of the Spirit that Christ has given us? Paul wrote the letter to the Ephesians while under the watch of Roman guards. Writing from captivity, Paul uses the imagery of a Roman soldier's armor to illustrate the principles of "putting on the full armor of God" (Ephesians 6:13). The "Armor of God" represents the spiritual resources that God provides His children to stand against the devil's "schemes" (Ephesians 6:11). The English word "methods" comes from this Greek word *methodeia*. Paul's teaching on the armor of God offers a practical framework for living out the Christian faith in the face of spiritual warfare. The armor of God also serves as a collection of essential truths that provide the believer with insight into the strength ("be strong"), balance (put on "full" armor), and support ("stand firm") Jesus offers to defend His followers against such attacks.

1. Paul lists various spiritual enemies we wrestle against in Ephesians 6:12: "rulers, authorities, cosmic powers over this present darkness, spiritual forces of evil in the heavenly places." **Acknowledge** what these terms suggest about the organized and strategic nature of our spiritual enemy.

_____

_____

_____

2. Respond to the relevance of these five warfare principles. Have you personally experienced spiritual warfare? If so, what did it look like, and how do these principles inform your response? ▼

_____

_____

_____

EXTRA

Five basic principles of spiritual warfare that can be derived from these passages:

- **Warfare Principle #1**: Satan is continually seeking to fracture the Church's unity, sow dissension, and corrupt all that is holy. We have a very real enemy who seeks to devour us (1Peter 5:8-9; James 4:7).

- **Warfare Principle #2**: Every follower of Christ has a formidable adversary. The Christian life is a battleground, not a playground (Genesis 3:15).

- **Warfare Principle #3**: Believers need to acknowledge their need to depend upon the Lord. Your strength is not sufficient apart from God (Proverbs 3:5-6; 1 Corinthians 15:57).

- **Warfare Principle #4:** Only spiritual weapons and spiritual disciplines will suffice for this battle (2 Corinthians 10:4; Hebrews 4:12; Psalms 91).

- **Warfare Principle #5**: Believers do not fight spiritual battles for victory. We fight from a position of victory. Jesus has already conquered the real enemy. We are beneficiaries of His triumph in our daily battles. (Genesis 3:15; Colossians 2:15).

THE TRUTH

MEDITATE   Fill in the blanks as you continue committing this week's verses to memory.

> "Stand firm therefore, having _____ your loins with truth, and having put on the _____ of righteousness, and having shod your feet with the preparation of the gospel of _____; in addition to all, taking up the shield of faith with which you will be able to extinguish all the _____ arrows of the evil one. And take the helmet of salvation, and the sword of the Spirit, which is the Word of God."
>
> *Ephesians 6:14-19*

ENGAGE

Praise God for the support of His Son, Spirit, Word, and Church. Confess the ways you turn to self-help processes and ask Him to expose all of those ways to you so you can trust in Him alone. Thank God for giving you His armor so you can stand firm against the devil's schemes. Ask Him to be your strength, balance, and support today and in every season of life.

THE TRUTH

Week 18 • Day 03
SPIRITUAL WARFARE

EXERCISE

READ *Ephesians 6:10-20*

☐ Want More? Read 2 Corinthians 3

1. **Highlight** the six different parts of the "Armor of God" below and note their use as offensive or defensive weapons. What does this tell us about the Christian's posture in spiritual warfare?

_____

_____

_____

2. **Explain** why Paul begins this list by exhorting believers to "be strong in the Lord and in the strength of His might" (6:10). Why is this the correct place to begin? Give one practical implication of this truth. ▼

_____

_____

_____

THE TRUTH

While writing his letter to the house churches of Ephesus, exhorting them to "take up the full armor of God," Paul is chained to a Roman soldier. Drawing from the imagery of a battlefield and a soldier's armor, Paul reminds his brothers and sisters in Christ that they are daily engaged in an ongoing conflict. He appropriately calls it "our struggle" from the beginning of the text (Ephesians 6:12). On an unseen battlefield, the followers of Christ face internal and external enemies who are actively involved in strategic attacks. The Church faces a formidable foe who never grows weary of destruction and has no ethics, morals, or rules of war (Proverbs 4:16, 1 Peter 5:8).

Paul's exhortation here utilizes each part of the soldier's armor to symbolize a different discipline or provision critical for spiritual warfare. Each is important, and all are required for a balanced defense. Note well the descriptor in the repeated command of the passage: "put on...take up... the full armor of God" (Ephesians 6:11, 13). The first piece of the armor mentioned is the **Belt of Truth** (Ephesians 6:14), the foundation of the entire armor of God. A Roman soldier's belt secured essential equipment while allowing increased mobility and core support. The Belt of Truth symbolizes the integrity and authenticity required to remain upright in a twisted world. By living out the truths of the Word of God, the disciple of Christ demonstrates the validity of their convictions and the legitimacy of the message of Christ (John 4). This call to reject duplicity ensures that our behaviors align with the words we speak about God in public. Truthful living fosters credibility and unity within the Church, as well as a consistent witness from the Church to a watching and listening world.

Next, Paul provides the imagery of the **Breastplate of Righteousness** (Ephesians 6:14). The Roman breastplate, or *Lorica Segmentata*, was an overlapping series of bronze or iron plates custom-fitted to cover the torso. Just as the Roman breastplate protected the soldier's vital organs from mortal wounds, the Breastplate of Righteousness preserves the heart and character of the follower of Christ. The overlapping plates of the Roman armor offered a high range of mobility that was not available within the constraints of rigid armor, yet left the soldiers' backs somewhat exposed. The soldier was always moving forward, rarely retreating. The righteousness of the breastplate is not the rigid and unforgiving yet fragile self-righteousness of legalism. The Breastplate of Righteousness illustrates the day-to-day obedience to God's commands, which is only possible due to the imputed righteousness of Jesus. Paul echoes this in Ephesians 5:3 when he warns that "there must not be even a hint of sexual immorality, or of any kind of impurity, or of greed." The decay of sin is like rust on a weapon, creating a vulnerability that the devil will leverage against a believer and the Church.

The third element in Paul's presentation is **"Feet Sandaled** with the readiness for the gospel of peace" (Ephesians 6:15). The Roman soldier wore sandals fitted with metal spikes, which offered increased stability and traction. The primary strength of the Roman army was its military strategy and unity among the ranks. A Roman unit advanced as a unified front. The cover and protection provided by the other soldiers is why the Roman breastplate did not require significant protection for the back. Just as these studded sandals anchored the Roman soldier's footing, the clear and consistent message of the gospel anchors the disciple of Christ and His Church. Jesus commanded His Church to move forward under His protection, unified in the mission of spreading His message of peace with His method of making disciples who make disciples (Matthew 28:19-20; Ephesians 4:3; John 17:21; Isaiah 52:7).

Paul instructs the believer to make use of the **Shield of Faith** (Ephesians 6:16). The scutum was a large shield capable of deflecting close-combat weapons, such as swords and spears, as well as projectile assaults from arrows. The Shield of Faith symbolizes a personal faith in God's perfect nature and sovereignty (Ephesians 3:20). Even when attacks are overwhelming, faith acts as a shield as follower of Jesus places their reliance on God. A Roman cohort could create a protective formation known as a testudo or "tortoise" with their large shields. As each soldier dug their spiked sandals into the ground and interlocked shields, they formed a mobile fortification. Like the Roman cohort, the interdependency and support of the Church, sustained by the Lord, can unite their shields to create profound security and forward movement.

Putting on the **Helmet of Salvation** (Ephesians 6:17) highlights one of the first acts of readiness in preparation for a battle. A Roman soldier donned his helmet as protection in the most dangerous moments. This well-fitted, secure helmet protected the brain and the function of senses like sight and hearing. For the believers, the Helmet of Salvation symbolizes the protective value of our thinking that assurance of salvation provides. The assurance of "no condemnation" in Christ (Romans 8:1) and "no separation" from Christ (Romans 8:39) gives the Spirit-filled believer the blessing of "no desperation" in the battle (Romans 8:2-38). As the conflicts of spiritual warfare occur on the battlefield of the heart and the mind, it is essential to guard the thoughts and senses from the flaming arrows of the enemy by the assurance of one's salvation. What enters through the eyes and the ears manifests in the mind and the heart.

Lastly, Paul draws the reader's attention to what he calls **"the Sword of the Spirit"** which symbolizes the Word of God (Ephesians 6:17). The Romans used the gladius as both a defensive and offensive weapon, as well as a standard tool. The Sword of the Spirit, which is God's Word, is the only offensive weapon listed in Paul's presentation of the Armor of God. Aware that the sinful heart and mind would attempt to wield Scripture with selfish intent and ego, Paul hastily reminds his readers of their dependence on the Spirit of God. Just as the Roman soldiers learned swordsmanship, the followers of Christ should familiarize themselves with God's Word. Jesus modeled this in His temptation by responding to Satan with specific Scriptures from verses He memorized from the book of Deuteronomy (Matthew 4:1-13). Knowledge and application of God's Word, along with dependence on His Spirit, are essential to counter the enemy's deceptions and attacks.

Paul summarizes his instructions with a call to prayer (Ephesians 6:18) and an encouragement to depend on the Spirit of God continually. This text reminds the early church in Ephesus, as well as the modern Church worldwide, that the Armor of God is not something they can obtain or maintain apart from God. The Armor of God is strengthened and sustained through spiritual growth and a commitment to fellowship with God through spiritual disciplines such as prayer, Bible study, and worship.

1. Acknowledge the core truths of the two repeated statements from Ephesians 6:10-20. Why does Paul repeat the phrases "full armor of God" and "stand firm?" What is he emphasizing?

_____
_____
_____

2. Respond to the list. Which piece of the armor do you find most challenging to "put on" or maintain in your daily life? Why? Which piece of the armor do you feel you rely on the most? How has it been effective for you?

_____
_____
_____

THE TRUTH

MEDITATE Fill in the blanks as you continue committing this week's verses to memory.

> "Stand firm therefore, having _____ your loins with _____, and having put on the _____ of righteousness, and having shod your feet with the preparation of the gospel of _____; in addition to all, taking up the _____ of faith with which you will be able to extinguish all the _____ arrows of the evil one. And take the helmet of salvation, and the sword of the _____, which is the Word of God."
>
> *Ephesians 6:14-19*

ENGAGE

Praise God for being Truth and Peace. Confess the ways you don't walk in the Armor of God and feel overwhelmed by the brokenness of the world. Thank Him for providing your belt of truth, sandaled feet, shield of faith, helmet of salvation, and sword of the Spirit. Ask Him to use you in battle to bring light to those trapped in darkness.

THE TRUTH

Week 18 • Day 04
SPIRITUAL WARFARE

EXAMINATION

READ
1 Peter 5:6-11

☐ Want More? Read 2Corinthians 4

WATCH
Week 18 - Spiritual Warfare

To watch the video, scan the QR code below by opening your phone's camera and holding your device so that the QR code appears on the screen. Click the link associated with the QR code, and choose this week's video. https://qrco.de/be3SWs

1. Walk through 1 Peter 5:6-11 and list the commands for you to obey.

_____
_____

2. Using the same verses (1 Peter 5:6-11), what are the things you can trust God to do?

_____
_____
_____

EXERCISE

READ   1 Peter 5:6-11

God's children are adopted into the Family of God (Romans 8:15), the Work of God (2 Corinthians 5:17-20), and the Kingdom of God (Romans 8:16-17). Yet many seem to forget that since the fall of man, the Kingdom of God is a Kingdom at war (Matthew 11:12, Luke 16:16). Verses such as 1 Peter 5:8 and James 4:7 illustrate the authenticity of spiritual warfare in the lives of God's children. During His temptation in the wilderness (Matthew 4:1-11), Jesus demonstrates the necessity of dependence on God and His Word. Although Jesus faced an intense spiritual attack, He resisted by standing on the truths of Scripture. First Peter 5 is a reminder for followers of Jesus to adopt a posture of submission and vigilance. "Therefore humble yourself under the mighty hand of God, that He may exalt you at the proper time" (1Peter 5:6). Within the pitfall of individualism, many unsuccessfully attempt to withstand temptation and spiritual attacks solely through self-reliance and willpower. Under the divine inspiration of God's Spirit, Peter reminds his audience that humility is a prerequisite for being under God's mighty hand.

Humility is also a requirement to accept support and wise counsel from one's brothers and sisters in Christ. Peter reminds the Church that, "the same experiences of suffering are being accomplished by your brethren who are in the world "(1Peter 5:10). Within the head and heart spaces of individualism, the enemy can more easily isolate those suffering through adversities and weakness. Much as a lion attempts to remove the young or weak from the protection of the herd. Jesus designed His Church to offer support (Ephesians 4:15-16), but this support is only effective when it is accepted. Lastly, Peter assures believers that this season of struggle is temporary. After enduring for "a little while," God "will himself restore you and make you strong, firm and steadfast" (1 Peter 5:10). Victory is inevitable because of His eternal power and grace.

MEDITATE Below, attempt to write out this week's verses from memory.

ENGAGE

Praise God for being dependable. Confess the ways you refuse the help God has provided you as you walk in your own ways. Thank Him for His provision and protection and for working everything for good. Ask Him to "restore you and make you strong, firm, and steadfast" (1 Peter 5:10).

Week 18 • Day 05
SPIRITUAL WARFARE

EXERCISE

READ *James 4:1-12*
☐ Want More? Read 2 Corinthians 10

EXEGESIS

Study James 4:1-12 using the **H.E.A.R.** method of inductive Bible study. Write at least one sentence for each letter below. Consult the notes from a study Bible if you need help.

HIGHLIGHT What I see:
___
___
___

EXPLAIN What it means:
___
___
___

ACKNOWLEDGE   The timeless truths:

_____
_____
_____

RESPOND   With specific action:

_____
_____
_____

While the **H.E.A.R.** method is the one that we will use to help ensure that a proper interpretation method is followed, there are other helpful plans to follow. As you become more comfortable we suggest trying other good Bible study methods.

The fourth chapter of James examines the origins and solutions to various conflicts, ranging from international disputes to interpersonal struggles. James chapter four identifies three main areas of contention: conflict with others, internal strife, and conflict with God. Disagreements among believers, such as congregational arguments and personal attacks, arise from a lack of harmony and the ungodly inclination to pass judgment on others. James argues that selfish desires and wrong motives drive the internal war within, are the root cause of external conflicts, and even misdirect prayers. Ultimately, James states that all conflict originates from a rebellion against God, manifested by befriending the world, succumbing to the flesh, and yielding to the devil. To find peace, James recommends three actions: surrendering to God, seeking closeness with Him through confession of sin, and practicing humility. By taking these steps, one can resolve conflicts with God, oneself, and others, leading to a life characterized by peace and righteousness.

EXAMPLE

In the late 1930's Nazi Germany continued moving in aggression against its enemies, but the United States chose to watch from a safe distance. Before the term Holocaust existed, the American people were aware that the Nazi party was imprisoning, abusing, and killing innocent men, women, and children. Despite mounting evidence of Hitler's territorial expansion, military threats, and murderous intent, most Americans chose to cling to the perceived security of neutrality. Such reluctance came at the tremendous cost of life and the attack upon Pearl Harbor.

Much like the hesitancy of the American citizens of the late 1930's, children of God are sometimes tempted to ignore the battle raging around them. Focused on their personal goals, plans, and comforts, one might wrongly assume that neutrality will result in safety. Yet they forget that this world faces an evil enemy with no rules of war, whose conquest is the destruction of all that is good. Satan and his army are not interested in natural resources or territories. The prize in this spiritual war is the eternal souls of humanity. Every follower of Jesus is engaged in spiritual warfare, even if they are not aware of it. Like the early days of World War II, ignorance or inaction only increases the injuries and losses suffered.

MEDITATE Practice reciting this week's verses from memory and be prepared to say them aloud to your d-group.

ENGAGE

Praise God for His righteousness. Confess the ways you walk in unrighteousness by befriending the world, succumbing to the flesh, and yielding to the devil. Thank God for rescuing you from the power of sin and gifting you with Christ's righteousness. Ask Him to enable you to walk faithfully by surrendering to God, seeking closeness with Him through confession of sin, and practicing humility.

ENCOURAGE

Use this checklist as a guide for your weekly d-group time. Refer to the discipler's guide at the front of the book for more encouragement and practical advice.

- Work through questions from the accountability page.

- Spend time praying specifics for one another.

- Take turns reciting the memory verses.

- Discuss answers to the questions throughout the week that are marked with this symbol. ▼

PRAYER REQUESTS

_____

_____

_____

_____

_____

_____

_____

ACCOUNTABILITY QUESTIONS

These questions are to be asked of one another in a spirit of accountability (Proverbs 27:17). They are intended to stimulate conversations of character and confession of sin in a safe environment that values honesty, vulnerability, confidentiality, and grace.

1. Have you spent quality time in your spiritual disciplines this week?
2. Have you taken advantage of opportunities to share your faith this week? Explain.
3. Have your words and actions been a good testimony this week to the gospel of Jesus?
4. Have your thoughts and speech been pure (cussing, criticism, negativity, etc.)?
5. Have you been sexually pure this week? Have you been exposed to sexually alluring material? (For those who are married: Have you prioritized quality romantic time with your spouse?)
6. Have you been a good steward of your finances? Have you lacked integrity in the handling of your finances?
7. Have you been honoring and generous in your meaningful relationships this week (Family, friends, etc.)?
8. Have you given in to any addictive behavior this past week? Explain.
9. Have you been completely honest with me?

I'm praying for the salvation of the following two people and prayerfully considering how to share Christ with them myself: _____

> "Therefore, confess your sins to one another, and pray for one another, so that you may be healed."
>
> *James 5:16a*

Week 19 • Day 01
SPIRITUAL FRUIT

ESSENTIAL TRUTH

The Holy Spirit works in us to be more like Christ. Spiritually speaking, every life bears fruit. The kind of fruit your life bears depends upon where your life is rooted. If one's life is rooted in the Spirit and the work of Christ, then fruitfulness will be in keeping with God's kingdom mission and values. The Spirit enables us to produce fruit in keeping with Christlikeness. Personal disciple-making cultivates "much" fruit.

1. Read the Essential Truth, identify two phrases that stand out to you, and write them below. Why do you believe these phrases are significant?

2. Using your own words, how does a believer produce fruit?

3. Consider the ways the Holy Spirit has worked in your life to make you more like Christ. List this fruit below.

_____
_____
_____

EXERCISE memory verses

> But the fruit of the Spirit is love, joy, peace, patience, kindness, goodness, faithfulness, gentleness, self-control; against such things there is no law."
>
> *Galatians 5:22-23*

The "fruit of the Spirit" described in Galatians 5:22-23 represents the righteous virtues cultivated in the life of a disciple of Jesus through the continued work of the Holy Spirit. The Apostle Paul reminds his readers that these qualities are not merely ideas or philosophical concepts but are the effect of the Holy Spirit's presence in the life of a child of God. While human carnality tends towards self-centeredness and sin, the Spirit gently molds the follower of Jesus into a more faithful image bearer of God (2 Corinthians 3:18). Spiritual fruit develops through continual submission to God's Word and ways, resulting in daily choices that better demonstrate the love and character of Jesus.

EXAMPLE

Famously remembered as the clergyman and hymnist who wrote "Amazing Grace," few know the incredible loss and adversity of John Newton's early life. Born in England in 1725, John lost his mother to tuberculosis when he was not yet 7 years old. At eleven, John went to sea with his father while working aboard a series of slaving ships. Surrounded by the dehumanization of the slave trade and the raucous environment of pirates and privateers, John followed a path of rebellion and moral depravity. Today, few realize that this famous Christian Hymn composer was once considered a notorious blasphemer and debaucher. While captain of an Atlantic slave trade vessel, Newton faced a violent storm. His desperate plea to God catalyzed a profound yet progressive conversion to Christ. The softening of John's heart did not happen overnight, but the continued work of the Holy Spirit progressively transformed a violent slave trader into a loving pastor and abolitionist.

While listening to "Amazing Grace" and aware of John Newton's story, it is impossible to overlook the tangible spiritual fruit that resulted from Jesus transforming a hate-filled blasphemer into a pastor, author, and hymnist. The testimonies Newton offered throughout his campaign to abolish slavery became the core content of the inspiring lyrics of "Amazing Grace" John Newton's story is a poignant reminder that genuine faith in Jesus yields tangible results.

THE TRUTH

MEDITATE   Write out this week's verses below as you spend time committing them to memory.

MORE   If you'd like to increase your time in Scripture, commit to this optional weekly Bible reading plan.
Read (or listen via an audio Bible)

- ☐ (Day 1) Philippians 1
- ☐ (Day 2) Philippians 2
- ☐ (Day 3) Philippians 3
- ☐ (Day 4) Philippians 4
- ☐ (Day 5) Galatians 5 & Ephesians 5

ENGAGE

Praise God for the Spirit at work within you. Confess the ways you root yourself in things of the world instead of the work of Christ. Thank Jesus for providing the way to the Father and giving your life identity, purpose, and hope. Ask God to be at work within you making you look more and more like His Son.

Week 19 • Day 02
SPIRITUAL FRUIT

EXERCISE

> READ *John 15:1-17*

☐ Want More? Read Philippians 2

1. How does Jesus describe Himself, the Father, and His disciples in this passage?
_____
_____
_____

2. Jesus connects love, obedience, and joy in this passage. What does that reveal about the life and call of a disciple of Jesus?
_____
_____
_____

Spiritual fruit in the life of a follower of Christ refers to the character traits and behaviors that are byproducts of following God and being progressively sanctified or set apart. Although the specific phrase "spiritual fruit" does not appear in scripture, the concept is a consistent theme throughout the Word of God. The Bible highlights several distinctions between "fruit" and "works." For example, Paul often emphasizes that fruit is not merely the outcome of external actions or the fleeting behavior modification of legalism and religion but is deeply rooted in an active personal relationship with Jesus.

The New Testament reveals various kinds of spiritual fruit. Referring to those "won to Christ" as fruit (Romans 1:13), the fruit of sanctification (Romans 6:22), and financial giving as fruit given to support ongoing ministry (Romans 15:26-28), to every good work as fruit that pleases God (Colossians 1:10), and to praise as a fruit of acknowledging God (Hebrews 13:15). However, when teaching about the Fruits of the Spirit text such as Galatians 5 are explicitly referring to the character of the disciple of Jesus. A Christ-centered character does not develop from a self-help "me-centered" culture but is crafted and gradually refined by abiding in the love of God.

Jesus' instruction in John 15 demonstrates that love is at the heart of spiritual fruit. This truth is echoed in Galatians 6, where love is listed as the first fruit of the Spirit. In John 15, Jesus describes Himself as the true vine and His disciples as the branches. Within the rich imagery of the vine, Jesus reminds His Church that just as the branch cannot produce fruit apart from the vine, neither can His followers produce fruit unless they abide in Him (John 15:4). Here, bearing fruit is revealed not solely as a matter of human effort, but as the natural product of a life connected to Christ. A healthy grape vine will produce grapes. A vine that doesn't produce fruit is referred to as ornamental, as its only value is decorative appearance. Likewise, a life that does not demonstrate the love of Christ and make disciples may have the outward appearance of spiritual maturity and health, but they are a branch that does not fulfill the vine's natural purpose.

In verses 9 through17, Jesus further enriches the imagery of the vine, describing love as the driving force behind bearing fruit. Jesus commands His followers to love one another as He has loved (John 15:12). This love was defined by sacrifice (John 15:13), obedience (John 15:14), knowledge of God (John 15:15), and trust in God (John 15:16-17). Such sacrificial love reflects the heart of Jesus' mission to seek and save the lost (Luke 19:10). The fruit of the Spirit grows from the budding blossom of love for God and others.

The love Jesus refers to throughout John 15 is more than a fleeting emotional state or a philosophical concept. Aware that His audience would devalue their views of love, Jesus presented His love as the high and Holy standard. By commanding His followers to "love one another as I have loved you," Jesus gives His Church little room to depreciate the purity of love. Where emotional sentiment or intellectual concepts of love are fragile constructs, the love that Jesus teaches His disciples withstands the harsh daily environments of this fallen world. Where busyness can hinder meaningful interactions, and insecurity fosters envy, love does not fail (1 Corinthians 13:8). The better one knows God, the better they can love others, for love is both the root and the fruit of a life lived in Christ.

1. What are the results of abiding in Jesus and how have you practically experienced this?

_____
_____
_____

2. In which ways do you feel called to abide in Jesus now, regardless of the pressure, stress, or suffering you are currently facing? ▼

_____
_____
_____

MEDITATE   Fill in the blanks as you continue committing this week's verses to memory.

> But the fruit of the _____ is love, joy, peace, _____ , kindness, goodness, faithfulness, gentleness, _____; against such things there is no law."
>
> *Galatians 5:22-23*

ENGAGE

Praise God for His love. Confess the ways you don't walk in obedience to His command to love others as He's loved us. Thank Him for equipping and enabling us to love, obey, and rejoice despite the struggles of the world. Ask Him to give you joy as you walk in obedience and love today.

Week 19 • Day 03
SPIRITUAL FRUIT

EXERCISE

READ *Galatians 5:13-26*

☐ Want More? Read Philippians 3

1. Contrast the idea of walking by the Spirit with walking by the flesh as seen in this passage.

___
___
___

2. In verse thirteen, Paul says that believers are called to freedom. What does the rest of the passage reveal about walking in freedom? ▼

___
___
___

WEEK 19

The New Testament consistently reminds disciples of Jesus that a life rooted in Christ will naturally produce fruit. Such spiritual fruit does not develop from strict adherence to religious statutes and customs but is an outgrowth of an authentic relationship with Jesus. Today's study of Galatians 5 offers a poignant reflection on this truth while highlighting the profound contrast between living according to the desires of the flesh and walking in step with the Spirit.

In his letter to the Galatians, the apostle Paul teaches about the nature of spiritual transformation, using the metaphor of fruit. In this text, Paul cautions the church in Galatia not to see their freedoms in Christ as an opportunity for self-indulgence. Instead, he encourages them to serve one another humbly in love. Aware of the continual struggle between the "flesh" and the "Spirit," Paul reminds his audience that "the whole Law is fulfilled in one word, in the statement, 'You shall love your neighbor as yourself.'" From the endless well of God's great love, the disciple of Christ will never grow thirsty.

Yet, those who abandon the love of Christ and His love for others choose instead to abide in wickedness. The wretched fruit of immorality, jealousy, and hatred springs from the dry, poisoned ground of one's depraved flesh. The desires of the flesh foster division, which both fractures community and stands in stark opposition to God's Kingdom. Those who follow the desires of the flesh will "bite and devour one another" (Galatians 5:15). The core of self-worship is the dehumanization and devaluation of others (James 1:14-15). Such works of the flesh are not overcome by merely following rules or aspiring to moral living. Instead, the works of the flesh are displaced as the Spirit of God destroys strongholds and transforms the believer's inner life (2 Corinthians 10:4, Titus 3:5).

By contrast, those who "walk by the Spirit" (Galatians 5:16) display a very different harvest than "the deeds of the flesh" (Galatians 5:19). Paul clearly describes this in Galatians 5:22 through 23, as he lists "the fruits of the Spirit" as love, joy peace, patience, kindness, goodness, faithfulness, gentleness, and self-control. Using "fruit" in the singular affirms that these qualities are inseparable attributes of a Spirit-led life. Like Jesus' analogy of the vine and fruit in John 15, Paul's imagery of fruit is also rooted in love. This love is not the product of human morality or effort, but springs from God's perfect and unwavering love. Joy and peace develop within a life anchored in Jesus' love (Philippians 4:7). The attributes of patience, kindness, and goodness demonstrate the transformation of believers through their relationships with others. At the same time, the Spirit's provision of faithfulness, gentleness, and self-control subdues the deeds of the flesh (2 Corinthians 10:4-5).

> But I say, walk by the Spirit, and you will not carry out the desire of the flesh."
>
> *Galatians 5:16*

1. Are there areas of your life where you are walking in the flesh? Write a confession to the Lord below and ask Him for help and transformation.

_____
_____
_____

2. How do you practically walk in the Spirit in your day-to-day life. How are you challenged to grow in this area?

_____
_____
_____

THE TRUTH

MEDITATE — Fill in the blanks as you continue committing this week's verses to memory.

> "But the fruit of the _____ is love, joy, peace, _____, kindness, goodness, faithfulness, gentleness, _____; against such things there is no law."
>
> *Galatians 5:22-23*

ENGAGE

Praise God for His provision in your life. Confess the ways you walk in the flesh and neglect His commands and purpose for your life. Thank Him for loving you in a way that saves and transforms you. Ask Him to deepen your love for God and others and enable you to walk in obedience.

THE TRUTH

Week 19 • Day 04
SPIRITUAL FRUIT

EXAMINATION

READ
Matthew 19:16-22

☐ Want More? Read Philippians 4

WATCH
Week 19 - Spiritual Fruit

To watch the video, scan the QR code below by opening your phone's camera and holding your device so that the QR code appears on the screen. Click the link associated with the QR code, and choose this week's video. https://qrco.de/be3SWs

1. How can you discern if you have fallen into the trap of seeking spiritual fruit apart from the vine?

2. List out some of the hurts, hang-ups, or issues that get in the way of you seeking a more consistent and deeper relationship with Jesus?

_____
_____
_____

EXERCISE

READ Matthew 19:16-22

Entire industries have developed around the Church's pursuit of personal growth, maturity, and development. While many of these studies, resources, and guides are excellent, the volumes of self-focused improvement and personal development reveal a disturbing shift away from a deep and continuous relationship with Jesus. It appears that while most want to experience the healthy attributes of spiritual fruit lived out in their lives, they perceive that this fruit is for sale in the produce aisle of a supermarket. The account of the rich young ruler (Matthew 19:16-22) demonstrates that the pursuit of spiritual fruit apart from a desire to walk with Jesus is not a new phenomenon.

Much like this young ruler, the current culture also desires the positive effects of spiritual fruit while assuming it can grow without (Jesus) the vine (John 15:5). While focused on the cultural morality and legality of keeping commands, this young man's heart clung to the idols of self-dependence, influence, and power provided by wealth (Proverbs 11:28, Psalms 52:7, Jeremiah 9:23-24). If his answer to Jesus were truthful, this rich young ruler would have appeared to have mastered moral character, humility, kindness, and gentleness. From the outside, he would have seemed to be a mastered man. Still he is the only person in the Gospel books to approach Jesus joyously, yet to leave sorrowful (Matthew 19:22).

This account serves as both a warning and a lesson: efforts to achieve authentic and lasting emotional and spiritual growth apart from Jesus ultimately lead to exhaustion and frustration (Proverbs 14:12). Genuine growth requires far more than following rules and upholding an outward image (Matthew 23:27). Ultimately, the incredible inward effects and outward behaviors (Spiritual Fruit) that result from sanctification (being set apart) are a byproduct of walking with Jesus. In many ways, the modern Church is asking Jesus to give them peace and joy and then leave them to their own devices. Such a request is both void of love and the realization that Jesus is the source of all good things.

MEDITATE Below, attempt to write out this week's verses from memory.

ENGAGE

Praise God for being the source of all good things. Confess the ways you are self-reliant instead of dependent on Jesus. Thank God for providing everything you need to live a faithful life. Ask Him to deepen your intimacy with Him and produce fruit in your life.

Week 19 • Day 05
SPIRITUAL FRUIT

EXERCISE

READ *Ephesians 5:6-16*
☐ Want More? Read Galatians 5 & Ephesians 5

EXEGESIS

Study Ephesians 5:6-16 using the H.E.A.R. method of inductive Bible study. Write at least one sentence for each letter below. Consult the notes from a study Bible if you need help.

HIGHLIGHT   What I see:
_____
_____
_____

EXPLAIN   What it means:
_____
_____
_____

ACKNOWLEDGE The timeless truths:
_____
_____
_____

RESPOND With specific action:
_____
_____
_____

While the **H.E.A.R.** method is the one that we will use to help ensure that a proper interpretation method is followed, there are other helpful plans to follow. As you become more comfortable we suggest trying other good Bible study methods.

Although God's Spirit can work through nearly any moment in time or medium, it is unlikely that one will discover practical tools to help develop authentic spiritual maturity through self-help processes. Just as modern agriculture attempts to streamline crop production through various methods, so too are modern disciples of Christ often tempted to "revolutionize" spiritual growth. However, your soul is not a head of lettuce. Just as sunlight is essential for a vine to produce fruit, God's presence is crucial to developing spiritual maturity. Without light, a vine cannot thrive. Where many within the modern Church believe there is a strategy or process to expedite their sanctification, there are no shortcuts to developing spiritual fruit. To nurture spiritual fruit, the disciple of Jesus must consistently position their lives in God's light. Like a houseplant pulling towards the window, the follower of Christ must draw near to God.

To nurture the growth of spiritual fruit, the children of God must step into the environment Jesus modeled for His first disciples. In this environment, the follower of Christ spends time bathing in the light of God through consistent time in God's Word and prayer from the posture of a humble and receptive heart. Through these seasons of conviction and confession, God prunes away the "unfruitful deeds of darkness." This sometimes-uncomfortable process makes way for the new growth of love, joy, peace, patience, kindness, goodness, faithfulness, gentleness, and self-control.

EXAMPLE

While pursuing continued space exploration, NASA and other similar organizations have invested significant resources and time into producing a sustainable food source. Early attempts at growing plants in space include the Skylab in 1973 and the Soviet Salut-7 Mission in the 1980s. With access to nearly infinite resources and the expertise of the greatest minds in botany and herbology, these groundbreaking experiments revealed significant challenges. Scientists faced poor root development due to microgravity and radiation-induced DNA anomalies. Despite difficulties and setbacks, teams continue to work on projects such as the Veggie system on the International Space Station. These extensive efforts demonstrate that although plants can grow off-world, they do not develop as healthily as those on Earth.

The continued efforts to cultivate a sustainable crop in the harsh environment of a space station are a good example of how the contemporary Church often turns to methods and models from modern business, education, or psychology. Although inadvertent, many modern "spiritual growth" processes are akin to cultivating plants in a space station. There are no artificial atmospheres or supplements that can replace a consistent walk with Jesus.

MEDITATE   Practice reciting this week's verses from memory and be prepared to say them aloud to your d-group.

ENGAGE

Praise God for His righteousness. Confess the ways you walk in unrighteousness by befriending the world, succumbing to the flesh, and yielding to the devil. Thank God for rescuing you from the power of sin and gifting you with Christ's righteousness. Ask Him to enable you to walk faithfully by surrendering to God, seeking closeness with Him through confession of sin, and practicing humility..

ENCOURAGE

Use this checklist as a guide for your weekly d-group time. Refer to the discipler's guide at the front of the book for more encouragement and practical advice.

- Work through questions from the accountability page.
- Spend time praying specifics for one another.
- Take turns reciting the memory verses.
- Discuss answers to the questions throughout the week that are marked with this symbol.

PRAYER REQUESTS

_____
_____
_____
_____
_____
_____
_____

ACCOUNTABILITY QUESTIONS

These questions are to be asked of one another in a spirit of accountability (Proverbs 27:17). They are intended to stimulate conversations of character and confession of sin in a safe environment that values honesty, vulnerability, confidentiality, and grace.

1. Have you spent quality time in your spiritual disciplines this week?
2. Have you taken advantage of opportunities to share your faith this week? Explain.
3. Have your words and actions been a good testimony this week to the gospel of Jesus?
4. Have your thoughts and speech been pure (cussing, criticism, negativity, etc.)?
5. Have you been sexually pure this week? Have you been exposed to sexually alluring material? (For those who are married: Have you prioritized quality romantic time with your spouse?)
6. Have you been a good steward of your finances? Have you lacked integrity in the handling of your finances?
7. Have you been honoring and generous in your meaningful relationships this week (Family, friends, etc.)?
8. Have you given in to any addictive behavior this past week? Explain.
9. Have you been completely honest with me?

I'm praying for the salvation of the following two people and prayerfully considering how to share Christ with them myself: _____

> "Therefore, confess your sins to one another, and pray for one another, so that you may be healed."
>
> *James 5:16a*

Week 20 • Day 01

BIBLICAL JUSTICE AND GIVING

ESSENTIAL TRUTH

Biblical justice teaches us: 1) God's heart leans towards the poor and oppressed, and 2) He judged the root of evil at the first coming of Christ and will judge the fruit of evil at His second coming. Biblical stewardship teaches us: 1) Our hearts should lean toward generosity and meeting needs, and 2) God has given us our time, talents, and treasures to invest for His glory. Because God owns everything, we are stewards, not owners, of the resources entrusted to us. Jesus taught that money easily becomes a rival god.

1. Read the Essential Truth, identify two phrases that stand out to you, and write them below. Why do you believe these phrases are significant?

_____
_____
_____

2. Using your own words, describe biblical justice and biblical stewardship.

_____
_____
_____

3. How do these ideas currently shape your life? How does your life look differently from these truths?

_____
_____
_____

EXERCISE

Each one must do just as he has purposed in his heart, not grudgingly or under compulsion, for God loves a cheerful giver."

2 Corinthians 9:7

Biblical generosity originates from a worshipful heart, which is aligned with God's purposeful work. In this sense, biblical generosity should significantly influence our relationship with people and finances. Second Corinthians 9:7 reminds the Church that the discipline of giving encompasses more than the sum of a financial contribution. Giving is an act of worship that allows the followers of Jesus to respond to their trust in God with gratitude for His faithful provision (Philippians 4:19; Matthew 6:11). Jesus modeled selfless giving by leaving the riches of heaven to offer His life in exchange for our eternal salvation. God's Word encourages His followers to provide for others intentionally from their treasures, time, and talents. Where some attempt to evaluate biblical generosity against a metric of social expectations or financial accounting, Scripture encourages a more heart-focused and holistic approach. Today's reading in Mark 12 demonstrates that the condition of the heart is the more accurate measure of generosity, not the quantity of the gift.

EXAMPLE

On January 10, 1901, an enormous oil gusher erupted from Spindletop Hill near Beaumont, Texas. The publicity of the "largest gusher the world has ever seen" transformed this small town into a hub of industry and enterprise. Seemingly overnight, many local shop owners and farmers became millionaires. Among those who prospered was George Washington Carroll. Having amassed an incredible wealth from the oil industry, Carroll used his newfound fortune to advance the Kingdom of God. Carroll's generosity is still evident today at Baylor University, as seen in the Science Hall, multiple chapels, libraries, and numerous mission efforts. He gave without reserve or regret, rarely keeping a record of his donations. Carroll's contributions fed and clothed the impoverished and advanced education, while consistently pointing to Jesus.

Towards the end of his life, Carroll was asked if he regretted his generosity after losing much of his fortune. He famously replied, "All I have is what I have given away." To the discussion of wealth, you might have heard someone say, "You can't take it with you." Even if it were possible to take material wealth to heaven, what value would this world's treasures hold in a place where gold is the standard material for road pavement? Long after his death, George Carroll continues to remind the Church that true wealth is what we freely give to serve others and glorify the Lord.

THE TRUTH

MEDITATE — Write out this week's verse below as you spend time committing it to memory.

MORE — If you'd like to increase your time in Scripture, commit to this optional weekly Bible reading plan.
Read (or listen via an audio Bible)

- ☐ (Day 1) Malachi 1
- ☐ (Day 2) Malachi 2
- ☐ (Day 3) Malachi 3
- ☐ (Day 4) Malachi 4
- ☐ (Day 5) Matthew 5

ENGAGE

Praise God for being your provider. Confess the ways you are selfish with your time, talents, and treasures. Thank God for His standard for generosity by not withholding good gifts from you. Ask Him to give you a vision and understanding for a worshipful life that is generous in all ways.

Week 20 • Day 02
BIBLICAL JUSTICE AND GIVING

EXERCISE

READ *Malachi 2:17-3:1-6*

☐ Want More? Read Malachi 2

1. **Highlight** below the two specific statements people make that weary the Lord in Malachi 2:17. What do they imply about God's justice or character?

___

2. List the specific groups of people against whom the Lord says He will be a swift witness in Malachi 3:5. **Explain** the common thread or characteristic among these groups.

___

Biblical justice is a divine mandate woven into the fabric of God's covenant with His people. God's commands for His children to pursue biblical justice flow directly from His heart (Deuteronomy 32:4). In this way, justice is not merely a social concept or fleeting sentiment, but a biblically and spiritually balanced expression of awareness and action.

Throughout the Bible, God explicitly commands His people to care for the vulnerable and marginalized (Exodus 22:1-11; Proverbs 31:8-9; Psalm 82:3; Luke 3:11). The Old Testament prophet Micah well expresses God's expectations when he wrote, "What does the Lord require of you but to act justly, to love mercy, and to walk humbly with God?" (Micah 6:8). The New Testament book of James reminds the Church that "pure and undefiled religion in the sight of our God and Father is this: to visit orphans and widows in their distress" (James 1:27). Likewise, passages such as Isaiah 1:17 and Jeremiah 22:3 command the children of God to oppose oppression and to care for the neglected. Biblical justice seeks to reconcile broken relationships and promote equality, consistently pointing to Jesus as the ultimate source of justice.

While grappling with concepts of biblical justice, some may find themselves intentionally or inadvertently questioning the character of God. Those who have personal experience with abuse, corruption, or oppression may struggle against their subjective views of God's character. To this point, the student of Scripture must acknowledge that God's ways are far greater than their own (Isaiah 55:8). Where Jonah saw Nineveh as a corrupt pagan people deserving of destruction, God saw Nineveh as the epicenter of the single greatest revival in history (Jonah 3:5-10). Jonah assumed to know the hearts and minds of the Ninevites, while God knew every hair on each of their heads (Luke 12:7).

Like Jonah or the Israelites of Malachi's day, most wish for God to be slow to anger and full of grace when confronting their personal sin (Jonah 2:1-10). However, they also expect God to swiftly and brutally punish those whom they perceive as wicked (Jonah 4:2). In so doing, one superimposes an imbalanced and finite view of "right-and-wrong" over God's divine justice. Within this distorted perspective, one falsely appoints oneself as both the author of justice and the prosecutor and judge. Thus, foolishly believing that God is their executioner. In Malachi 2:17, the Israelites accuse God of favoring the wicked due to His delayed judgment. The grumblings of Jonah and the Israelites of Malachi's time still resonate today among God's followers who focus on suffering while wickedness appears to prosper. However, Malachi's writings emphasize that God's justice operates according to His perfect timeline.

The book of Malachi further reminds the children of God that divine justice transcends human understanding (Malachi 3:1-6). Malachi 3:1 foretells the arrival of John the Baptist ("My messenger"), who would prepare the way for Jesus, the "Messenger of the Covenant." This incredible prophecy demonstrates God's strategy to address sin at its core. Jesus' life, death, and resurrection reconciled humanity to God and continues to facilitate the sanctification of both individuals and communities. Malachi challenges his readers to trust in God's justice, both in His timing and His ways. Ultimately, the justice of God is fulfilled in the person of Jesus Christ and His mission to seek and save the lost (Luke 19:10). In short, hide your watch—do not seek to time God's justice—because God "will" judge wickedness in the future. To this end, followers of Jesus should strive to carry out the justice Jesus modeled through selfless service to others (1 John 3:17-18) and the proclamation of the gospel. While exploring the topics of biblical justice and stewardship, remember that the spare change in your pocket is not capable of ending world hunger. Still, it is capable of demonstrating the gospel as you feed a few.

1. **Acknowledge** how the theological statement "For I, the Lord, do not change" provides comfort and assurance to the "sons of Jacob" despite the impending judgment and purification. What is the theological significance of God's immutability in the context of His covenant promises and warnings?

_____
_____
_____

2. **Respond** to the image of God's refining fire and launderer's soap (Malachi 3:2). How do these two concepts apply to our personal spiritual growth and the purity of the church today? ▼

_____
_____
_____

THE TRUTH

MEDITATE Fill in the blanks as you continue committing this week's verse to memory.

> "Each one must do _____ as he has purposed in his heart, not _____ or under compulsion, for _____ loves a cheerful giver."
>
> *2 Corinthians 9:7*

ENGAGE

Praise God for His unchanging nature. Confess the ways you have allowed the world to shape your understanding of justice, instead of the Word of God. Thank Him for His divine justice. Ask God to purify your heart and attitude so you will be just and generous with everything He has given you.

Week 20 • Day 03
BIBLICAL JUSTICE AND GIVING

EXERCISE

READ *Malachi 3:7-12, Matthew 6:1-4*

☐ Want More? Read Read Malachi 3

1. How does your understanding of God's character shape your understanding of His divine justice?

___

2. Matthew 6:1-4 warns against generous giving for the purpose of being noticed by others. What is the danger in that, and how do you avoid it? ⊙

___

The way God's Word entwines the concepts of financial stewardship and giving against that of spiritual maturity indicates that the handling of resources is an indicator of one's heart and relationship with God (Luke 12:48; Acts 4:32). How a disciple of Jesus manages their financial resources (**stewardship**) demonstrates their convictions (**testimony**), while allowing them the opportunity to invest into the Kingdom of God (**giving**). Malachi commands the children of God to "return to God" in both the worship of their hearts and in proportion to the generosity with which God had blessed them (Malachi 3:7-12). In Malachi 3:7, the Lord promises, "Return to Me, and I will return to you." For nearly a generation, Israel had neglected God's statutes. Through this season, their lack of generosity and stewardship indicated their waning loyalty and love for God (Psalm 112:9; Matthew 10:42).

Even the most faithful followers of Jesus tend to wrestle with varying levels of legalism as they attempt to navigate the intertwined and controversial subjects of biblical justice, stewardship, and giving. It is essential to acknowledge that the discussion is not primarily about the size of the gift given to God's work or the value of one's wealth, but rather about the condition of the heart. Jesus demonstrates this by pointing out the incredible gift of the widow's two mites compared to the offering of the wealthy (Luke 21:1-4). Although her meager gift might seem insignificant compared to the lavish gifts of the rich, Jesus tells His followers that "this poor widow put in more than all of them." Unlike legalism, which prioritizes the amount of a gift, God's concern is the attitude of the giver. Legalism fixates on the quantity of a gift, but God focuses on the quality of the giver's heart. The One who created and sustains everything (Colossians 1:16-17) does not need your financial contributions (Psalm 50:10) or your skills (Luke 19:40). On the other hand, we need to give God our treasure and talents to pursue a proper, healthy relationship with Him.

Biblical texts such as Deuteronomy 8 remind the children of God that all time, talents, and treasures originate from God Himself. Every moment, every skill, and every opportunity comes directly from God. The capacity to labor, create, and collect wealth depends on God's provision (Proverbs 12:11; Deuteronomy 8:18). When Jesus' followers refuse to acknowledge God's blessings, they can easily fall into the trap of believing they are self-sufficient. The Psalmist reminds us, "The earth is the Lord's and everything in it" (Psalm 24:1). Ultimately, biblical stewardship proves sound theology by accepting God's power and provision over one's life and possessions. In this way, stewardship is a "test" (Malachi 3:10).

Malachi demonstrates that the test of stewardship is not one-sided. Malachi 3:10

invites the children of God to test God's faithfulness: "Test Me in this... and see if I will not throw open the floodgates of heaven." Because God is sovereign, this is not a manipulation of God but rather an opportunity to trust in Him. Through acts of generosity and service, followers of Christ are invited to participate in God's work. It is through obedient acts of generosity that God promises blessings. These blessings may sometimes come in the form of material wealth, but they are truly found in the abundance of God's presence, provision, and peace.

In the parable of the sheep and goats, Jesus specifically describes meeting the needs of the thirsty, hungry, and sick (Matthew 25:31-40). He then explains that "to the extent that you did it for one the least of these brothers and sisters of Mine, you did it for Me." The calling to support the poor and care for the vulnerable is a consistent theme throughout the Word of God (Proverbs 19:7; Matthew 25:35-40). The proper stewardship of resources requires active participation in God's work of justice and restoration. When Jesus' followers give to God, their hearts become more aligned with His. Jesus underscored this vital connection, reminding His disciples in Matthew 6:21 that "where your treasure is, there your heart will be also." Pursuing biblical justice and giving is a spiritual discipline that tests one's faith in God and, in turn, God's unwavering faithfulness.

1. Respond to Jesus' teaching in Matthew 6:1-4. How can you ensure that your acts of giving and service are motivated by a desire to honor God alone, rather than seeking human recognition or approval? ▼

_____

_____

_____

2. Respond personally to Malachi 3:10. In what area of your life (not just finances) might God be inviting you to "test" His faithfulness through an act of obedience or generosity this week?

_____

_____

_____

MEDITATE Fill in the blanks as you continue committing this week's verse to memory.

> "Each one must do _____ as he has _____ in his heart, not _____ or under compulsion, for _____ loves a _____ giver."
>
> 2 Corinthians 9:7

ENGAGE

Praise God for being all-sufficient. Confess the ways you rely on yourself instead of trusting Him to do what only He can do. Thank God for making you new through salvation and giving you time, talents, and treasures to be used for His kingdom. Ask God to deepen your desire to know Him and to be on mission for Him, so you may respond faithfully and obediently.

Week 20 • Day 04
BIBLICAL JUSTICE AND GIVING

EXAMINATION

READ
Matthew 6:19-24 ☐ Want More? Read Malachi 4

WATCH
Week 20 - Biblical Justice and Giving

To watch the video, scan the QR code below by opening your phone's camera and holding your device so that the QR code appears on the screen. Click the link associated with the QR code, and choose this week's video. https://qrco.de/be3SWs

1. Examine what specific contrasts Jesus draws between earthly treasures and heavenly treasures? How does Jesus connect the location of one's treasure to the condition of one's heart in verse 21?

2. Reflect on Jesus' warning about serving two masters in Matthew 6:24—how might this principle challenge believers to evaluate their current financial decisions and priorities?

_____
_____
_____

EXERCISE

READ   Matthew 19:16-22

God's command to provide for the needy and to support the work of His Church is not seated in a place of recognition, moral grandstanding, or virtue-signaling. Outlined countless times throughout His Word, the act of giving is always contextualized as an expression of worship and obedience (Proverbs 3:9-10, Hebrews 13:16). In Matthew 6, Jesus reminds His audience that "when you give to the poor, do not sound a trumpet before you, as the hypocrites do in the synagogues and in the streets, so that they may be honored by men." Within these verses, Jesus emphasizes that the actual value of giving is not public display, earthly rewards, or personal attention. The righteous rewards of giving are set in the unseen faithfulness and honor of God.

God's Word commonly references the giving of finances, time, and resources within the context of **spiritual giftings** (Romans 12:6-8), **spiritual disciplines** (2 Corinthians 9:6-7), and clearly as a **command** (Deuteronomy 15:11). Jesus says that "for where your treasure is, there your heart will be also" (Matthew 6:21). If you wish to evaluate the loyalties of your heart look no farther than the treasures you surround yourself with. One's financial priorities often reveal what they value the most. By contrasting the eternal riches of God's everlasting Kingdom with that of the fleeting and failing financial systems of this world, Jesus challenges His followers to evaluate the state of their hearts. Saying that, "No one can serve two masters; for either he will hate the one and love the other, or he will be devoted to one and despise the other" (Matthew 6:24).

Giving from a righteous heart is also a response of God's generosity. Everything one possesses is ultimately from God (James 1:17). As stewards of God's blessings, Jesus tells His followers to give joyfully, freely, and to advance God's Kingdom. Jesus' teachings shift the focus of His Church from the mechanical question of "how much" they should give to the heart-focused question of "why," while reminding His disciples that giving is an act of faith.

MEDITATE Below, attempt to write out this week's verse from memory.

ENGAGE

Praise God for His love towards you. As you look around at the treasures your surround yourself with, confess the loyalties of your heart. Thank Him for giving you purpose in life and choosing to use you when He doesn't need to. Ask God to enable you to give joyfully, freely, and to advance His Kingdom.

THE TRUTH

Week 20 • Day 05
BIBLICAL JUSTICE AND GIVING

EXERCISE

READ   *Luke 12:22-34*
☐ Want More? Read Malachi 5

EXEGESIS

Study Luke 12:22-34 using the H.E.A.R. method of inductive Bible study. Write at least one sentence for each letter below. Consult the notes from a study Bible if you need help.

HIGHLIGHT   What I see:
___
___
___

EXPLAIN   What it means:
___
___
___

ACKNOWLEDGE   The timeless truths:

_____
_____
_____

RESPOND   With specific action:

_____
_____
_____

While the **H.E.A.R.** method is the one that we will use to help ensure that a proper interpretation method is followed, there are other helpful plans to follow. As you become more comfortable we suggest trying other good Bible study methods.

In His omniscience, God is aware of every need. In His love, God delights in providing for His children. Jesus often instructed His disciples to trust in God's provision and to seek His Kingdom above all else (John 14:1). Jesus sends out His disciples twice in Luke's Gospel, forbidding them from bringing extra supplies or finances. In doing so, Jesus fostered an environment in which His disciples grew in their faith and dependence on God. In this scenario, the entire early Church was also allowed to grow in their reciprocated faithfulness and generosity as they supported Kingdom builders (missionaries and pastors). The faith developed during this season of training would enable Jesus' first disciples to move beyond the limitations of their self-sufficiency, to trust in God's provision as they carried out Jesus' commission to make disciples of all nations.

Jesus' commission for His Church to make disciples still requires His followers to rest in the knowledge that God will provide for every need. Such faith allows modern disciples of Jesus to live with open hands and a loosened grip on their earthly plans and possessions. Instead of hoarding treasures that will perish, Jesus instructs His followers to give freely and generously. Such giving reflects God's heart for those in need by presenting a testimony of generosity. A closer examination of Luke 12 reveals that true security does not come from amassing wealth, but from the eternal treasure found in serving God as Kingdom builders.

EXAMPLE

The life of Henrietta Green serves as a cautionary tale of a life consumed by financial fears. "Hetty" was a wealthy financier who had inherited a fortune worth hundreds of millions in today's market. Despite her incredible wealth, Hetty lived in continuous fear of financial loss. It is said that Hetty wore the same dress every day, lived in small efficiency apartments, and avoided heating her home. The relentless efforts to preserve her wealth extended to every aspect of daily life. Hetty even refused to pay for proper medical care for her son, which led to the amputation of his leg.

While prudence with money is wise, Hetty's story reveals the danger of not trusting the Lord. Through the corrective lens of Scripture, biblical stewardship seeks to honor the Lord in how we make and spend money. From one extreme, an unhealthy obsession with finances erodes both personal well-being and relationships. Yet from the other extreme, the abandonment of work and financial management leaves one unable to support themselves or offer to the building of God's kingdom. Luke 12 reminds followers of Jesus to let go of their fears and worries and to rest in God's care and purposeful work. Yet, like Hetty Green, many within the Church continue to approach finances with fear and obsession, or complete abandonment. If you trust God with your eternal soul and are committed to growing in spiritual maturity, why would you not trust God with your finances?

MEDITATE Practice reciting this week's verse from memory and be prepared to say it aloud to your d-group.

ENGAGE

Praise God for His omniscience. Confess the ways you don't trust God to know or provide for your needs. Thank Him for supplying all good things and faithfully meeting the needs of His people. Ask God to convict your heart of the ways you should step forward in obedience so He may be glorified in your trust and generosity.

ENCOURAGE

Use this checklist as a guide for your weekly d-group time. Refer to the discipler's guide at the front of the book for more encouragement and practical advice.

- Work through questions from the accountability page.

- Spend time praying specifics for one another.

- Take turns reciting the memory verses.

- Discuss answers to the questions throughout the week that are marked with this symbol. ⏷

PRAYER REQUESTS

ACCOUNTABILITY QUESTIONS

These questions are to be asked of one another in a spirit of accountability (Proverbs 27:17). They are intended to stimulate conversations of character and confession of sin in a safe environment that values honesty, vulnerability, confidentiality, and grace.

1. Have you spent quality time in your spiritual disciplines this week?
2. Have you taken advantage of opportunities to share your faith this week? Explain.
3. Have your words and actions been a good testimony this week to the gospel of Jesus?
4. Have your thoughts and speech been pure (cussing, criticism, negativity, etc.)?
5. Have you been sexually pure this week? Have you been exposed to sexually alluring material? (For those who are married: Have you prioritized quality romantic time with your spouse?)
6. Have you been a good steward of your finances? Have you lacked integrity in the handling of your finances?
7. Have you been honoring and generous in your meaningful relationships this week (Family, friends, etc.)?
8. Have you given in to any addictive behavior this past week? Explain.
9. Have you been completely honest with me?

I'm praying for the salvation of the following two people and prayerfully considering how to share Christ with them myself: _____

> "Therefore, confess your sins to one another, and
> pray for one another, so that you may be healed."
> *James 5:16a*

Week 21 • Day 01
DISCIPLE MAKING

ESSENTIAL TRUTH

Passing on the spiritual blessings we have received from those who guided us profoundly increases our spiritual capabilities (equipment) and deepens our connections (endearment). The desire to invest our lives intentionally in others as we walk alongside them provides a clear indication of growth toward maturity in Christ. Disciples of Jesus make disciples for Jesus.

1. Read the Essential Truth, identify two phrases that stand out to you, and write them below. Why do you believe these phrases are significant?

___

___

___

2. What does it mean to "walk alongside" someone in their spiritual journey, and how can you practice this intentionally in your daily life?

___

___

___

EXERCISE `memory verse`

"Having so fond an affection for you, we were well-pleased to impart to you not only the gospel of God but also our own lives, because you had become very dear to us."

1 Thessalonians 2:8

In 1 Thessalonians 2, Paul reminds the early church of Thessalonica that his motivations were not like those of others who leveraged beliefs for attention, adoration, power, or profit. Due to his past as a Pharisee (Acts 23:6), Paul well understood the temptations and potential trappings associated with religious leadership (Matthew 23:27). As such, Paul reminds his audience that He and his companions did not receive profit, nor attempt to raise themselves above others. Rather than seeking personal gain or ambitious aspirations of grander, Paul mirrored the selfless and authentic love of Jesus. Throughout His ministry, Jesus graciously and patiently met His disciples in their strengths and in their weaknesses. Jesus' teachings emphasized love to the point of citing the word over 70 times throughout the gospel books. In contrast, He never once spoke positively about the hypocrisy, legalism, and self-focused intentions associated with the religious systems of His day.

Somewhere between his conversion to Christ on the road to Damascus (Acts 9:1-19) and his incredible ministry to make disciples of all nations, Paul grasps the astonishing value of God's love. He realized that the motivation to invest in the gospel is not one of fulfilling lofty goals, achieving success, or gaining attention. Paul learned that "having so fond an affection" (love) is the pure and purposeful Christ-centered motivation "to impart to you not only the gospel of God but also our lives, because you had become very dear to us" (1 Thessalonians 2:8).

EXAMPLE

Born in 1867, Marie Curie developed into an inquisitive young woman who went on to become the first female recipient of the Nobel Prize. Marie's discoveries in physics and nuclear chemistry set the foundation for the modern uses of radiation and atomic power. Eight years later, alongside her husband, Pierre Curie, the couple would receive an unprecedented second Nobel Prize for their continued contributions to chemistry. Marie's discoveries of polonium and radium revolutionized science, paving the way for advancements in medicine, agriculture, deep space exploration, and nuclear energy.

However, Marie Curie's investment went beyond her scientific achievements. Marie intentionally mentored her daughter, Irène Joliot-Curie, cultivating Irène's curiosity and instilling in her the rigorous disciplines of science. This mentorship culminated in her daughter also receiving a Nobel Prize in Chemistry in 1935 for the breakthrough discovery of artificial radioactivity. Without Marie's loving dedication to her daughter and her passion for science, countless modern advancements in nuclear physics may have been delayed or even lost. When focusing primarily on personal development and professional success, a young disciple can easily overlook Jesus' command to invest in the lives of others. To a large extent, a follower of Jesus develops significantly as they nurture the message and method of Jesus in the lives of those God places in their path.

MEDITATE Write out this week's verse below as you spend time committing them to memory.

MORE If you'd like to increase your time in Scripture, commit to this optional weekly Bible reading plan.
Read (or listen via an audio Bible)

☐ (Day 1) 1 Thessalonians 1
☐ (Day 2) 1 Thessalonians 2
☐ (Day 3) 1 Thessalonians 3
☐ (Day 4) 1 Thessalonians 4
☐ (Day 5) 1 Thessalonians 5

ENGAGE

Praise God for using people to reveal Himself to you. Confess the ways you want to walk in self-sufficiency instead of depending on the community He created you to live within. Thank Him for providing spiritual growth through the power of the Holy Spirit.

Week 21 • Day 02
DISCIPLE MAKING

EXERCISE

READ *1 Thessalonians 2:1-6 & 2 Timothy 1:1-5*

☐ Want More? Read 1 Thessalonians 2

1. As you read through the two passages above, **Highlight** the various action verbs below that make up Paul's investment in others.

_____
_____
_____

2. Explain what it mean to be "approved by God" (1 Thessalonians. 2:4) in the context of disciple making or sharing faith? How does this approval impact Paul's motivation?

_____
_____
_____

The Gospel accounts of Jesus' ministry provide the Church with numerous examples of His consistent investment in His followers (Matthew 4:19). By sharing daily life with His disciples, Jesus prepared them for the powerful and purposeful work of making disciples of all nations. Where the contemporary Church has often allocated "discipleship" to the dynamics of the modern classroom environment, the model Jesus gave His Church to follow is far more personal and organic. A follower of Christ may learn the definition of sanctification, but it is not until someone lovingly holds them accountable for their confessed sin that they begin to be set apart and grow in holiness. Personal disciple making is more about "training in righteousness" (2 Timothy 3:16) than mere teaching about right behaviors.

As an Apostle and early Church planter, Paul followed Jesus' ministry model. Like Jesus, Paul intentionally nurtured those he discipled within the context of authentic love and compassion. When addressing the church of Thessalonica, Paul demonstrated that his intentions were not tainted by deceit, impurity, or self-serving motivations (1 Thessalonians 2:3). Inspired by the Spirit of God, he emphasized the importance of integrity multiple times (2 Corinthians 1:12; Ephesians 4:25; Titus 1:7). Paul's gospel ministry focused on serving Jesus instead of pleasing men. Paul reminded his readers that God "examines our hearts" (1 Thessalonians 2:4). Following in the footsteps of Jesus (1 John 2:6), His disciples should filter their intentions through His compassionate and selfless investment in others. By acknowledging that they are not the hero in another's story, the disciple of Jesus can avoid the pitfalls of selfishness and personal gain. Jesus is the hero in every story. His disciples are just the guides.

Current surveys and forecasts suggest that between 70% and 80% of young people leave Christian corporate worship shortly after graduation. As the modern Church strives to regain relevancy and influence, those who comprise the Church are rarely examining themselves. Through the humbling lenses of self-evaluation, explore how you intentionally spend your time with your immediate family and community. Ask yourself, "How have I selflessly, compassionately, and intentionally invested the life of Christ into those around me?" As a follower of Jesus, it is never too late to start. In Paul's first letter to the Thessalonians, Paul described how he focused his daily life and profession around imparting both the Gospel and his own life (1 Thessalonians 2:8). Paul then emphasized the diligence and purpose required to make disciples like Jesus modeled (1 Thessalonians 2:9). Followers of Jesus are commanded to share and multiply the blessings of the Gospel into other people's lives with both their words and actions (Matthew 25:14-30).

Paul compared the work of personal disciple making to that of a mother or father (1 Thessalonians 2:7, 11). The faithfulness of spiritual parenting is evident in one's speech and actions (Matthew 5:16). Behaviors are an expression of belief (James 2:14-17), and as such, disciple-makers must consistently strive to align their lives with Jesus. Paul's letters demonstrate how his speech aligned with his actions, proving that his counsel was grounded in the truth of Christ. Unlike the disconnected environment of a lecture or classroom, disciple-making requires personal patience, persistence, and grace in a more intimate, up-close relationship. Just as Jesus individually invested in His first disciples, He continues to equip His modern disciples to carry out His command to make disciples of nations in the same up-close and personal way. However, while focused on the grand scale of reaching "all nations" (Matthew 28:19), the follower of Christ cannot neglect the geographically expanding implications of texts like Acts 1:8. Jesus purposefully clarified that the mission to make disciples begins in Jerusalem (those closest to you) and then extends to the farthest reaches of the world.

The benchmark of success for a disciple of Jesus is measured by the lives they impact spiritually. The purposeful work of the Church, as Jesus designed it, is to share the good news of Jesus and to invest in the lives of those who come to faith so they might grow in spiritual maturity to the point of repeating the process. In this regard, every follower of Jesus should be committed to the arduous yet rewarding work of intentionally nurturing faith in the lives of a few others.

1. Acknowledge the truth Paul implied by his use of the term "sincere faith" (literally "unhypocritical faith") in 2 Timothy 1:5. How does the passing down of faith through generations demonstrate its authenticity and power?

_____

_____

_____

THE TRUTH

2. Respond personally to the ministry methodology of Paul and Jesus. How can you cultivate similar "spiritual parent-child" or "mentor-mentee" relationships within your local church? Who are the "Pauls" and "Timothys" in your life? Discuss with your group. ▼

___

___

___

___

MEDITATE Fill in the blanks as you continue committing this week's verse to memory.

"Having so fond an _____ for you, we were well-pleased to _____ to you not only the _____ of God but also our own lives, because you had become very dear to us."

1 Thessalonians 2:8

ENGAGE

Praise God for His Church. Confess the ways you seek worldly things for help and growth. Thank Jesus for training His disciples so they would go and make disciples in the same way. Ask God to give you joy exactly where you are today and to provide the next step needed in your walk with Him.

Week 21 • Day 03
DISCIPLE MAKING

EXERCISE

READ *1 Thessalonians 2:7-12, 2 Timothy 1:6-8*
☐ Want More? Read Read 1 Thessalonians 3

1. As you read through the two passages above, **Highlight** some action verbs below that depict Paul's investment in others. List at least two metaphors Paul uses to communicate the disciple-making relationship.

_____
_____
_____

2. **Explain** what Paul might have intended to convey with the metaphors that you chose to highlight above? Define spiritual parenting in your own words.

_____
_____
_____

Jesus' Great Commission to make disciples applies to all of His followers (Matthew 28:18-20). Sadly, many within the modern Church have assigned the high and holy calling of disciple-making to church programs or paid staff. By doing so, numerous believers have neglected Jesus' teachings and have missed their calling and purpose. The homes, hobbies, and workplaces of every believer represent a tailored mission field. It is easy to overlook that a place of work is about more than making money, and a school is about more than receiving an education. These seemingly mundane environments outside the home represent a space where disciples of Jesus have the required access, relationships, and opportunities to share the gospel and invest in others. The home is particularly vital, providing parents with unmatched time and avenues to disciple their children.

By design, Jesus intends disciple-making to be a purposeful and personal investment into the lives of others. When stepping beyond extensive programmatic processes and focusing on a few select individuals, a disciple-maker discovers an environment where they can form authentic and adaptive relationships. Paul's relationship with Timothy and the church in Thessalonica serves as a profound example of such spiritual parenting. Through First Thessalonians 2 and Second Timothy 1, Paul demonstrates his heart for nurturing believers in faith and godly living. These texts remind the Church that disciple-making is about more than imparting information in the formal sense of teaching. The model of disciple-making that Jesus gave His followers is about demonstrating Christ-like character while walking alongside others as they grow in their faith.

Paul understood that, much like parenting, disciple-making demands personal sacrifice founded upon authentic love. In today's reading, Paul likened himself to both a mother who tenderly nurtures her children and a father who protects and encourages his spiritual children (1 Thessalonians 2:7-12). Both metaphors are necessary to describe the disciple maker's job adequately. Paul demonstrated that authentic disciple-making requires affection and care that extends beyond a rigid commitment to completing a curriculum or checking a box. Paul told the church in Thessalonica that he had given his very life to them, much like a father who has invested his years nurturing his children.

Paul consistently demonstrated throughout his letters that those he had discipled had become "very dear" to him (1 Thessalonians 2:8). As a follower of Jesus, one cannot simply hand off the incredible privilege of making disciples to another leader or an impersonal external program. True disciple-making requires time, effort, and genuine connection. The life-on-life nature of disciple-making demonstrates the importance of accountability and authenticity. By following Jesus' model, Paul did not merely point others toward a lofty moral goal; he modeled "training" others in sanctification. By living out his conviction, his life was a witness, saying, "You are witness, and so is God, how devoutly and upright and blamelessly we behaved towards you believers" (1 Thessalonians 2:10). Paul's letter to the ancient church in Thessalonica still reminds the Church today that daily speech and behaviors are often the most powerful sermons. As Robert Fulghum aptly put it, "Do not worry that children never listen to you; worry that they are always watching you."

Paul's goal for investing his life into others was clear: help them "walk in a manner worthy of God who calls you into His own kingdom and glory" (1 Thessalonians 2:12). Paul reminded Timothy to "kindle afresh the gift of God" as to not live within a spirit of fear, but with power, love, and self-discipline (2 Timothy 1:6-8). Jesus was fully aware of the fear and self-doubt present in His first disciples as He gave them the Great Commission to make disciples. These men were not highly educated, accomplished, influential, or wealthy, but Jesus had personally invested in their lives. Before ascending, Jesus promised His first disciples that He would be with them "always, even to the end of the age" (Matthew 28:20). As you complete this leg of your journey as a disciple-maker in training, do not be fearful. Boldly obey Jesus' marching orders for you to share the wealth of your spiritual life with others in small, reproducible groups, all the while claiming His promise that He is "with you" in a special way as you make disciples for Him. As you prayerfully prepare to lead your own Disciple group and intentionally share the gospel with your family and coworkers, know that you do not have to have all the answers. Jesus is with you always.

1. Respond personally to both the equipment and endearment God has given you through this D group? List below some of the "wealth" received from your time together that you would like to "share" with others for the sake of the gospel.

_____
_____
_____

1. Who are the people in your life with whom you are "sharing your life" for the sake of the gospel? What does that practically look like?

_____
_____
_____
_____

MEDITATE   Fill in the blanks as you continue committing this week's verse to memory.

" Having so fond an _____ for you, we were well-pleased to _____ to you not only the _____ of God but also our own lives, _____ you had become very _____ to us."

1 Thessalonians 2:8

ENGAGE

Praise Jesus for His sacrifice for you. Confess the ways you seek to earn His love and favor and neglect the reality that it has been freely given to you. Thank God for giving you people to lock arms with as God teaches, stretches, and uses you. Ask Him to enable you to walk in a manner worthy of the gospel.

THE TRUTH

Week 21 • Day 04
DISCIPLE MAKING

EXAMINATION

READ
Mark 9:31-37 ☐ Want More? Read 1 Thessalonians 4

WATCH
Week 21 - Disciple Making

To watch the video, scan the QR code below by opening your phone's camera and holding your device so that the QR code appears on the screen. Click the link associated with the QR code, and choose this week's video. https://qrco.de/be3SWs

1. Reflecting on Paul's relationship with Timothy, what specific qualities do you see in Paul's investment in Timothy's life? ▼

_____
_____
_____

2. In what areas of your spiritual walk do you need to show more patience to yourself and others? How does Jesus' patience and grace towards His first disciples encourage you?

_____
_____
_____

EXERCISE

READ   Mark 9:31-37

This week's study focuses on the authentic life-on-life investment that is critical to making disciples for Jesus. While examining the accounts of Paul and Timothy, one might conclude that intentionally pouring into the lives of a few is an easy endeavor. Yet when discussing Paul's analogy of spiritual parenting (1 Thessalonians 2:1-6), as well as the volumes of biblical text in which Paul and other Apostles correct and chastise the waywardness and sinfulness of local churches (Galatians 6:1, 1Corinthians 5:1-13, 2 Thessalonians 3:6, 14-15) the student of scripture must acknowledge that disciple-making relationships are not always easy.

While pouring into His first disciples, Jesus consistently demonstrated the need for patience and compassion (Mark 8:14-21). Like a parent, Jesus continued to commit Himself to the growth of His disciples, even as they struggled to understand His mission (Mark 8:31-33), doubted His authority (Mark 4:35-41), and even abandoned Him (Mark 14:50). Despite an evident lack of comprehension, Jesus consistently guided those He discipled with incredible grace and compassion. In Mark 9:31-37, Jesus transformed a debate among His disciples about personal greatness into an opportunity to teach about humility and service. He stated, "If anyone wants to be first, he shall be last of all and servant of all" (Mark 9:35).

Much like His first disciples, many who comprise the modern Church seemingly hold too tightly to the world's definitions of greatness and self-importance. This fatal flaw within the sinful nature of humanity leaves its destructive mark on every relationship. Although personal disciple-making offers incredible rewards, like parenting, it can be challenging. To illustrate the need for patience and humility, Jesus embraced a child, representing those who were considered powerless in society. Saying, "Whoever welcomes one of these little children in my name welcomes me" (Mark 9:37). Through this action, Jesus further emphasized the Kingdom value of serving others selflessly. Later in John 13, Jesus would set the expectation of a disciple-maker as He washed the feet of His disciples. Investing the love of Jesus in the lives of others is rarely as easy and straightforward as one wishes, but it is the Kingdom method Jesus modeled for His Church.

MEDITATE   Below, attempt to write out this week's verse from memory.

ENGAGE

Praise God for His Spirit within you. Confess the ways you deny the power of the Holy Spirit by focusing on your own limitations. Thank God for providing everything necessary to walk boldly in the work He has called you to. Ask Him to deepen your understanding of His presence and power, and to trust His work to be accomplished through His power as you step forward in obedience.

Week 21 • Day 05

DISCIPLE MAKING

EXERCISE

READ *John 21:15-17*
☐ Want More? Read 1 Thessalonians 5

EXEGESIS

Study John 21:15-17 using the **H.E.A.R.** method of inductive Bible study. Write at least one sentence for each letter below. Consult the notes from a study Bible if you need help.

HIGHLIGHT   What I see:
_____
_____
_____

EXPLAIN   What it means:
_____
_____
_____

THE TRUTH

ACKNOWLEDGE The timeless truths:

_____
_____
_____

RESPOND With specific action:

_____
_____
_____

While the **H.E.A.R.** method is the one that we will use to help ensure that a proper interpretation method is followed, there are other helpful plans to follow. As you become more comfortable we suggest trying other good Bible study methods.

As you face the biblical reality that Jesus commissioned you to make disciples in the mission fields of your home, hobbies, and profession, you may have to confront feelings of doubt, regret, or fear. At first glance, making disciples of all nations is overwhelming, but you are not alone. Jesus' first disciples faced similar emotions just before He delivered the Great Commission. Aware of Jesus' mission, message, and method, Matthew 28:17 says, "they worshiped Him; but some were doubtful." Aware of their doubt, Jesus assures His followers that He is with them through every step of their journey (Matthew 28:20; John 14:16-17).

When reading the New Testament, it is easy to forget that the Apostles came from common backgrounds and vocations. As such, they had grown up within a religious system and culture that taught that most of them were unfit and below the calling of a priest or rabbi. However, Jesus did not select His first disciples from the well-studied and groomed ranks of the Pharisees or Sadducees. Jesus chose instead to select seemingly ordinary men and women from the average environments of their workplaces, from the common intersections of daily living. Although a higher education in a theological seminary is an incredible gift, it is by no means required to follow Jesus' Commission to make disciples.

WEEK 21

In John 21, the apostle John brings his readers back to a post-resurrection scene from the common background and vocation he shared with Peter, as both were fishermen. As Peter worked through the regret of denying Jesus multiple times and the incredible reality of Jesus' resurrection, he returned to his trade as a fisherman. Perhaps, like Peter, you are doubting your calling, regretting your past, or scared of what life looks like after this D-group. As you face these difficult emotions, consider the scene and significance of John 21:15-17.

Throughout Jesus' ministry, Peter confronted the clear and present reality of his lacking genealogy, his limited education, and obvious character flaws. It was here on a beach, after a night of fishing, that Jesus asked Peter three times, "Do you love Me?" With each response, Jesus gives clear and undeniable instructions to "feed my lambs," "shepherd My sheep," and "tend My sheep." There is no better life than the life of Christ. It is never too late to begin investing in your family and others for the sake of Christ. There is no season of life in which you will feel "capable" of this great work. But remember, you are not alone. Jesus has given you a completed Bible, His indwelling Holy Spirit, and the support of His Church. Jesus planned His Church the way He wanted it, and He wants His Church the way He planned it. Jesus saves sinners (His Message). And, disciples make disciples (His Method). It is never too late to start this great work.

> "But you are a chosen race, a royal priesthood, a holy nation, a people for God's own possession, so that you may proclaim the excellencies of Him who has called you out of darkness into His marvelous light."
>
> *1 Peter 2:9*

EXAMPLE

The ministry of Charles Spurgeon has impacted millions through his sermons, books, and theological influence. Often referred to as the "Prince of Preaching," Spurgeon's legacy can be traced to the investment of his grandfather, James Spurgeon. Under the encouraging eye of his grandfather, Charles was immersed in a spiritually rich environment of prayer, sermon preparation, and the daily rhythms of ministry. James Spurgeon was a faithful pastor in Stambourne, England, for 54 years and "trained" young Charles to ask theological questions and develop a deep love for the Word of God. With access to his grandfather's extensive library of Puritan works, Charles became a voracious reader and student of both theology and church history.

James modeled ministry in action by taking young Charles to visit the sick and to share the gospel with those who did not yet know Jesus. Later in life, Charles Spurgeon would point to James's constant reminder of the power and purity of the gospel message as one of his greatest inspirations. Upon recognizing Charles's incredible gifts as a preacher, his then-aged grandfather once told him, "You can preach the gospel better than I can, but not a better gospel." James Spurgeon committed to investing the love of Jesus into the life of his grandson. James's faithful training of his grandson is a testament to Jesus' method of personal disciple-making. As Charles Spurgeon later wrote, "This is the perpetual commission of the Church of Christ; and the great seal of the Kingdom attached to it."

MEDITATE Practice reciting this week's verse from memory and be prepared to say it aloud to your d-group.

ENGAGE

Praise God for His Spirit within you. Confess the ways you deny the power of the Holy Spirit by focusing on your own limitations. Thank God for providing everything necessary to walk boldly in the work He has called you to. Ask Him to deepen your understanding of His presence and power, and to trust His work to be accomplished through His power as you step forward in obedience.

ENCOURAGE

Use this checklist as a guide for your weekly d-group time. Refer to the discipler's guide at the front of the book for more encouragement and practical advice.

- Work through questions from the accountability page.

- Spend time praying specifics for one another.

- Take turns reciting the memory verses.

- Discuss answers to the questions throughout the week that are marked with this symbol. ▼

PRAYER REQUESTS

_____
_____
_____
_____
_____
_____

ACCOUNTABILITY QUESTIONS

These questions are to be asked of one another in a spirit of accountability (Proverbs 27:17). They are intended to stimulate conversations of character and confession of sin in a safe environment that values honesty, vulnerability, confidentiality, and grace.

1. Have you spent quality time in your spiritual disciplines this week?

2. Have you taken advantage of opportunities to share your faith this week? Explain.

3. Have your words and actions been a good testimony this week to the gospel of Jesus?

4. Have your thoughts and speech been pure (cussing, criticism, negativity, etc.)?

5. Have you been sexually pure this week? Have you been exposed to sexually alluring material? (For those who are married: Have you prioritized quality romantic time with your spouse?)

6. Have you been a good steward of your finances? Have you lacked integrity in the handling of your finances?

7. Have you been honoring and generous in your meaningful relationships this week (Family, friends, etc.)?

8. Have you given in to any addictive behavior this past week? Explain.

9. Have you been completely honest with me?

I'm praying for the salvation of the following two people and prayerfully considering how to share Christ with them myself: _____

> "Therefore, confess your sins to one another, and pray for one another, so that you may be healed."
>
> *James 5:16a*

Made in the USA
Coppell, TX
27 February 2026